Visual Security Studies

The present volume engages visuality in security from a variety of angles and explores what the subfield of Visual Security Studies might be.

To structure this experimentation, and to encourage a more careful and multifaceted approach to visuality and security, the main conceptual move in this volume is to envision three different transversal meeting points between security and visuality: visuality as a modality (active in representations and signs of security), visuality as practice (active in enacting security), and visuality as a method (active in investigating security). These three approaches structure the book together with three areas in which we see visuality as especially pertinent in relation to security: in security technologies that (en)vision security and are themselves the objects of visions of security; in spectacles of security and security spectatorship; and in ways of making security visible.

In this way, the volume works to sensitize International Relations research to visual forms of knowledge and practice by examining visual aspects of security. At the same time, it allows for debate on how this particular modality of the sensible not only affects what is visible and what is not, but also how authority and truth-claims come about, and how they are compared and evaluated. Through engagement with security via the 'language' or 'code' of the visual, it is possible to interrogate how scholars in the field understand visuality as well as the economy, grammar, and performativity of visual articulation and the production of knowledge. The volume also examines how visuality can be used as a method in doing research, and as a way of presenting research results.

Visual Security Studies is not a new theory of security or its study; instead, the present volume suggests that visuality should be envisioned as an aspect of security studies that can be incorporated into pre-existing approaches. The aim is to highlight how much of contemporary practice is visual and to foster an increased attentiveness to visuality in security politics, security practice, and to the possibilities of employing visual research methods in security scholarship.

This book will be of much interest to students of critical security, media studies, surveillance studies, visual sociology, and IR in general.

Juha A. Vuori is acting Professor of International Politics at the University of Turku, and an Adjunct Professor of International Politics at the University of Tampere. He is the author of *Critical Security and Chinese Politics* (Routledge, 2014) and co-author of *A History of the People's Republic of China* (in Finnish, 2012).

Rune Saugmann Andersen is a post-doctoral fellow at University of Tampere and holds a PhD from the Center for Advanced Security Theory (CAST), University of Copenhagen.

Series: Routledge New Security Studies
Series Editors:
J. Peter Burgess
École Normale Superieur (ENS), Paris

The aim of this book series is to gather state-of-the-art theoretical reflection and empirical research into a core set of volumes that respond vigorously and dynamically to new challenges to security studies scholarship. This is a continuation of the PRIO New Security Studies series.

Security Expertise
Practice, power, responsibility
Edited by Trine Villumsen Berling and Christian Bueger

Transformations of Security Studies
Dialogues, diversity and discipline
Edited by Gabi Schlag, Julian Junk and Christopher Daase

The Securitisation of Climate Change
Actors, processes and consequences
Thomas Diez, Franziskus von Lucke and Zehra Wellmann

Surveillance, Privacy and Security
Citizens' perspectives
Edited by Michael Friedewald, J. Peter Burgess, Johann Čas, Rocco Bellanova and Walter Peissl

Socially Responsible Innovation in Security
Critical Reflections
Edited by J. Peter Burgess, Genserik Reniers, Koen Ponnet, Wim Hardyns and Wim Smit

Visual Security Studies
Sights and Spectacles of Insecurity and War
Edited by Juha A. Vuori and Rune Saugmann Andersen

For more information about this series, please visit: www.routledge.com/Routledge-New-Security-Studies/book-series/RNSS

Visual Security Studies
Sights and Spectacles of Insecurity and War

Edited by Juha A. Vuori and
Rune Saugmann Andersen

LONDON AND NEW YORK

First published 2018
by Routledge
2 Park Square, Milton Park, Abingdon, Oxon OX14 4RN

and by Routledge
711 Third Avenue, New York, NY 10017

Routledge is an imprint of the Taylor & Francis Group, an informa business

© 2018 selection and editorial matter, Juha A. Vuori and Rune Saugmann Andersen; individual chapters, the contributors

The right of Juha A. Vuori and Rune Saugmann Andersen to be identified as the authors of the editorial matter, and of the authors for their individual chapters, has been asserted in accordance with sections 77 and 78 of the Copyright, Designs and Patents Act 1988.

All rights reserved. No part of this book may be reprinted or reproduced or utilized in any form or by any electronic, mechanical, or other means, now known or hereafter invented, including photocopying and recording, or in any information storage or retrieval system, without permission in writing from the publishers.

Trademark notice: Product or corporate names may be trademarks or registered trademarks, and are used only for identification and explanation without intent to infringe.

British Library Cataloguing-in-Publication Data
A catalogue record for this book is available from the British Library

Library of Congress Cataloging-in-Publication Data
A catalog record for this book has been requested

ISBN: 978-1-138-22992-1 (hbk)
ISBN: 978-1-315-38758-1 (ebk)

Typeset in Times New Roman
by Wearset Ltd, Boldon, Tyne and Wear

Contents

List of illustrations vii
Notes on contributors viii
Acknowledgements xi

1 Introduction: visual security studies 1
 RUNE S. ANDERSEN AND JUHA A. VUORI

PART I
Visions of security technology/technological security vision 21

2 Scalia.warhead1: securitization discourses in hacktivist video 23
 ADAM FISH

3 The gaze, the drone *dispositif*, and necro-biographies: a brief conceptual intervention 38
 MICHAEL J. SHAPIRO

4 CCTV oddity: on the archaeology and aesthetics of video surveillance 52
 PAOLO CARDULLO AND JAMES STEVENS

PART II
Security spectacles and spectatorship 69

5 The humanity of war: iconic photojournalism of the battlefield, 1914–2012 71
 LILIE CHOULIARAKI

6 World Drug Day and visual rituals of security in
   West Africa   91
   ADAM SANDOR

7 Collaging Iranian missiles: digital security spectacles and
   visual online parodies   114
   SAARA SÄRMÄ

PART III
Making security visible   131

8 Leonardo's security: the participant witness in a time of
   invisibility   133
   FRANK MÖLLER

9 Making norms visible: police uniforms and the social
   meaning of policing   150
   XAVIER T. GUILLAUME, JUHA A. VUORI, AND
   RUNE S. ANDERSEN

10 Auto-photographing (in)securities: former young female
   soldiers' post-war struggles in Monrovia   171
   LEENA VASTAPUU

11 Visual security: patterns and prospects   189
   ROLAND BLEIKER

   Index   201

Illustrations

Figures

2.1	US Sentencing Commission Website transformed into a video game	32
2.2	Still from Anonymous Operation Last Resort featuring Zinn quote	33
3.1	Brandon Bryant	48
3.2	Tariq	48
3.3	Soccer ball and plane	49
3.4	Jirga in Datta Khel	50
4.1	#OCTV stills, #OCTV composite	57
4.2	#OCTV by night, OCTV stills	60
4.3	Sniffing devices, Deptford.tv	62
4.4	CCTV Sniffing, 2011	63
5.1	Frank Hurley, 'Death the Reaper' (combined negatives), 1917	77
5.2	US National Archives, Hiroshima, 1945	79
5.3	Flag-draped US soldiers' coffins, 2005, Department of Defense	82
5.4	US Department of Defense, Bagram Air Base, Afghanistan, 2005	83
5.5	Abu Ghraib prison, 2004	86
6.1	Officers in uniform light up the seized drugs	104
6.2	The spectacle gets out of hand	105
6.3	The bonfire	106
9.1	From colour-use in police uniforms to policing as a system of the sensible	157

Table

1.1	The transversal approaches to visuality and the thematic division of the volume	6

Contributors

Rune S. Andersen is a post doc at the University of Tampere and holds a PhD from the Center for Advanced Security Theory (CAST), University of Copenhagen. His interdisciplinary research has been published in journals such as *Security Dialogue*, *European Journal of International Relations*, and *Journalism Practice*. Andersen has led multiple workshops on video as a research method, and published his research video in *Audiovisual Thinking*.

Roland Bleiker is Professor of International Relations at the University of Queensland, where he coordinates an interdisciplinary research programme on Visual Politics. His research explores the political role of aesthetics, visuality and emotions. Recent publications include *Divided Korea: Toward a Culture of Reconciliation* (University of Minnesota Press, 2005/2008), *Aesthetics and World Politics* (Palgrave Macmillan, 2009/2012) and, as co-editor with Emma Hutchison, a forum on 'Emotions and World Politics' in *International Theory* (Vol. 3/2014). Bleiker's new book *Visual Global Politics* has come out with Routledge in 2018.

Paolo Cardullo holds a PhD in Visual Sociology at Goldsmiths University of London. His thesis was around the affective geographies of gentrification in East Greenwich. He is currently an Associate Lecturer in Sociology (Goldsmiths) and a visiting research fellow at the Centre for Urban and Community Research (CUCR). He is among the 'first' AHRCCHASE Digital Scholars.

Lilie Chouliaraki is Professor of Media and Communications at the London School of Economics. She has published extensively on the nature of mediated public discourse, particularly on the link between mediation, social action, and cosmopolitan citizenship. Lilie is the author of award-winning books such as *The Ironic Spectator* (2012) and *The Spectatorship of Suffering* (2006/2011).

Adam Fish is a cultural anthropologist, video producer, and senior lecturer in the Sociology Department at Lancaster University. He is the author of *Technoliberalism* (Palgrave Macmillan, 2017), and co-author of *After the Internet* (Polity, 2017). In 2017–2018 he is a Leverhulme Research Fellow conducting research titled 'Opening the Droncode: The Privatisation of Urban Airspace'.

Contributors ix

Xavier T. Guillaume teaches at the Rijksuniversiteit Groningen. He has published books, articles and chapters (not necessarily in that order).

Frank Möller is a senior research fellow at the Tampere Peace Research Institute, Faculty of Social Sciences, University of Tampere, Finland, and co-convenor of the ECPR Standing Group on Politics and the Arts. He is the author of *Visual Peace: Images, Spectatorship, and the Politics of Violence* (Palgrave Macmillan 2013) and the co-editor of *Art as a Political Witness* (Budrich 2017).

Adam Sandor holds a PhD in Political Science from the University of Ottawa. Drawing on field research in Burkina Faso, Ghana, Senegal, Mali, and Niger, his research examines the governance of cross-border threats in West Africa. Adam is currently a Post-Doctoral Researcher with the Centre FrancoPaix en résolution des conflits et missions de paix based at the Université du Québec à Montréal (UQÀM). His research has been published in *African Studies Review* and the *Journal of Intervention and Statebuilding*. His current research focus is on how illicit economic practices impact local peace efforts in the Sahel.

Michael J. Shapiro is Professor of Political Science at the University of Hawai'i, Manoa. His most recent book is *The Political Sublime* (Duke University Press, 2018).

James Stevens launched Backspace, the proto cybercafe on Clink Street, London, in 1996. Backspace is an accessible place to explore creative networking and critical media in public. This was modelled online by digital native Dorian Moore and became a touchstone to a thousand web coders and inventors, inspiration for the technology spaces and businesses that boomed in the years that have followed. He teamed up with Julian Priest in 2000 to present wireless network primer Consume which advocated the open wireless networking that today thrives at OWN, based in Deptford, London.

Saara Särmä is a feminist, an artist, and a researcher in International Relations at the University of Tampere, Finland, from where she received a doctorate in 2014. Saara's doctoral dissertation, *Junk Feminism and Nuclear Wannabe – Collaging Parodies of Iran and North Korea*, focused on internet parody images and memes, and developed a unique art-based collage methodology for studying world politics. She is interested in the politics of visuality, feminist academic activism, and laughter in world politics. Currently she is working on developing further the visual collage methodology as both a research and a pedagogical tool, and experimenting with collective possibilities of collaging.

Leena Vastapuu is a postdoctoral researcher at the Tampere Peace Research Institute (TAPRI). She earned her doctoral degree from the University of Turku in 2017 and is the author of *Liberia's Women Veterans: War, Roles and Reintegration*, illustrated by Emmi Nieminen (Zed Books, 2018).

Through her writing, teaching, consulting, and voluntary work she tries to make sense of the world.

Juha A. Vuori is acting Professor of International Politics at the University of Turku, and an Adjunct Professor of International Politics at the University of Tampere, both in Finland. He is the author of *Critical Security and Chinese Politics* (Routledge, 2014). His articles have appeared in journals such as *European Journal of International Relations*, *Security Dialogue*, *Surveillance and Society*, *Global Discourse*, and *Asian Journal of Political Science*.

Acknowledgements

The idea that has become the present volume began its germination in the 'visuality cluster' of the International Collaboratory on Critical Methods in Security Studies (ICCM). We would like to thank the whole collaboratory, especially Claudia Aradau, Jef Huysmans, Andrew Neal, and Nadine Voelkner for organizing the ICCM, and Alex Heck, Can E. Mutlu, and Gabi Schlag for the inspiring times and ideas shared in the ICCM visuality cluster. Although formally only contributing to our own chapter in the volume, we most certainly have been greatly influenced in our overall vision by our fellow 'Colourboratory' member, Xavier T. Guillaume.

The volume benefited from two workshops held at the University of Copenhagen in November 2012, and at the University of Turku in December 2014. We would like to thank James Der Derian and Carsten Bagge Laustsen for their insights during the first workshop, and the participants of the PhD courses organized in conjunction with both workshops. Also thanks to Yannis Skarpelos, who gave a presentation in the first workshop. We would also like to acknowledge Margarita Rosselló Ramón and Eero Tuorila for their help in the technical editing of this volume. Our appreciation also goes to Andrew Humphrys and Hannah Ferguson for commissioning the work and aiding in the editing work at Routledge, to J. Peter Burgess as the series editor, and to the anonymous reviewers of the proposal and sample chapters. All remaining errors and inadequacies are our own.

We are grateful for financial support from the Nordic International Studies Association (NISA), the Danish Politological Research School Polforsk, the Centre for Advanced Security Theory and Department of Political Science at the University of Copenhagen, the subject of Political Science at the University of Turku, and the subject of International Politics at the University of Tampere. We appreciate and gladly acknowledge the support we have received.

This has been a project long in the works, which means that some of it has been previously published. Lilie Chouliaraki's chapter has appeared in a slightly different form in *Visual Communication* in 2013, sections of Michael J. Shapiro's chapter appear in his book *Politics and Time: Documenting the Event*, and a different version of Leena Vastapuu's chapter appears in *Liberia's Women Veterans: War, Roles and Reintegration*. We thank the previous publishers for the permission to publish these contributions here as well. The images that appear in the volume either are from the authors, used under the principle of fair use, or are in the public domain. In all cases where images are not from the authors we have made every effort to acquire all necessary permissions. If someone feels that their copyright has not been acknowledged, they should contact the editors so that such errors can be rectified in future editions.

1 Introduction
Visual security studies

Rune S. Andersen and Juha A. Vuori

In the opening of *Writing and Difference*, Derrida (2002: 1) describes the structural project with a bold claim: 'What is at stake, first of all, is an adventure of vision.' Fifty years later, what he termed the 'structuralist invasion' continues to occupy parts of the social sciences through post-structuralist camps as well as visual and aesthetic turns, and the adventure of vision is still ongoing.

As part of this adventure, a Visual Security Studies is emerging as a subfield of (critical) Security Studies. In W. J. T. Mitchell's terms, this new subfield is an 'interdiscipline', that is, 'a site of convergence and conversation across disciplinary lines' (Mitchell 1995: 540). Visual security studies is thus indebted to multiple disciplines, even though it is primarily nested in and descending from security studies. Indeed, the importance of visuality for security and conflict is indicated by the rising numbers of scholarly works devoted to visual aspects of security within disciplines such as international relations and security studies, media and visual culture studies, urban geography, surveillance studies, anthropology, and sociology. It is possible to interrogate the economy, grammar, and performativity of visual articulations and the production of security by engaging them via the languages, codes, modalities, media, and emotional registers that connect with visuality. As a multidiscipline, scholars from different fields that touch upon the visual production of contemporary security bring with them different understandings of visuality and of how visualities intersect with (in)security, just as they do in regard to security (Bourbeau 2015).

To give but a few examples of developments in such connected fields, media studies has paid increasing attention to topics at the heart of traditional security studies. The journal *Media, War and Conflict* is the clearest expression of this sustained interest. Here, visualities of security are often seen in a wider contemporary media landscape, rather than as a separate modality of knowledge. Important recent work has, inter alia, studied the changes in the digital mediation of crises, disasters, and wars (Seib 2008; Andén-Papadopoulos and Pantti 2011), as well as the roles played by institutions and citizens in such mediation (Chouliaraki 2006, 2013). In a similar vein, war and conflict have become important research topics for visual culture studies with a number of works devoted to the visual cultures of the post-9/11 invasions of Afghanistan and Iraq, and the way in which these impact and interact with larger cultural currents in Western culture (Mirzoeff 2005; Mitchell, W. J. T. 2011). More historically minded explorations have interrogated how the visual colonial experience and the visual cultures of Western art continue to inform visualities as well as scopic regimes of war and conflict (Mirzoeff 2011). Focusing on the mundane of urban life, surveillance studies has since its inception cultivated an acute attention to the workings of the electronic eye of the surveillance apparatus (Lyon 1994). Together with sociological and criminological insights, these studies have produced both works on visual knowledge production, and in a more Foucauldian tradition, on the structuration of society through visual surveillance practices (Finn 2012; for such concerns in visual security studies see, e.g. Andersen and Möller 2013).

Such examples are important for visual security studies when it combines insights from multiple fields in regard to understanding the role visuality can play in the expanded field of security studies. They can allow leveraging some of the previous research gains by paying attention to disciplines that are more advanced in their engagements with visuality. In this way, VSS builds on the pictorial turn in the social sciences, the related aesthetic turn in international relations research (Bleiker 2001), and innovative research programmes in security studies. The incorporation of first the use of security language (e.g. Buzan *et al.* 1998) and then practices of enacting security (e.g. Huysmans 2014) into the study of security have taught us much about the politics of security during the past quarter of a century. From these viewpoints 'security' is a modality (Hansen 2000: 296) or a rationale (Huysmans 2006: 147) that can operate in the absence of 'security words'. These kinds of studies have highlighted the negative side of security, and participated in elucidating how the logic of considering security to be inherently positive is faulty. Rather than a positive or a good for all, the increase of security for some often means its sacrifice for others (Bigo 2008: 124). In the everyday, and beyond security speech, this field explores security practices that focus on bodily movements such as saying and doing, both explicit and tacit knowledges, and objects (Bueger 2016), as well as networks of security actants (Schouten 2014). Visual security studies do and can benefit from such viewpoints by paying attention to institutional practices of visuality, affects and emotions, and media environments in the investigation of visual security practice.

As already suggested above, the critical study of security has emphasized the ambiguity of international security. Security, accordingly, is something that we cannot fully grasp. This is the case whether it be understood in more abstract terms as states of being, sets of relations, modes of reasoning and acting, identities and understandings, or more concretely connected to episodes of violence conceptualized as rebellions, wars, systematic repression, and so on. Visuality is deeply implicated in events, relations, and identities, in how we get to know them, and in how we can critically engage them. This volume works to sensitize research dealing with visualities of security and the international to visual forms of knowledge through a series of adventures in visual security. These open up what visuality might mean for the study of security and explore how different conceptions of visualities are implicated in security practice and politics. It allows for debate on this particular modality of the sensible (Barthes 1973; Rancière 2004): how it affects what is visible and what is not, how it affects the ways in which knowledge, authority, and truth-claims come about, are compared, and evaluated, and how it intervenes in security and the daily experience of it. This hopefully opens up for further ocular investigations and critiques of security, its politics, and its practice. It is in this sense that we quote Derrida to the effect that what we put at stake is 'an adventure of vision': the aim of this project goes in line with Derrida's remark upon the structuralist project, to effect 'a conversion of the way of putting questions to any object posed before us', with that object being security (Derrida 2002: 1).

Indeed, despite its parentage in international security studies, VSS is not a new theory of security or its study; instead, VSS is here envisioned as an aspect of security studies that can be incorporated into pre-existing approaches. The aim is to highlight how much of contemporary practice is visual and to foster an increased attentiveness to visuality in security politics, security practice, and the possibilities of employing visual research methods in security scholarship.

To encourage a more careful and multifaceted approach to visuality and security, the main conceptual move in this volume is to envision three different transversal meeting points between security and visuality: visuality as a *modality* (active in representations and signs of security), visuality as *practice* (active in enacting security), and visuality as a *method* (active in investigating security). These three approaches structure the book, together with three areas in which we see visuality as especially pertinent in relation to security: in security *technologies* that (en)vision security and are themselves the objects of visions of security; in *spectacles* of security and security spectatorship; and in ways of *making security visible*.

In fostering such encounters, the present volume brings together scholars from a number of disciplines to engage with visuality in security (for a similar multidisciplinary engagement with security as such, see Bourbeau 2015). What is shared across these different disciplines is the problem of the irreducibility of images to words (and vice versa), the problem of their non-equivalence. In Foucault's (2007: 10) words from his oft-cited meditation on Velázquez's *Las Meninas*, it is 'in vain' that we use words to describe images (or vice versa) since 'what we see never resides in what we say'. Different semiotic modalities (Jewitt 2011) provide for different affordances (Kress 2010) as vehicles of political communication, identification, governance, and social sorting. The investigation of multimodal political communication and practice has become an ever more pertinent problem for research and teaching across disciplines. Images, whether still or moving, captured, rendered, or drawn always contain a 'surplus of meaning' compared to verbal interpretations of them. Yet this surplus and this irreducibility is politically productive, whether we think of it in the day-to-day meetings between security infrastructures and citizens, or in the representations of politics. The task for research is to find ways to work with these issues rather than deny them, 'to treat their incompatibility as a starting point [...] instead of as an obstacle to be avoided' (Foucault 2007: 10).

A number of crises as well as general developments in security politics during the last few decades make it apparent that visualities of various kinds are important to security and its study. The prominence of video in the activities of the now-notorious Islamic State group is but one example here. Beyond using video as a visual medium for their recruitment and other propaganda purposes, visual artefacts and references are used by the group quite effectively as well. The black flag with a white shadada is ubiquitous in their videos and practical operations, and works to bring together and unite separate groups in a diffuse network spanning different regions (on flags, see Andersen *et al.* 2016). At the same time, ISIS leverages visual references to US practices in Guantánamo – dressing prisoners to be executed in orange jumpsuits made infamous by that prisoner camp – which gives a sense not only of how important visual mediation is to the constitution of security and its actors, but also how the visuality of security and conflict 'become "not things we think about, but things we think with" and think through' (van Veeren 2010: 1725, drawing on Gillis) in day-to-day world politics.

Indeed, rather than listing a few other contemporary examples of visual representations that have greatly influenced world politics, we can try the road of falsification: think of a major conflict or security issue where visuality is *not* important; or think of contemporary security issues without their visual imprint – Islamic State without propaganda videos, the Iraq war without falling statues and the 'ghost of Abu Ghraib' (W. J. T. Mitchell 2011), the Iranian nuclear issue without the satellite images of 'secret' underground production facilities at Natanz, or the crisis of European refugee politics without images of overcrowded vessels and drowned children's still bodies on the shores of the Mediterranean.

Such examples display how visualities often take centre stage in the constitution and conduct of security. This has been facilitated by the profound changes in the media landscape where previously separate media and formats have moved online and converged (Deibert 1997; Jenkins 2004). This allows online visual media to play a key role in the practice, the politics, and the protest against security. In this new media environment, the mediation of security not only combines previously separate formats and modalities (e.g. image, sound, and text) but is increasingly driven by the algorithmic mining of user data rather than editorial concerns. This erodes long-established hierarchies of who gets to speak about security and how (Andersen 2015). The online mediation of security allows for expansion of the kinds of visuals as well as the range of actors capable of producing them. The visualization of conflict is no longer only dependent on embedded media professionals, or images released by officials. Private individuals can gain global circulation for their images of conflict and insecurity through online mediation. Yet, the present exploration of the visuality of security is not intended to be about the changing media landscape, and concomitant changes to the sociopolitical constitution of security. As indicated by the three meeting points outlined above, visualities of security are far from only about the representation of something as security (see also Andersen *et al.* 2015). Studies in the visuality of security, thus, is better understood as an analytical sensibility (see Moore and Farrands 2013; Vuori 2013; Andersen *et al.* 2015). The importance of such a sensibility is highlighted by recent changes to the mediated constitution of security, but it predates and is not conceptually dependent on changes in the media, as many of the chapters in this volume show.

Three transversal approaches to visuality in security

There is a multiplicity of disciplines at work in any sustained effort to understand the intersection of visuality and security (Bleiker 2014, 2018). At the same time, there is a multiplicity of scopic regimes at work in security practices. Both make it difficult to provide strict guidance on how to begin an adventure into the visual investigation of security – on how to engage the visualities at play in the translation, contestation, or (re)appropriation of the ambiguous symbol of security into practices, policies, and identities. Indeed, what these multiplicities do is to point to the need of a flexible and open approach. Accordingly, rather than seeking to set strict boundaries for the emerging discipline, we take the adventurer's approach in the present volume to try to explore what visual security studies might be (cf. Aradau and Huysmans' 2014 approach of experimentation; or Law's 2004 concept of telling stories).

While the study of objects that represent security (photographs, cartoons, etc.), and the politics of that representation, have been the subject of most of the scholarship devoted to combining security with the visual (e.g. Möller 2009; Hansen 2011a, 2011b, 2016), we make three moves that open up for a broader range of visual practices to become part of the subject matter of visual security studies. First, we think visuality as not only about objects that represent security in some way ('images of security'), but second, also as about how sight and appearance is part of all the bureaucratic routines, everyday encounters, and minuscule decisions that have been studied under the umbrella of security practices ('visual practices of security'). Third, we contend that visual security research can be about not only the study of 'security things' that can be seen (whether emphasizing images or the practices that produce visual experiences), but also about the use of visual modalities in investigation as such. Researching security through other modalities than text ('visual research practice') affords different forms of engagement with both images of security and practices of security that are not themselves necessarily visual.

In addition, we have divided the chapters of the present volume into three thematic parts: (I) visions of security technology/technological security vision, (II) security spectacles and spectatorship, and (III) making security visible. When combined with the epistemological division, the chapters can be placed in a three-by-three table (Table 1.1). The first section approaches visuality in security through the theme of technology. Here, visuality is thought to play 'a vital role in both the conduct and rationalization' (Gregory 2010: 266) of security practices, including the use of military violence. Visual modalities are not assumed to be innocent parts of security practice, but a part of techno-cultural systems, and 'mangles' (Pickering 1995) or 'entanglements' of science,

Table 1.1 The transversal approaches to visuality and the thematic division of the volume

	Transversal approaches to security		
	Visuality as a modality (of security representations and signs)	**Visuality as a practice** (in enacting security)	**Visuality as a method** (for investigating security)
Section I: *Visions of security technology / technological security vision*	Scalia.warhead1	The gaze, the drone *dispositif*, and necro-biographies	CCTV oddity
Section II: *Security spectacles and spectatorship*	The humanity of war	World Drug Day and visual rituals of security in West Africa	Collaging Iranian missiles
Section III: *Making security visible*	Leonardo's security	Making norms visible	Auto-photographing (in)securities

art, and security (Forsyth 2014: 128). Much of security is 'constructed visibility' (Rajchman 1991). The second section approaches visuality in terms of security spectacles, whether these are journalistic photographs or spectacular political events organized by authorities, and what it means to be a spectator of such spectacles. The theme questions the assumed veracity of photography and the visual as evidence. It also explores how the spectator has been emancipated in this sense. The third section engages visuality from the viewpoint of how it makes security – whether its norms, positions, or personal experiences of it – visible. The theme explores how obscure photographs can bring forth ethical implications of objects and witnessing them, how visuality can make norms visible, and how visualization can be used as a basis for interviewing informants in research processes.

Images of security: visuality as a modality of representation

The representation of security has long been regarded as a form of international/security politics in itself. Conceived of as images, visual representation has been addressed as to its capabilities of representing security, as communicative acts, and via the terms of the practices dominating the production of security-relevant images, as detailed below. The attention to the politics and performative aspects of images is an important approach to what visual security studies might concern itself with, and the one that has been most thoroughly addressed so far (see e.g. Hansen 2011a; Schlag and Heck 2013; Andersen *et al.* 2015).

Shapiro's (1988) 'politics of representation' is one of the first works in international relations that thoroughly addresses images from the viewpoint of how they represent that which they depict. Research on the role of images and visuality in critical studies of security has tended to see images as powerful in contemporary politics. Such studies have often followed Shapiro's analysis in looking at the role of images in constituting some representations of politics as natural and true. This kind of visual production of truth can work through different mediums and practices, but the majority of such studies have focused on photographs. To view photographs in such a way, calls for 'a politicized reading practice, one which situates the images in order to discern their complicities with prevailing power and authority as well as their challenges' (Shapiro 1988: 131). This, importantly, is achieved by bringing in the Barthesian notion of 'code' as a set of common understandings by which the viewer and the visual artefact interact, the codes themselves 'performing a kind of captioning' of the image by telling the viewer what to see and how to see (Shapiro 1988: 150).

Indeed, from the viewpoint of representation, images should be studied as a sphere of security practice: since visual artefacts have political implications, they should be taken seriously as an object of security analysis – the pictorial power of security representations matters (Andersen *et al.* 2015). Most often, the assumptions of special powers inherent in images are not taken autonomously by analysts. They reflect views of how society relates to the images that are part of it, i.e. the prevalent discourses about images. As such, pictorial power is not something that is pre-given; visual power remains something seen as culturally constituted in most accounts. As most analysts of visuality come out of traditions affiliated with poststructuralist and linguistic lines of thought, they are well aware of the constructedness of such pictorial power (e.g. Hansen 2011a). Yet, they frequently appear more interested in asserting that pictorial power abounds in contemporary visual culture than in trying to investigate its constructedness. Therefore, paradoxically, while the processes of images making the cultural and contingent look natural are frequently studied, the wider societal discourse about images as powerful is rarely assessed.

In critical IR and (critical) security studies, the study of visuals as representations has manifested itself, for example, in explorations of visual artefacts in terms of how they enact the international (Campbell 2004), question security practices (Möller 2007), or take part in securitizing (Vuori 2010). Yet, visuals have also been studied in terms of how visual signs differ from and relate to verbal or other categories of signs/texts. Indeed, a number of works have developed frameworks for studying images as acts of representation, from Hansen's (2011a, see also 2011b) cartoon-based theorization of 'the image' in securitization processes to Andersen's (2015) work on security articulation made with video. In the present volume, Adam Fish (Chapter 2) begins the investigation of visuality as a modality in technological visions of security with an analysis of the hacktivist collective Anonymous' online videos and their use of universalizing macrosecuritization speech acts performed in word and image. The hacktivist group has established itself through a plethora of iconic visuals, and has deployed online videos on a number of its campaigns. Here, Fish shows how video can visualize securitization and operate in the framing of an issue. In his case the use of video as a visual modality facilitates the presentation of internet freedom as globally threatened by, for example, presenting it in comparison with thermonuclear war. Yet, the openness and controversy of such modalities is apparent in the petitions that some hacktivists made to stop using militarized imagery in the collective's videos.

Indeed, what images do, or how they speak politically, has been approached differently in the literature on security visuals. Variety in such views has both ontological and methodological implications (Andersen *et al.* 2015); methodological choices are not without consequence as 'methods create worlds' (Aradau and Huysmans 2014) and the use of a certain method in a certain situation may be a political act with concomitant effects. Here, some have emphasized the ambiguity and polysemy of images, which requires spoken or written discourse for images to have specific political meanings, such as securitization (Möller 2007). Others have pointed out how neither words nor images can speak without intertextual linkages to other words and images (Hansen 2011a). Yet, there have also been approaches that argue for the 'auto-activity' of images to, in a way, speak for themselves (Schlag and Heck 2013). Visual security, in this case, refers to the idea that because images have performative power politically, they should be taken seriously as an object of security analysis. Visual artefacts can be viewed here as the tip of the security politics/rationale/practice iceberg.

Different genres of images have been viewed by studies of visual security to have varying effects. Placed on a continuum, artefacts have been taken from working as tools for maintaining spectacular domination to working as vehicles of critique and demystification. For example, 'mainstream' film and news images have often been portrayed as complicit in dominant and repressive security practices. This is the case in Der Derian's (2009) outline of the visual integration of the theatre of war in home theatre entertainment, or in Campbell's (2003) investigation of what he terms 'cultural governance'. Such a view is also present in Mirzoeff's (2005) account of imagery of the 2003 Iraq war, and in Weber's (2008) critique of the representation of 9/11 in *United 93*. Similar thoughts feature – albeit less unambiguously – in Shapiro's (1988) exposure of the stereotyping practices of representation found in the production of foreign policy.

On the other side, artistic images and relatively 'slow' photojournalistic work have been brought to critical security studies as vehicles with which to resist domination by security practices and spectacular representations of security practice in mainstream news and films. In Möller's (2007) analysis of how artistic photography can perform desecuritization, images are seen in a Foucauldian optic to possess an ever-present surplus of meaning that always offers some space for resistance. Later, Andersen and Möller (2013) credit art photography with the ability to introduce critical everyday seeing. Between these two poles, Lisle's (2011) work on aftermath photography allows for some critical intervention by photography but maintains that such photography remains ambiguously trapped between documenting and aestheticizing the traumatic past.

In the present volume, Lilie Chouliaraki (Chapter 5) examines the practice where the controversies over whether images are aestheticizing spectacles or provide for critical spectatorship have been most pronounced: war photojournalism. She conceives of the different modalities involved in war photojournalism as 'war imaginaries'.[1] Photographs of battlefields are imagined as constitutive dimensions of public morality and to carry specific visions of humanity. Such dimensions and visions suggest how we should relate to the spectacles of war and security presented to us as spectators. How bodies, landscapes, and moral agency are presented in images of battlefields have a bearing on how those outside such spaces have mundane encounters with them. Examining visuals over a century provides for opportunities to reflect on societal changes in the war imaginary, and the stated legitimation of warfare as such.

Rather than dominant imaging practices enacted in the mundanity of photojournalism, Frank Möller (Chapter 8) explores in his chapter how the position of the spectator of security spectacles can be acted on through obscure art photography that makes security visible by pointing to its obscurity. Many security sites and practices are made to disappear, but this disappearance may be countered by the spectators' imagination that makes material security objects reappear. Möller directly engages the question of the agency of images vis-à-vis that of spectators, arguing that obscure photography of security sites can move security spectators from the subject position of a (passive, observing, neutral) viewer towards the direction of the subject position of a participant witness who self-critically reflects upon the conditions depicted in a given image.

In this way, the chapters in this transversal theme explore the rich diversity of analyses that can stem from looking at images of security, whether these are staged in online productions or rendered in photographic film. They show how specific spectator positions and attitudes are enacted in security spectacles but can also be questioned by spectacles that put on display how security is made visible, and how the scale of image analysis can vary from interrogations of individual speech acts to considerations of regimes of visualization. Rather than suggesting a formula for making 'security sense' of images, the chapters thus point to the variety of questions that can be examined, from the operations of the individual spectacle to how ways of imagining security operate on our relation to security and war.

Enactments of security: visuality as practice

The study of practice in international relations and security studies is interested in the embodied habits and ways of doing in the everyday that share practical understandings (McCourt 2016). As such, practice approaches draw on field theories, network analysis, and actor network theories to get a grasp of commonsensical routines of social interaction (Bueger 2016). These theories dissolve the dichotomy between the material and the ideational, whereby words and material things can be investigated as equals. Material objects and artefacts can be considered both meaningful and as actants in political assemblages. The various materials of practice are where human actors often think from (Pouliot 2010).

When visuality is thought of as connected to security practice, it quickly becomes apparent that most practices that make up and enact security are visual in one form or another: bodily movements, knowledges, and objects involved in security practices are more often than not visual. Here, rather than (re)presenting security discourses visually, visual practices are operative, for example, in making things and political norms visible or obscure, on display or hidden, and in the enactment of social sorting. At the same time, much of the various kinds of 'capital' considered relevant in the study of security practice can either be communicated or appears visually (in, for example, types of dress, hairstyle, and so on). Such a vantage point to visuality examines security as sites, encounters, enactments, or institutions and thereby provides for the study of visual modalities that are not limited to individual or sequential visual forms or shapes (drawings, photographs, videos, etc.), but that are an inevitable aspect of all material security practices. In this way, visuality can be an entry-point into the logics of security practice.

Fields, communities, actor-networks, and assemblages are among the concepts used to engage security practice overall (Bueger 2016: 128). From the visualities of security point of view, the focus is on the role of the visual in the development of techniques of knowledge, and the configuration of elements into in/security assemblages. Investigations into these can, for example, examine how vision and (in)visibility is an integral part of practices and modulations of the social, the political, and of security (Haggerty and Ericson 2006), and is central to the cultural governance of war (Campbell 2003). This type of conceptualization presents visualities as implicated in ways of knowing, and treats them as spheres to be known. Examples here include how the colouring of uniforms worn by security officials (Guillaume *et al.* 2016), or how the prohibitions on photography in an expanding range of public places (Simon 2012) contribute to security practices. Such practices do not securitize and point to threats as such. Rather, they attempt to direct understandings of security through the manipulation of what the security apparatus looks like, and by controlling representations of it.

In regard to how security is made in fields of practice (Bigo 2002), the habituses (practical knowledges inscribed through collective experiences) and doxas (practical knowledges of larger configurations) involved in them can be approached through their visual aspects: how does visuality affect how social agents are socialized prior to joining security institutions, how they are socialized within an institution, and how visuality affects their position within and between social fields (Davidshofer *et al.* 2017: 214). Here, the practice of wearing a security uniform is very much an everyday and embodied experience. Uniforms are involved in a number of practices, and serve a number of functions. In the present volume, Xavier Guillaume, Rune S. Andersen, and Juha A. Vuori (Chapter 9) examine the use of colour in police uniforms as a visual modality of signs that make security norms visible. Indeed, to wear a uniform endows agents with social capital, inserts certain norms into social situations, and invites certain interpellations in social spaces; to wear certain colours in one's dress is a way not only to distinguish oneself from others, but at times also to make certain rights, duties, or norms visible, and to relate agents to both social fields and other actors.

When practice is viewed as a community (Adler 2008), the visual can be examined as an aspect of the practical learning, interaction, and ways of doing involved in producing communities of security expertise and politics. In the present volume, Adam Sandor's chapter (Chapter 6) explores a haptic and embodied experience of visual security practice as spectacle in his examination of the World Drug Day in West Africa. Securitization theory allows for an investigation of the performative visual rituals that are the spectacle of burning seized drugs. Such practices produce communities of security spectators and display the effectiveness of drug enforcement. Sandor shows how ritual performances can compose an important genre of visual security practice. His analysis points to how in West African politics, political elites have become very adept at strategizing meaning in spectacular rituals that play to multiple simultaneous audiences, including the international security and development donor community.

In terms of practice as relationality, visual security practice highlights the role of objects and technologies involved as actants in material semiotics (Law 2009). Technological vision and visions of technology are highly involved in various actant networks and relations of practice that make up much of today's security assemblages. Concomitantly, the technologization of security practice has involved a number of visual aspects. In the present volume, Michael Shapiro (Chapter 3) provides a critical view on one of these. He engages the technological gaze in the context of the use of drones. Drones are crucial actants in the 'manhunts' that have become a prevalent security practice in the borderlands and peripheries of today's militarized conflicts. The expectation in these kinds of practices is that the drone provides for a unidirectional technological security vision from the drone to its target. Yet, Shapiro explores the disruptive effects the return of such a technological gaze can have on those that operate the drones. Such a reverse view has been a topic in film and television that question the seemingly disembodied practices of operational looking in contemporary battlespaces.

As such a tripartite division of ways to approach practice (field, community, and network) indicates, the way in which practice is understood also impacts how the visual is comprehended as an aspect of it (cf. Bueger and Gadinger 2014). Security scholars need to include visuality as an aspect of dividing the sensible within practices and discourses of security, as visuality is implicated in practices that 'not only detect objects and people but also produce' them with certain statuses and as 'surveillant subjects' (Harris 2006: 102). Thus far, the segregation of visual security as a subfield of security studies has often limited it to the study of 'visual artefacts' such as images, paintings, and other objects made to look at. The study of visuality in conjunction with security practices aims exactly at bridging this divide by expanding the scope of visual analytics of security. It is interested in how security practices are mediated through visual objects, devices, and techniques (cf. Davidshofer *et al.* 2017: 205) rather than how visuals represent or make security meaningful. Accordingly, practices of looking and displaying are central to the analyses in this theme, emphasizing how norms and political motives are never alien to the quotidian visual encounter between citizen and police, subject and state, the targeted and the one doing the targeting. Rather than expecting to find questions of visual security only in practices of representing security politics, thus, the analyses demonstrate how visuality is key to everyday security practice.

Visual investigations of security: visuality as method

Visual methods are under development across both the social and natural sciences, as visual technologies enable new ways of producing and processing visual data. Visual anthropology has perhaps the longest tradition of visual analysis, and is a well-established discipline within the social sciences, with its own conferences, graduate programmes, and journals. But sociology and media studies also have productively engaged visual modes of doing research, using visual media to interrogate research topics that are not necessarily themselves visual – e.g. using images or films to make research subjects reflect on ageing (Pink 2013) . For a number of years this type of work has been occasionally popping up in research on international relations and security issues with studies using, e.g. video production tools (Weber 2007; Andersen 2015), collaging (Florman 2002), or photography (Möller 2013; Balomenou and Garrod 2015) to develop research methods that use visual media to interrogate IR and security. Thus far, most of this work has been concerned with phenomena that are already visual such as the integration of digital visual media into war (Stahl 2007; Der Derian and Gara 2009; Der Derian *et al.* 2010), into propaganda and national identity (Weber 2011), and into security debate (Saugmann Andersen 2012). Indeed, in most of this work, audiovisual media has been used to present research points rather than as a method or research tool (Stahl 2007; Der Derian *et al.* 2010; Weber 2007, 2011), even if researcher-made films necessarily transgress that line in the editing and production of visual work.

Given the lack of institutional recognition of non-textual work and of visual publication outlets in security and IR,[2] a film-and-book publication of the same research ideas, in the tradition of Berger's (1972) eminent visual study of 'ways of seeing', has been the predominant survival strategy of researchers interested in working through visual means. This double strategy, of course, requires uncommon resources. The double-publication strategy enables peers to regard the visual work as a mere illustration or dissemination of scholarly work, a stark contrast to the work being done in, e.g. the International Visual Sociology Association.

New work by emerging scholars, and the transversal theme of visuality as method in the present volume, seeks to explore the possibilities of doing rather than presenting research visually. Drawing inspiration from the traditions of visual anthropology and visual sociology, this work is not necessarily published in visual format – as discussed in Leena Vastapuu's chapter in the present volume (Chapter 10) on female ex-combatants. Indeed, publishing the images that are used in a visual research strategy may at times be detrimental to the scholarly aims and ethics – yet, all the while, the treatment of images can still be a key part of the research process. In her chapter, Saara Särmä (Chapter 7) draws on feminist thinking about collaging as a way of forming 'a compelling composition that brings to mind connections not visualized using our standard methodologies' (Sylvester 2007: 572) and pushes this thinking by actually using visual collaging to interrogate Western perceptions of Iranian missile tests. In their turn, Paolo Cardullo and James Steven (Chapter 4) manipulate the issue of visibility and invisibility to great effect when they let people in surveilled university buildings take control over the surveillance apparatus to produce images that they are comfortable with.

Visual social science methods literatures often point to the possibilities for using images as vehicles of participation. These ideas draw from work in educational, anthropological sciences, as well as marketing studies, where images are often part of participatory research strategies, making images and image processing tools through which research subjects *participate* (see e.g. C. Mitchell 2011; Denov *et al.* 2012; Balomenou and Garrod 2015). Images can be used in a participant mode in a situation where it is not the visual end-product that is important, but rather the process of studying the people making it and/or reflecting upon it.

Such image use in anthropological and ethnographic research is often targeted at studying social dynamics and cultural understandings by letting the researcher work with research subjects as they are involved in producing and processing visual data (Haw and Hadfield 2011: chap. 7). Here, images are at times somewhat problematically regarded as a transparent medium transmitting the message of participants and researchers as 'visually verifiable data' without disruptive distortions. The idea is that researchers can understand what research subjects communicate in images, and vice versa. While this epistemology allows for transcription of video and audio to reflect this data without distortion, as emphasized in Mitchell's review (C. Mitchell 2011: 153, 80) it sits rather poorly with ideas about images as political, as having different epistemic strengths and weaknesses than verbal representation, and drawing on different registers of understanding than text-based politics. The visual sociologist Luc Pauwels has pointed to the semiotically problematic naïveté of letting this understanding guide the use of images in research:

> [t]he visual works in social science have [...] tended to overemphasize the iconic (the high 'resemblance' of the depiction to the depicted) and indexical (the perceived "natural" or 'causal' link with the depicted object) aspects of camera images at the expense of developing a visual language and a methodology to produce and process visual data.
> (Pauwels 2010: 547)

While using images in a 'participation mode', Vastapuu's chapter shows that regarding images as transparent is by no means a precondition for using photography to interrogate how security questions intervene and figure in the everyday life of the marginalized. The political and epistemic ambiguity and instability of images, in contrast, can be a vehicle that empowers image creators in their interaction with institutionally privileged researchers, and in making the understandings and concerns that relate to security visible. Conversely, as Särmä's collaging of the visual spectacles of online parodies of missile test images shows, research strategies can also leverage such ambiguity to question the 'normal' operation of images by replacing taken-for-granted juxtapositions and contexts for new and unexpected ones. For semiotician and art scholar Arthur Asa Berger such interruptions – cuts, transitions, juxtapositions – are devices that 'are analogous to punctuation in writing; they are the means by which the director indicates (though not overtly) to the viewers how they should relate scenes to one another' (Berger 1989: 84). Perverting the indications of the 'directors' of surveillance assemblages, Cardullo and Steven's intervention into the technological surveillance assemblages operating in our everyday shows that the ambiguity and opacity of images can also be productive when manipulated, hacked, or played with by the researcher.

The chapters thus make a compelling case for a visual security studies to employ visual methodologies in its inquiry into the meeting points between security and visualities. While drawing on the visual methodology literature in the social sciences, the chapters engaging such methods in relation to security and the political deployment of images and visual assemblages call for special attention to the questions of the transparency/opacity of images and the uses of ambiguity and instability in images and visual assemblages. These are areas where the study of visualities in relation to the intensely political deployment and manipulation of images can help advance the visual social science literature.

Together, the approach taken in the volume and the chapters that constitute it produce a sketch of a kind of adventurer's map for visual security studies. Roland Bleiker (Chapter 11) concludes the volume by reflecting on the implications of taking such a journey.

Notes

1 The chapter was published in *Visual Communication* in 2013.
2 Seb Kaempf and Roger Stahl's website The Vision Machine is perhaps the only site dedicated to publication of non-textual work.

References

Adler, E. (2008). The Spread of Security Communities: Communities of Practice, Self-Restraint, and NATO's Post-Cold War Transformation. *European Journal of International Relations*, 14(2), pp. 195–230.

Andén-Papadopoulos, K. and Pantti, M. (2011). *Amateur Images and Global News*. Bristol, UK/Chicago: Intellect.

Andersen, R. S. (2015). *Remediating Security. A Semiotic Framework for Analyzing How Video Speaks Security*. Copenhagen: University of Copenhagen, Department of Political Science.

Andersen, R. S., Guillaume, X., and Vuori, J. A. (2016). Flags. In: M. B. Salter, ed., *Making Things International 2: Catalysts and Reactions*. Minneapolis, Minnesota University Press, pp. 137–152.

Andersen, R. S. and Möller, F. (2013). Engaging the Limits of Visibility: Photography, Security and Surveillance. *Security Dialogue*, 44(3), pp. 203–221.

Andersen, R. S., Vuori, J. A., and Mutlu, C. E. (2015). Visuality. In: C. Aradau, J. Huysmans, A. Neal, and N. Voelkner, eds., *Critical Security Methods: New Frameworks for Analysis*. London and New York: Routledge, pp. 85–117.

Aradau, C. and Huysmans, J. (2014). Critical Methods in International Relations: The Politics of Techniques, Devices and Acts. *European Journal of International Relations*, 20(3), pp. 596–619.

Balomenou, N. and Garrod. B. (2015). A Review of Participant-Generated Image Methods in the Social Sciences. *Journal of Mixed Methods Research*, 10(4), pp. 335–351.

Barthes, R. (1973[1964]). *Elements of Semiology*. Trans. Lavers, A. and Smith, C. New York: Hill and Wang.

Berger, A. A. (1989). *Seeing Is Believing: An Introduction to Visual Communication*. 4th edn, New York: McGraw-Hill Education.

Berger, J. (1972). *Ways of Seeing*. London: British Broadcasting Corporation and Penguin.

Bigo, D. (2002). Security and Immigration: Toward a Critique of the Governmentality of Unease. *Alternatives*, 27(1), pp. 63–92.

Bigo, D. (2008). International Political Sociology. In: P. D. Williams, ed., *Security Studies: An Introduction*. London and New York: Routledge.
Bleiker, R. (2001). The Aesthetic Turn in International Political Theory. *Millennium*, 30(3), pp. 509–533.
Bleiker, R. (2014). Visual Assemblages: From Causality to Conditions of Possibility. In: M. Acuto and S. Curtis, eds., *Reassembling International Theory: Assemblage Thinking and International Relations*. Houndmills, Basingstoke & New York: Routledge.
Bleiker, R. (2018). *Visual Global Politics*. London: Routledge.
Bourbeau, P. ed., (2015). *Security: Dialogue Across Disciplines*. Cambridge: Cambridge University Press.
Bueger, C. (2016). Security as Practice. In: M. D. Cavelty and T. Balzacq, eds., *Routledge Handbook of Security Studies*, 2nd edn, Abingdon: Routledge, pp. 126–135.
Bueger, C. and Gadinger, F. (2014). *International Practice Theory: New Perspectives*. Basingstoke: Palgrave.
Buzan, B., Wæver, O., and Wilde, J. de. (1998). *Security: A New Framework for Analysis*. Boulder, CO: Lynne Rienner.
Campbell, D. (2003). Cultural Governance and Pictorial Resistance: Reflections on the Imaging of War. *Review of International Studies*, 29, pp. 57–73.
Campbell, D. (2004). Horrific Blindness: Images of Death in Contemporary Media. *Journal for Cultural Research*, 8(1), pp. 55–74.
Chouliaraki, L. (2006). *The Spectatorship of Suffering*. Thousand Oaks, CA: SAGE Publications.
Chouliaraki, L. (2013). *The Ironic Spectator: Solidarity in the Age of Post-Humanitarianism*. Cambridge/Malden, MA: Polity.
Davidshofer, S., Jeandesboz, J., and Ragazzi, F. (2017). Technology and Security Practices: Situating the Technological Imperative. In: T. Basaran, D. Bigo, E.-P. Guittet, and R. B. J. Walker, eds., *International Political Sociology: Transversal Lines*. Abingdon: Routledge, pp. 205–227.
Deibert, R. (1997). *Parchment, Printing, and Hypermedia: Communication in World Order Transformation*. New York: Columbia University Press.
Denov, M., Doucet, D., and Kamara, A. (2012). Engaging War Affected Youth through Photography: Photovoice with Former Child Soldiers in Sierra Leone. *Intervention*, 10(2), pp. 117–133.
Der Derian, J. (2009). *Virtuous War: Mapping the Military-Industrial-Media-Entertainment Network*, 2nd edn, New York: Routledge.
Der Derian, J. and Gara, P. (2009). *Virtous War*. www.youtube.com/watch?v=oqgxw911YMQ. [Accessed 5 April 2017].
Der Derian, J., Udris, M., and Udris, D. (2010). *Human Terrain*. Udris Film, Global Media Project, Oxyopia Films.
Derrida, J. (2002). *Writing and Difference*. Translated by A. Bass. Reprint. Chicago, IL: University of Chicago Press.
Finn, J. (2012). Seeing Surveillantly. Surveillance as a Social Practice. In: A. Doyle, R. Lippert, and D. Lyon, eds., *Eyes Everywhere: The Global Growth of Camera Surveillance*. London & New York: Routledge.
Florman, L. (2002). The Flattening of 'Collage'. *October*, 102(October), pp. 59–86.
Forsyth, I. (2014). The Practice and Poetics of Fieldwork: Hugh Cott and the Study of Camouflage. *Journal of Historical Geography*, 43, pp. 128–137.
Foucault, M. (2007). *The Order of Things: An Archaeology of the Human Sciences*. London: Routledge.

Gregory, D. (2010). Seeing Red: Baghdad and the Event-ful City. *Political Geography*, 29(5), pp. 266–279.

Guillaume, X., Andersen, R. S., and Vuori, J. A. (2016). Paint it Black: Colours and the Social Meaning of the Battlefield. *European Journal of International Relations*, 22(1), pp. 49–71.

Haggerty K. D. and Ericson R. V. (2006). *The New Politics of Surveillance and Visibility.* Toronto: University of Toronto Press.

Hansen, L. (2000). The Little Mermaid's Silent Security Dilemma and the Absence of Gender in the Copenhagen School. *Millennium: Journal of International Studies*, 29(2), pp. 285–306.

Hansen, L. (2011a). Theorizing the Image for Security Studies: Visual Securitization and the Muhammad Cartoon Crisis. *European Journal of International Relations*, 17(1), pp. 51–74.

Hansen, L. (2011b). The Politics of Securitization and the Muhammad Cartoon Crisis: A Post-structuralist Perspective. *Security Dialogue*, 42(4–5), pp. 357–369.

Hansen, L. (2016). Reading Comics for the Field of International Relations: Theory, Method and the Bosnian War. *European Journal of International Relations*, First On line.

Harris, C. (2006). The Omniscient Eye: Satellite Imagery, 'Battlespace Awareness' and the Structures of the Imperial Gaze. *Surveillance and Society*, 4(1–2), pp. 101–122.

Haw, K. and Hadfield, M. (2011). *Video in Social Science Research: Functions and Forms*. New York: Routledge.

Huysmans, J. (2006). *The Politics of Insecurity – Fear, Migration and Asylum in the EU.* London & New York: Routledge.

Huysmans, J. (2014). *Security Unbound: Enacting Democratic Limits*. Abingdon & New York: Routledge.

Jenkins, H. (2004). The Cultural Logic of Media Convergence. *International Journal of Cultural Studies*, 7(March), pp. 33–43.

Jewitt. C. ed. (2011). *The Routledge Handbook of Multimodal Analysis*. London & New York: Routledge.

Kress, G. (2010). *Multimodality: A Social Semiotic Approach to Contemporary Communication*. London & New York: Routledge.

Law, J. (2004). *After Method Mess in Social Science Research*. Abingdon/New York: Routledge.

Law, J. (2009). Actor Network Theory and Material Semiotics. In: B. S. Turner, ed., *The New Blackwell Companion to Social Theory*. Oxford: Wiley-Blackwell, pp. 141–158.

Lisle, D. (2011). The Surprising Detritus of Leisure: Encountering the Late Photography of War. *Environment and Planning D: Society and Space*, 29(5), pp. 873–890.

Lyon, D. (1994). *The Electronic Eye: The Rise of Surveillance Society*. Minneapolis, MN: University of Minnesota Press.

McCourt, D. M. (2016). Practice Theory and Relationalism as the New Constructivism. *International Studies Quarterly*, 60(3), pp. 475–485.

Mirzoeff, N. (2005). *Watching Babylon. The War in Iraq and Global Visual Culture*. New York & London: Routledge.

Mirzoeff, N. (2011). *The Right to Look : A Counterhistory of Visuality*. Durham, NC: Duke University Press.

Mitchell, C. (2011). *Doing Visual Research*. Los Angeles, CA/London: SAGE.

Mitchell, W. J. T. (1995). Interdisciplinarity and Visual Culture. *Art Bulletin*, 77(4), pp. 540–544.

Mitchell, W. J. T. (2011). *Cloning Terror: The War of Images, 9/11 to the Present.* Chicago, IL: The University of Chicago Press.

Moore, C. and Farrands, C. (2013). Visual Analysis. In: L. J. Shepherd, ed., *Critical Approaches to Security: An Introduction to Theories and Methods.* Abingdon: Routledge, pp. 221–235.

Möller, F. (2007). Photographic Interventions in Post-9/11 Security Policy. *Security Dialogue,* 38(2), pp. 179–196.

Möller, F. (2009). The Looking/Not Looking Dilemma. *Review of International Studies,* 35(4), pp. 781–794.

Möller, F. (2013). *Visual Peace: Images, Spectatorship, and the Politics of Violence.* New York: Palgrave Macmillan.

Pauwels, L. (2010). Visual Sociology Reframed: An Analytical Synthesis and Discussion of Visual Methods in Social and Cultural Research. *Sociological Methods & Research,* 38(4), pp. 545–581.

Pickering, A. (1995). *The Mangle of Practice: Time, Agency and Science.* Chicago, IL: University of Chicago Press.

Pink, S. (2013). *Doing Visual Ethnography.* 3rd edition. London: SAGE.

Pouliot, V. (2010). *International Security in Practice: The Politics of NATO-Russian Diplomacy.* Cambridge: Cambridge University Press.

Rajchman, J. (1991). *Philosophical Events: Essays of the 80s.* New York: Columbia University Press.

Rancière, J. (2004). *The Politics of Aesthetics: The Distribution of the Sensible.* London/ New York: Continuum.

Saugmann Andersen, R. (2012). The Battlefield of (In)Visibility. *Audiovisual Thinking: A Journal of Academic Videos* 4.www.audiovisualthinking.org/videos/issue04_the_battlefield_of_invisibility/. [Accessed 5 April 2017]

Schlag, G. and Heck, A. (2013). Securitizing Images: The Female Body and the War in Afghanistan. *European Journal of International Relations,* 19(4), pp. 891–913.

Schouten, P. (2014). Security as Controversy: Reassembling Security at Amsterdam Airport. *Security Dialogue,* 45(1), pp. 23–42.

Seib, P. (2008). *The Al Jazeera Effect: How the New Global Media Are Reshaping World Politics.* Washington, DC: Potomac Books.

Shapiro, M. J. (1988). *The Politics of Representation.* Madison, WI: University of Wisconsin Press.

Simon, S. (2012). Suspicious Encounters: Ordinary Preemption and the Securitization of Photography. *Security Dialogue,* 43(2), pp. 157–173.

Stahl, R. (2007). *Militainment, Inc.: Militarism and Popular Culture.* Documentary. Northampton, MA: Media Education Foundation.

Sylvester, C. (2007). Anatomy of a Footnote. *Security Dialogue,* 38(4), pp. 547–558.

Veeren, E. van. (2010). Captured by the Camera's Eye: Guantánamo and the Shifting Frame of the Global War on Terror. *Review of International Studies,* 37(4), pp. 1721–1749.

Weber, C. (2007). *I Am an American: Portraits of Post-9/11 US Citizens.* www.opendemocracy.net/article/i_am_an_American_portraits_of_post_9_11_us_citizens. [Accessed 5 April 2017].

Weber, C. (2008). Popular Visual Language as Global Communication: The Remediation of United Airlines Flight 93. *Review of International Studies,* 34(S1), pp. 137–153.

Weber, C. (2011). *I Am an American Filming the Fear of Difference.* Bristol and Chicago, IL: Intellect.

Vuori, J. A. (2010). A Timely Prophet? The Doomsday Clock as a Visualization of Securitization Moves with a Global Referent Object. *Security Dialogue*, 41(3), pp. 255–277.
Vuori J. A. (2013). Pictoral texts. In: M. B. Salter and C. E. Mutlu, eds., *Research Methods in Critical Security Studies: An Introduction*. New York: Routledge, pp. 199–202.

Part I
Visions of security technology/technological security vision

2 Scalia.warhead1
Securitization discourses in hacktivist video

Adam Fish

Introduction

The hacktivist collective Anonymous frames the fight for 'internet freedom' as a 'battle' to be won for universal human rights. Corroborating interviews and video analysis, this chapter investigates Operation Last Resort, a 2013 political project to avenge the death of internet activist Aaron Swartz. The video associated with Operation Last Resort features militarized images and includes universalizing speech acts about global existential threats. For example, The Operation Last Resort video makes a metaphor out of imagery of global thermonuclear war, thus framing internet freedom as globally threatened.

Anonymous is not a peaceful social movement, but does the military symbolism contradict their efforts in Operation Last Resort? As a leaderless collective, Anonymous does not have a central ideology but rather self-organizes for timely causes that range from resisting surveillance to rape culture – while at other times engaging in their own efforts in cyber-bullying and other trolling activity. This impulsive responsiveness makes it impossible to discuss a single 'Anonymous ideology'. But while lacking a consistent ideology outside of a somewhat vague 'internet freedom', many operations do have powerfully executed visions. For the video producers, hacktivists, and social media campaigners associated with Operation Last Resort there was an agreement about 'internet freedom' and related issues – the suicide of Aaron Swartz, the draconian sentence he faced because of the Computer Fraud and Abuse Act, and the intellectual property regime that led to his arrest. The actors in Operation Last Resort were convinced that the exercising of networked supported freedoms were at risk. This conviction manifested in the most intense images the editors could muster – images of war, warheads, and mortal explosions. Such imagery is not outside of the symbolic repertoire of Anonymous, which has included everything from the absurd to the terrifying as well as the profound. For example, videos produced by Anonymousworldwar3 to support operations supporting global revolution and #OperationPalestine are steeped in visuals of protesting individuals and heaving masses being violently repressed by militarized forces. The symbolism shared by virtually all Anonymous videos, the slogan 'We do not forgive, we do not forget, expect us', is itself aggressive and ominous.

These violent and menacing images, I would argue, are not contradictory. It is impossible for a decentralized social movement without a central ideology to be paradoxical, with few core ethics to violate. But if there is a core morality it is about freedoms online, which Anonymous defends vigorously, with every weapon at their disposal, including visions of certain death – a death mirrored in the suicide of Swartz, a defender of the only possible organizing principle: internet freedom. Yet, while it is erroneous to forgive Anonymous for using this violent imagery, it is also impossible to blame a leaderless living network peopled by names masked by pseudonyms. Individuals responsible for message continuity and ethicality are not to be found. Visually graphic threats to life create strong emotional responses and that is what we see in the video associated with Operation Last Resort.

With images of globally universal threats such as nuclear war, it is possible to read the video from Operation Last Resort as an example of macrosecuritization (Buzan and Wæver 2009) – a discourse that frames threats as universal and requiring rapid military responses. Anonymous's macrosecuritization discourse appears inclusive and cosmopolitan, hailing video viewers anywhere in the world to participate in activism. However, the use of militant macrosecuritization discourses in masked and ominous videos, I argue, creates not inclusion but exclusion. Furthermore, Anonymous uses macrosecuritization propaganda to inspire themselves and terrify their enemies, but in doing so they help to position the internet into the discursive framework of state militaries and cybersecurity experts. Not all within Anonymous agree that the use of military imagery is the optimal way of resisting the militarization of the internet. While it was dominated by a macrosecuritization discourse, a desecuritization process followed Operation Last Resort as former participants sought to counter the military macrosecuritization discourse with an online petition that rejected the military imagery. Desecuritization requires not discussing issues in terms of security but instead shifting the dialogue to agonistic politics (Buzan *et al.* 1998).

Introducing Anonymous

The politically active participants of Anonymous self-organize to conduct direct action and digital civil disobedient operations. Their communicative actions include hacks, distributed denial of service (DDOS) attacks, and propagandistic press releases and videos. Anonymous has since 2009 waged an online war with the Church of Scientology, supported WikiLeaks and Arab Spring activists, and hacked and released the emails of Sarah Palin, a US politician and former vice-presidential candidate, and military subcontractor HBGary. The values Anonymous defends – digital freedom of speech and association, cryptographic anonymity, etc. – are made possible because of the packet-switching and binary data capacities of the internet and computers. Anonymous translates these technological feature-sets into political values. Their organizational patterns mirror the decentralized internet itself. Like other cyberactivists and hacktivists before them, a defence of specific code, computer, and network practices is a defence of the means of their sociality and survival. For Anonymous the internet is a model of and for freedom; it is the means and the reason for liberty. It is an existential necessity that the internet remains (or regains) its decentralization, openness, and anonymity. They defend the qualities and freedoms for others too but because of the existential importance, Anonymous deploys polemic, militarizing, and universalizing discourses around the global battle for internet freedom. Using analysis of videos made by Anonymous and interviews with their authors, this chapter identifies and theorizes the implications of an activist discourse that securitizes (Buzan *et al.* 1998) the internet in terms of conflict and war.

Anonymous uses military language and imagery while describing themselves as horizontally formed and leaderless. Informants in my research describe their formation as a 'nomadic war machine' (Anonymousworldwar3) and their organization as a 'rhizome' or a 'hive mind' (see also Wiedemann 2014). While scholarship shows that centralized leadership does emerge in Anonymous, the task of describing the relative horizontality of Anonymous's organizational structure will not be examined in this chapter (Coleman 2014). Instead, I focus on 'Anonymous' as constituted by a shared visual and symbolic system with a specific securitizing discourse. This project of symbolic analysis is assisted by the works of Deseriis (2012), who describes Anonymous as an 'improper name' or a shared pseudonym and attendant set of symbols that enable collective identification and recognition. The Anonymous pseudonym empowers those without voice with an agency that emerges from outside institutionalized forms of power. This process results not in collectivities but 'co-dividual' and 'trans-individual' subjectivity characterized by multiplicity and fragmentation in its political projects (Deleuze and Guattari 1986: 16–27). Anyone who has tracked or participated in Anonymous operations will know the collective as a fractious multiplicity of individuals forgoing individualism.

'Anonymous' is a pseudonym anyone can adopt and provides the conditions for 'generativity, democracy, and instability' (Coleman 2010). That generativity is expressed in YouTube videos, where anyone can make or acquire from YouTube the general elements – an ominous soundtrack, one of several clips of an individual in a Guy Fawkes mask, a text-to-speech voice program – and produce an Anonymous video. And while the improper name and shared symbols create some cohesion they also produce a destabilizing multiplicity. This variety is exacerbated by the bewildering proliferation on YouTube of accounts mirroring or reproducing Anonymous videos of varied quality. Frenetically edited and populated with layered HTML5-based digital artefacts requesting participation and promising diversions, capable of disappearing at any moment because of deletion or a red flag campaign, the images are unstable and fragmented. This instability is a necessary result of anonymity advocated in Anonymous's approach to privacy. The fragmental nature of Anonymous and the fractionality inherent in 'improper names' provides challenges to Anonymous's universalizing and securitizing claims about the threats to 'internet freedom'. Furthermore, their militant and foreboding imagery about the present techno-dystopia works against their inclusive and universalizing discourse.

Securitization and macrosecuritization

Aaron Swartz was a computer prodigy. As an internet freedom activist, he believed in the necessity for data and research to be open and freely accessible. Frustrated with the gatekeeping and firewalling of academic scholarship by for-profit publishing houses, he wrote a script that downloaded millions of journal articles from JSTOR on a computer hidden in a closet of a library at MIT. He was caught, prosecuted, and faced potentially twenty years in prison. Instead of being incarcerated, Swartz, who suffered from depression, took his own life in his apartment in New York City on 11 January 2013. Both online and off, people grieved the loss of a passionate and articulate information activist.

In 2013, activists amassed under the improper name Anonymous, and initiated Operation Last Resort to avenge the death of Swartz, which they attributed to harassment and overzealous enforcement of outdated computer crime laws. Like all major Anonymous operations, Operation Last Resort was a visual spectacle, which included the hijacking of a MIT website to make a Swartz tribute, hacking and releasing the names and contact information for 4000 banking executives (Robertson 2013), and the usurping of the US Sentencing Commission website (ussc.gov), a website of the Department of Justice (Blue 2013). Most controversially, as part of Operation Last Resort, Anonymous claimed to have distributed encrypted government files pertaining to US Supreme Court Justices and threatened to release the decryption keys if the government did not reform the draconian laws that Anonymous believed had led to the death of Swartz. In press releases and videos, Anonymous called these decryption files 'warheads' and each referenced a US Supreme Court Justice, for example, 'Scalia. warhead1'. What are the implications of cyberactivism being framed in such explosive and military terms? The answer to this question depends upon who is receiving the security.

Security for a system administrator working for the Department of Justice is different from the way security is framed by Swartz or the hackers working under the Anonymous moniker who want to reform the Department of Justice. In the first case, security is about firewalling and encryption to protect the privacy and values associated with contacts, contracts, and finances. For the latter, security is something to be penetrated through SQL injections in activism for judicial reform, radical transparency, and accountability. Government computer scientists' technical discourse reveals a concern with building bugless and difficult-to-crack programs. The work of such computer scientists is to defend the interests of states and corporations. For Anonymous it is the state, judicial systems, information corporations, and their supportive cast of sysadmins who require anti-security measures. Security for Anonymous is living in a world of privacy, judicial equity, and governmental accountability. In the cases that this is not possible, rightful retaliations require the penetration of state informational security. Thus for Anonymous or the state, 'security' has variable referents (Nissenbaum 2005). Security is relative to who is securitizing. In light of the leaks of Edward Snowden about the suspicionless mass surveillance conducted by the

NSA and GCHQ it should be apparent that states and corporations are not the most responsible institutions to defend internet-based liberal freedoms. Before Snowden's revelations, Anonymous and Swartz were calling for greater awareness of the global state security apparatus. But in doing so, Anonymous used the very securitization discourse that emphasized military imagery their opponents used about *them*.

Securitization refers to the speech acts that interpret problems not as political but as security threats (Buzan *et al.* 1998; see also Sandor in this volume). Securitization positions contentious issues as best addressed through the defence, aggression, and containment approach of the security apparatus. Securitization militarizes positionalities with aggressive interventions. As speech acts, securitization is intimately intertwined with media systems. Thus, securitization is mediatization, which is defined by how issues formerly autonomous from media practices are prefigured as mediated actions (Couldry 2008). In the twenty-four-hour television and internet news cycle, for instance, political campaigns are impossible to disambiguate from their media performances, plannings, propaganda, and ambitious manipulations. Before the internet, a securitizing actor had to be in a position of authority, able to persuade political or economic elites of an imminent threat through private or mass mediated channels (Vuori 2010: 257). In order to successfully securitize an issue it was necessary to be interviewed on television or radio news, write an op-ed for a newspaper, or make a filmic documentary and inject the securitizing interpretation into the public sphere where it could gain traction. After the internet, securitization speech acts could be spoken and distributed, often accompanied by evocative visual and aural symbol systems, by individuals formerly without access to the means of mainstream media production. Obviously, access to internet production and broadband distribution does not automate successful securitization. The biased link structures of internet intermediaries such as search engines as well as the filtering algorithms of social media platforms create and affirm hierarchies of power and promotion online (Hindman 2009). Nevertheless, the internet provides an opportunity for more securitizing actors. But this does not mean that securitization by visual means is more accurate – only more proliferated. With the so-called media democratization of citizen journalism, a news cycle geared towards sensational fearmongering, and actual instabilities caused by global warming, political revolution, and economic crises, we are awash with securitization. A hegemonic media culture of short clips, soundbites, and ephemeral Snapchat videos distributes abbreviated and often sensationalistic visual signs. Anonymous is particularly literate in these regards, framing threats to liberties online in securitizing terms on a scale more global than previous securitization discourses articulating meso-level threats to the state.

Networked securitization videos may propagate by means of viral replication, or what I call 'mirroring', wherein Anonymous supports download and reupload and thereby propagates versions of Anonymous videos (Fish 2016). Others in the emergent freedom of information movement (Beyer 2014) practice mirroring as well. The Pirate Bay (TPB) is mirrored from sites like baymirror.com and piratebaymirror.com to connect users with servers located wherever they can avoid prosecution. WikiLeaks mirrors its leaked content in protected jurisdictions in eleven countries (Wikileaks.info). Mirrors are a result of the copy and paste functionality of computers and the distribution scale of the network of networks. Mirroring is not static but pseudoanonymous, ephemeral, and nodal occurrence. Mirrors enable Anonymous to explore the 'possibilities of viralization' as THXi330, an Anonymous videomirror producer wrote to me. Mirroring is an entangled practice, both 'an offensive maneuver in a propaganda campaign and a defensive maneuver to remain visible in a contested and privatized networked public sphere' (Fish 2016). Mirroring as well as other new media practices afford to actors novel paths to the propagation of securitization discourses.

Using grand, vague, polemic, and militarizing speech acts, Anonymous securitizes the internet. While the referent for securitization is the internet, this indigenous securitization constellates around the discourse of 'internet freedom', which Anonymous sees as a universal human right threatened by corporations and government surveillance. Anonymous's audience is any internet video and television news viewer who sees their videos and propaganda projects. Collectively, their videos have received over 100 million views and have been rebroadcast on major international television networks around the world. In their view, binary and packet-switching technologies are capable of promoting equity through border-transcending communication and are threatened by government and corporate surveillance under the auspices of national security and free services. The enemy of internet freedom fighters consists of the nebulous nexus of information imperialists and unscrupulous Silicon Valley firms linked in a corporatocracy. Internet freedom fighter on the one hand and informational corporatocracy on the other generate a securitization constellation where each constructs the other as the central threat (Buzan and Wæver 2009: 259).

Securitizations require vague floating signifiers like the 'internet' and 'freedom' (Levi-Strauss 1950; Barthes 1957). The two terms co-constitute and reinforce each other without referencing a more material 'transcendent signified' (Derrida 1976: 20; 1978: 278–280). Anonymous has a co-constituting Other, the pan-state cybersecurity apparatus, which it fundamentally opposes through its exploitation of the floating signification of 'internet freedom'. Securitization is one discursive strategy in what participants see as a 'battle' for the 'future' of 'freedom', the 'internet', 'democracy', and other empty but nevertheless meaningful signifiers. Despite being an improper name referring to anyone in a subjective state of pseudoanonymity, Anonymous as a signifier is more material than 'internet freedom'. Communicating in an evocative and excessive manner in a multisensorial medium, video is central to the securitization practices of Anonymous. Video is one component of a hacktivist toolkit that includes politically motivated cracking of state and corporate secrets, supporting whistleblowers, conducting journalistic investigations, and others. These efforts are on behalf of internet freedom, a broadly universal securitization discourse or more precisely a macrosecuritization discourse (Buzan and Wæver 2009).

While securitization refers to securitization discourses with a meso-level referent, such as threats to the nation, macrosecuritization refers to macro-order securitization processes. Macrosecuritizations are defined by securitizing actors performing universalizing speech acts about global existential threats for potentially receptive audiences (Buzan and Wæver 2009). Anonymous's securitization move has a global referent in the internet, and gathers in other securitization discourses, and thus is an example of macrosecuritization. The Cold War, climate change, and the War on Terror – issues that can potentially affect all of humanity – are examples of large-scale macrosecuritization discourses. The macrosecuritization of internet freedom absorbs lower order informational securitizations such as privacy, surveillance, freedom of speech, freedom of assembly, social commodification, rights to the digital commons, national cybersecurity, malware, viruses, etc.

On the one hand, securitization describes the discourses that frame problems on a meso-level in terms of national security. Examples of informational securitization are nations like Iceland, Brazil, or Germany framing the defence of their informational sovereignty, post-Snowden, in nationalistic terms. Macrosecuritization, on the other hand, is a meta-discourse that transcends the meso-level discourses of the nation state by presenting threats as solvable only though transnational interventions. An internet-centric example of macrosecuritization discourse was US Secretary of State Hillary Clinton's 2011 speech on 'internet freedom', a discourse that macrosecuritizes and universalizes a technoliberal vision of the central role of communication technologies within democracies. 'Freedom', 'democracy', and, increasingly the 'internet' are words that summon audiences into macrosecuritization assemblages. Anonymous embeds these terms and their threats into globally networked semiotics systems.

As either 'hackers on steroids' as Fox News called Anonymous, or noble vigilantes fighting against neoliberal informationalism, Anonymous frames the fight for the internet in terms that securitize the debate, as a 'battle' to be won for universal human rights. Anonymous's version is not an exclusive universalism that claims moral superiority and the right to violently intervene. Their inclusive universalism claims that internet freedom is not only more a human right than an absolute wrong but is moreover a negative liberty endogamous to all. Inclusive universalisms like internet freedom link to 'existing order universalism' by claiming that the institution of the globally free and open internet is threatened by government and corporate powers (Buzan and Wæver 2009: 261). Existing order and inclusive universalisms are marks of cosmopolitanism as opposed to the communitarianism associated with exclusive universalisms that emphasize difference. Anonymous, however, is an improper name whose graphic symbolism, technical competencies, and macrosecuritizing discourses are less inclusive and more communitarian than some Anonymous supporters and journalists admit. While some videos do indeed 'go viral', the Anonymous video in question is collectively created, visually intense, and fails to follow traditional storytelling forms – and therefore has a poor chance of developing a robust audience and succeeding in universalizing their macrosecuritization.

In most ways, Anonymous's discourse is inclusive cosmopolitanism, hailing any internet video viewer anywhere in the world to participate in information activism. The use of militant macrosecuritization discourses in masked and ominous videos, I argue, creates not inclusion but exclusion. Anonymous is not the decentralized and leaderless 'rhizome' it is often described as being by itself and journalists. Centralized and individualized power accrues to managers of private IRC chatrooms and Anonymous servers. Discussion and planning of highly technical actions like hacking and cracking happen in private IRC chatrooms and are not open nor subject to democratic participation and deliberation. Despite the rhetoric of cosmopolitanism, inclusion, and universalism, Anonymous's militant macrosecuritization discourse, paired with its private planning, exhibit communitarianism and the visual symbolism of exclusion. As opposed to hacking and cracking, video production is a more inclusive practice; anyone can make an Anonymous video. More prominent and sophisticated videos directly linked to operations are usually produced by more experienced Anonymous editors competent with IRC and video production software. The semi-inclusiveness of this production practice is tempered by Anonymous's symbolism and the militant and polemical rhetoric that attracts small and rabid groups and not inclusive majorities.

As I will describe below, Anonymous appropriates macrosecuritizing tropes of war and battle. It is in their very monikers. For example, a key informant's YouTube pseudonym is Anonymousworldwar3. Another, THXi330, says, 'My anon vids are one face of this vehicles/weapons/bulletproof defense to make a dialogue with the "real" world.' Anonymousworldwar3 describes Anonymous 'as an instance of the "nomadic war-machine" as developed by Deleuze and Guattari within this rhizomatic context.' They continue to say: 'What we need is a large "army" of scientists telling the "old world" what the future could be/is most likely to look like, thereby making it happen in the long run.' The framing of internet freedom within a macrosecuritization discourse, however, may work against the goals of Anonymous. Despite their bravado, Anonymous does not have the capacities to enact a successful cyberwar against the state for their version of internet freedom. But, then again, they are leaderless, so there exists little accountability for contributing to a cyberwar discourse.

In fact, their macrosecuritization of the internet may have the opposite effect of preserving what remains of the open, decentralized, and encrypted services on the internet. Anonymous's ominous symbols of cackling white masks, cyborg voices, and rocketing warheads can be used by those with actual political, economic, and infrastructural power over the governance of the internet to persecute Anonymous while defending the expansion of their closed and centralized powers. The number of hackers presently incarcerated or in court is testament to the statutory pursuit of these actors (Fish and Follis 2015). Anonymous's macrosecuritization of internet freedom would be met and defeated by a more powerful macrosecuritization rival – the state and para-state security apparatus. Indeed, to fight this system a more nomadic war-machine is needed.

Methods

Using social media, I have tracked Anonymous since 2009 when they first gained public attention because of their protests against the Church of Scientology. Like a lot of people, I have watched hundreds of videos of all genres, lengths, and technical skill. I sent a questionnaire to a list of eighty highly active Anonymous YouTube producers. Fourteen responded and I conducted follow-up interviews with several. Of these, one key informant, THXi330, has made seven videos that have been viewed over 283,500 times. These project participants are indicative of the small population of competent Anonymous YouTube producers capable of visually evocative and political video production.

I corroborate my interview data from these and other informants with a textual analysis of Operation Last Resort as well as the video that shares that name. The video was uploaded on a YouTube account called Aarons ArkAngel, a reference to information activist and martyr Aaron Swartz. Anonymous YouTube producer Aarons ArkAngel made two videos that have received over 1,614,000 views. I selected Operation Last Resort because it is expressive of a militaristic language indicative of macrosecuritization discourse within Anonymous. Operation Last Resort is symptomatic of macrosecuritization but it is not indicative of all Anonymous videos. Operation Last Resort is considered controversial by many within Anonymous. The controversy reveals the fragmentation and communitarianism of Anonymous, which conflicts with their inclusive macrosecuritizing discourse.

Operation last resort

On 25 January 2013 visitors to the United States Sentencing Commission website, ussc.gov, were not greeted by the droll and bureaucratic website but instead witnessed a ten-minute video framed in black and green text decrying the abuse of judicial overreach. Two days later @OpLastResort tweeted a video game cheat code – a sequence of buttons to get secret powers – claiming that they had transformed ussc.gov into a video game 'in which the visitor could control a missile-enabled Nyan Cat and shoot chunks of text off the government page' (Figure 2.1) (Brad 2013). With antagonistic language, CGI military footage, and a globalizing gaze onto the earth from a missile in outer space (see also Shapiro, and Cardullo and Stevens in this volume), Aarons ArkAngels' video accompanying this disruption, Anonymous Operation Last Resort, epitomizes macrosecuritization visual culture and technological vision.

The video begins with a scene from *War Games*, the 1980s movie about a young hacker who hacked into the North American Aerospace Defense Command (NORAD) and began a global thermal war when he thought he was playing a video game. Over a military simulation video of a tank in a desert location aiming a battery of missiles, the Anonymous narrator in a dark computerized British accent claims to have 'armed' warhead 'US-DOJ-LEA-2013.aes256'. The voice asserts to 'have enough fissile material for multiple warheads. Today we are

32 Adam Fish

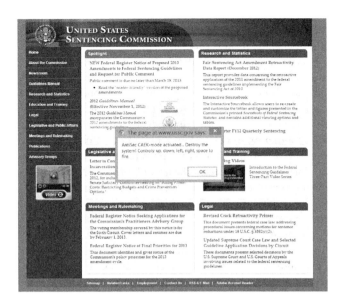

Figure 2.1 US Sentencing Commission Website transformed into a video game (screen capture by Adam Fish).

launching the first of these. Operation Last Resort has begun …' They threaten to release 'fissile' and 'warhead' files that contain sensitive information on individuals in the Justice Department. Publicizing a list of alleged encryption keys to the so-called 'warhead files', Anonymous used the Twitter hashtag #warhead1 for Twitterers to follow. The last three minutes of the nine-minute video features a clip edited for continuity of a realist CGI animation of the launching of a nuclear warhead into space while the narrator says: 'If we are forced to reveal the trigger key to this warhead, we understand there will be collateral damage' before continuing with a list of demands that will prevent the firing of the warhead, including judicial reform in the wake of the death of Swartz. The voice continues within a discourse of informational macrosecuritization: 'Furthermore there must be a solemn commitment to the freedom of the internet, this last great common space of humanity, and to the common ownership of information for the common good.' As the warhead disengages from its rocket engines and swivels to turn and point back at Earth a Howard Zinn quote appears – 'Protest beyond the law is not a departure from democracy; it is absolutely essential to it' – on the right of the screen, while the left features the words 'We do not forgive, we do not forget, expect us' rotating around the headless Anonymous logo superimposed on a globe (Figure 2.2). As the missile rockets to the Earth, the narrator intones in an absolutist fashion: 'We do not expect to be negotiated with, we understand that due to the actions we take we exclude ourselves from the system within which solutions are found.' The warhead re-enters Earth's atmosphere and detonates over an oceanic

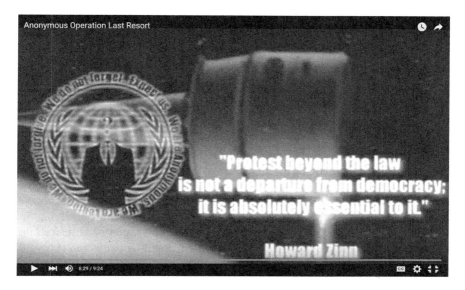

Figure 2.2 Still from Anonymous Operation Last Resort featuring Zinn quote (screen capture by Adam Fish).

target, and the video ends in a bright flash of white with the narrator threatening, 'There will be change or there will be chaos.'

Visual, text, and speech acts of macrosecuritization are numerous in this ten-minute video. These include signs of globalization, such as the Earth, and its universal threats, such as nuclear war. In this video, Anonymous, its decryption keys and 'warhead' files, are represented by this nuclear warhead that threatens the globe. The Earth, then, from the producer's perspective, would be the judicial system needing reform, through violence if necessary. Seeing that nuclear holocaust would negatively impact all life on Earth, casting the enemies to internet freedom and judicial reform in the Earth's role leaves little room for non-guilty Earth inhabitants. The paradox of using globe-destroying weapons to achieve local solutions is the result of absolutist macrosecuritizations that posit inclusive universality but are in actuality exclusive. This mixed metaphor fragments an audience that reflects the divisions within Anonymous and shows the communitarian complications for their cosmopolitanism.

In the end, the so-called warhead files were neither the keys to actual nuclear warheads nor incriminating documents. Like the movie *War Games*, war had not actually been waged but rather the language had been used to make a political point. This example of macrosecuritization mixes iconography of space, technology, and nuclear war with a defiant narrative claiming to be beyond the law. Like the missile in the video, Anonymous and the internet are above nation-state jurisdictions. The importance of the fight for internet freedom makes the seriousness of war necessary. In this battle, war is a metaphor and in metaphorizing internet rights in terms of war the internet is macrosecuritized.

This video is an example of what Anonymous calls 'PR', public relations, or 'propaganda':

> So the video is basically the main part of Anon's PR work and the main medium to influence public opinion and thus politics. So basically, video is the most important and efficient medium for propaganda out there, hence we try to use it as extensively and good as we can,

said Anonymousworldwar3. Video is conceptualized as the 'public relations' division of larger operations. To speak to Anonymous videos in terms of macrosecuritization, the concept of propaganda is useful. Propaganda is the media materialization and visual modality of securitization.

Early theories of propaganda securitized the discourse of messaging in wartime by discussing propaganda as a psychological weapon used to weaken the mental stamina of an enemy while encouraging domestic patriotism (Laswell 1927; Doob 1935). Utilizing securitization discourse, Doob (1935) described propaganda in terms of 'guns' and 'ammunition'. Lee and Lee (1939) explained propaganda as using: card stacking, or binary or fundamentalist arguments, and bandwagon techniques, or the use of inclusive 'glittering generalities' to imply general support (as cited in Curnalia 2005: 243). Like Anonymous's use of 'warhead' lingo, propaganda speaks in connotative as opposed to denotative terms. Later media effects theorists such as Ellul (1965) believed that propaganda sought to create uncritical objects incapable or unwilling to critically consider the information being offered.

The militant language used in the videos, the images of war and violent protest, the desire to frighten foes and inspire friends, make Anonymous videos suitable examples of early theories of propaganda. But while Anonymous videos are propaganda, they do not, as Ellul (1965) contends, seek to produce zombie objects but rather critically self-aware subjects. For Anonymous, propaganda does not begin, as Snow says, when 'critical thinking ends' (2003: 22). Unlike Ellul's concept of propaganda, Anonymous is like Soviet filmmaker Sergei Eisenstein who designed his moving pictures to produce an 'awakening which puts the spectator's emotional and intellectual activity into operation to the maximum degree' (Aumont 1987: 59). These videos are forms of 'political mimesis' that seek to move the bodies of the viewers to action (Fish 2016; Gaines 1999). Anonymous is not a hegemonic but rather a counter- or anti-hegemonic movement for radical as opposed to incremental change.

Desecuritization

The absolutism and militancy of the macrosecuritization discourse of Anonymous in general and Operation Last Resort in particular instigated a desecuritization discourse within some factions of Anonymous. Desecuritization refers to attempts to reframe the referent outside of a securitization discourse (Buzan *et al.* 1998). The desecuritization discourse was evident on a change.org petition that received 120 signatures. The petition claimed that Operation Last Resort

> breaks the basic core ideals of anonymous. Not to mention has signs of a complete fraudulent false flag perpetrated by the very people holding us back. We are not condemning those participating, only distancing ourselves from the message of this operation which goes too far.
>
> (Falzone nd)

The petition's author continued:

> The metaphorical speaking style in this video release is not clear to average mainstream TV audience. For them, we are now criminals. They see threats, claims that we will not negotiate, and metaphors with military equipment and apocalyptic wargames [*sic*].

Falzone and the signers of his petition broke with what cosmopolitanism existed within Anonymous. These moves enabled a challenge to the macrosecuritizing discourse of Operation Last Resort. In the end, Operation Last Resort was a successful crack and release of the names of 4,000 bankers and the takeover of a government website but it failed to institutionalize the macrosecuritization of the internet because of the exclusive macrosecuritization visualities it deployed.

Once demilitarized systems like the internet are remilitarized how will demilitarization again be achieved? Situated by the securitization rhetoric of militarization, the internet can be discursively controlled by those whose singular focus is state military. While at times Anonymous fashions itself as a 'nomadic war machine' they will likely be defeated in military combat by state defence administrators and their subcontractors who have multiple billion-dollar budgets and secret jurisprudence defending their operations. Anonymous uses macrosecuritization propaganda to inspire themselves and terrify their enemies, but in doing so they help to position the internet into the discursive framework of state militaries and cybersecurity experts. Desecuritization requires not discussing issues in terms of security but instead shifting the dialogue to agonistic politics (Wæver in Vuori 2010: fn 6, 258). In a limited manner, the petition above attempts this desecuritization.

Macrosecuritization is political but also existential for Anonymous and others whose very sociality depends upon the implementation of certain interpretations of the internet as being open and decentralized. For Anonymous, informational macrosecuritization makes sense because liberalized informational infrastructures are constitutively necessary for the very survival of those making the speech acts. Desecuritization valorizes peace and compromise, assuming that securitization is an unnecessary move. In critical situations, agonistic debate adopts conflictual intonations, particularly if decisions impact the survival of sociality. Militancy, in some instances, is needed.

Macrosecuritization discourse is evident in Anonymous videos such as Anonymous Operation Last Resort but some Anonymous supporters recognize that the militarization rhetoric is counter-productive. For example, THXi330 puts 'war' in scare quotes in a written interview, and says that what is needed instead are 'new effective strategies'. They say

> Just now Anonymous in Spain are planning a "war" against this mad order. Lulz is end in Spain, and we need bring it back to make a real revolution, but not by the way of weapons (is impossible and no admissible), au contraire, we need think new effective strategies [*sic*].

A close reading of their videos shows that Anonymous acquires mainstream media attention from these vivid videos and the dark iconography of war and espionage. But the nuanced, reflexive, unmasked 'human face' of Anonymous is not present in the videos, as such pragmatic moves would not likely garner media attention. The 'lulz' of ironic reflexivity and playful engagement would defuse the warhead rhetoric of macrosecuritization. In this way, as scholars we need not fall into a reciprocal securitization of our own devising. By taking the securitizing visual cues too seriously, we forget the importance of play, irony, and the lulz in theory and Anonymous.

The mobilization of the critical infrastructure of the internet for revolutionary social movements may not require macrosecuritization. Perhaps the use of metaphors more attuned to the material and afforded specifics of the internet as an informational and networked system would be more befitting. As Hardt and Negri claim (2000), within the systems of socially extractive communicative capitalism exists the power for revolutionary reversal. But first a revolutionary language not repurposing colonized metaphors but rather radicalizing emergent properties needs to be written. In their hacks and video mirroring practices, Anonymous has innovated a number of infrastructurally specific resistance practices. Now they need to turn their attention to hacking not only networks but visual language itself.

References

Aumont, J. (1987). *Montage Eisenstein*. London: BFI.
Barthes, R. (1957). *Mythologies*. New York: Hill & Wang.
Beyer, J. (2014). The Emergence of a Freedom of Information Movement: Anonymous, Wikileaks, the Pirate Bay and Iceland. *Journal of Computer-Mediated Communication*, 19(2), pp. 141–154.
Blue, V. (2013). Anonymous Hacks US Sentencing Commission, Distributes Files. ZDnet. www.zdnet.com/article/anonymous-hacks-us-sentencing-commission-distributesfiles/ [Accessed 5 April 2017].
Brad. (2013). Operation Last Resort. Know Your Meme. http://knowyourmeme.com/memes/events/operation-last-resort#fn46 [Accessed 5 April 2017]
Buzan, B. and Wæver, O. (2009). Macrosecuritization and Security Constellations: Reconsidering Scale in Securitization Theory. *Review of International Studies*, 35(2), pp. 253–276.

Buzan, B., Wæver, O., and Wilde, J. de. (1998). *Security: A New Framework for Analysis*. Boulder, CO: Lynne Rienner.
Coleman, G. (2014). *Hacker, Hoaxer, Whistleblower, Spy: The Many Faces of Anonymous*. London: Verso.
Coleman, G. (2010). The Aesthetic Face(s) of Anonymous, Savage Minds, http://savageminds.org/2010/12/15/aesthetic-face-of-anonymou/ [Accessed 5 April 2017].
Couldry, N. (2008). Mediatization or Mediation? Alternative Understandings of the Emergent Space of Digital Storytelling. *New Media & Society*, 10(3). pp. 373–392.
Curnalia, R. (2005). A Retrospective on Early Studies of Propaganda and Suggestions for Reviving the Paradigm. *The Review of Communication*, 5(4), pp. 237–257.
Deleuze, G. and Guattari F. (1986). *Kafka: Toward a Minor Literature*. Translated by D. Polan. Minneapolis, MI: University of Minnesota Press.
Derrida, J. (1976). *Of Grammatology*. Baltimore, MD: Johns Hopkins University Press.
Derrida, J. (1978). *Writing and Difference*. London: Routledge & Kegan Paul.
Deseriis, M. (2012). Improper Names: Collective Pseudonyms and Multiple-Use Names as Minor Processes of Subjectivation. *Subjectivity*, 5(1), pp. 140–160.
Doob, L. (1935). *Propaganda: Their Psychology and Techniques*. New York: Holt and Company.
Ellul, J. (1965). *Propaganda: The Formation of Men's Attitudes*. New York: Vintage.
Falzone, J. (nd). Cease Operations in the Name of Anonymous Ideals. Change.org. www.change.org/p/anonymous-operation-last-resort-cease-operations-in-the-name-of-anonymous-ideals [Accessed 5 April 2017].
Fish, A. (2016). Mirroring the Videos of Anonymous: Cloud Activism, Living Networks, and Political Mimesis. *The Fibreculture Journal*, 26(191), pp. 85–107.
Fish, A. and Follis L. (2015). Edgework, State Power, and Hacktivism. *Hau: Journal of Ethnographic Theory*, 5(2), pp. 383–390. www.haujournal.org/index.php/hau/article/view/hau5.2.022 [Accessed 5 April 2017].
Gaines, J. M. (1999). Political Mimesis. In: J. M. Gaines and M. Renov, eds., *Collecting Visible Evidence*. Minneapolis, MI: University of Minnesota Press.
Hardt, M. and Negri, A. (2000). *Empire*. Cambridge, MA: Harvard University Press.
Hindman, M. (2009). *The Myth of the Digital Divide*. Princeton, NJ: Princeton University Press.
Lasswell, H. (1927). The Theory of Political Propaganda. *The American Political Science Review*, 21(3), pp. 627–631.
Lee, A. and Lee E. (1939). *The Fine Art of Propaganda*. New York: Harcourt Brace.
Lévi-Strauss, C. (1950). Introduction à l'oeuvre de Marcel Mauss. In: M. Mauss, *Sociologie et Anthropologie*, Paris: Les Presses universitaires de France.
Nissenbaum, H. (2005). Where Computer Security Meets National Security. *Ethics and Information Technology*, 7(2), pp. 61–73.
Robertson, A. (2013). Anonymous Posts Banking Industrial Data Dump in Ongoing Aaron Swartz Protest. The Verge. www.theverge.com/2013/2/4/3950732/anonymous-posts-banking-industry-details-in-aaron-swartz-protest [Accessed 5 April 2017].
Snow, N. (2003). *Information War: American Propaganda, Free Speech and Opinion Control Since 9–11*. New York: Seven Stories Press.
Vuori, J. A. (2010). A Timely Prophet? The Doomsday Clock as a Visualisation of Securitisation Moves with a Global Referent Object. *Security Dialogue*, 41(3), pp. 255–277.
Wiedemann, C. (2014). Between Swarm, Network, and Multitude: Anonymous and the Infrastructures of the Common. *Distinktion: Scandinavian Journal of Social Theory*, 15(3), pp. 309–326.
Wikileaks.info. Mirrors (nd), http://wikileaks.info/

3 The gaze, the drone *dispositif*, and necro-biographies
A brief conceptual intervention[1]

Michael J. Shapiro

The gaze: Lacanian and Foucauldian versions

In his lectures, *The Four Fundamental Concepts of Psycho-Analysis*, Jacques Lacan famously distinguishes the eye and the gaze (1979: 67–78). Articulating the gaze in psychological discourse and focusing on its return, Lacan sees it as something traumatic for subjects, a sense of being seen that disrupts the scopic field in a way that undermines their confidence in being in control of perceptions. As he characterizes it, the gaze is

> that which performs like a phantom force.... In our relation to things, in so far as this relation is constituted by the way of vision, and ordered in the figures of representation, something slips, passes, is transmitted, from stage to stage, and is always to some degree eluded in it – that is what we call the gaze.
>
> (73)

Lacan tells a story about the emergence of his idea of the gaze as psychically disruptive:

> I was in my early twenties ... and at the time, of course, being a young intellectual, I wanted desperately to get away, see something different, throw myself into something practical.... One day, I was on a small boat with a few people from a family of fishermen ... as we were waiting for the moment to pull in the nets, an individual known as Petit-Jean ... pointed out to me something floating on the surface of the waves. It was a small can, a sardine can.... It glittered in the sun. And Petit-Jean said to me – *You see that can? Do you see it? Well it doesn't see you!*

Petit-Jean's remark prompted Lacan to reflect on the potential return of the gaze, which he saw as something alienating subjects from themselves by causing them to see themselves as objects of the gaze of others, thereby rendering the field of vision traumatic (89). What is experienced is a sense of a returned gaze that does not coincide with the place from which the subject sees (103). The resulting trauma for the subject, induced by the recognition that it is not an autonomous agent but is rather caught up in a decentred scopic field, is represented in exemplary moments in Kathryn Bigelow's film *The Hurt Locker* (2008). The invading US soldiers in Iraq in her film manifest disorientation when they sense that – as a harried and ill-at-ease Sergeant J. T. Sanborn (Anthony Mackie) exclaims – there are lots of eyes on them. Sanborn and the others in his patrol are effectively relays of the military gaze who are unprepared for its return.

Within a Lacanian frame, the return of the gaze by Iraqis renders the soldiers less sutured to the weapons they use and thus less certain to implement the targeting directed by the military apparatus. However, to complete the way in which the Iraqi civilian as image functions for US soldiers within eye-shot, we have to heed another register within which the militarized gaze is deployed – Michel Foucault's rendering of the gaze, which is elaborated in his investigation of the 'medical gaze'. For Foucault, the medical gaze is not merely the doctor's look. Rather, it locates the patient/subject (the target of the gaze) in an epistemological field associated with a new form of governance. When the hospital (or 'clinic') became a concrete institutionalization of the state's concern with public health, the patient became a source of knowledge to be used rather than simply a client seeking to be cured. The patient became but a series of signs whose deciphering would provide for the management of the health of the population as a whole, and medicine had become 'a task for the nation' (whereas prior to the development of the teaching hospital, medicine was about an individual healing relationship between doctor and patient (Foucault 1973)). As the medical gaze displaced the healer's look, the patient was displaced by the 'population'. No longer an object of a healing look, she/he had become an object of knowledge to be interpreted within a complex health *dispositif*, which included government bureaucracies, health professions, scientific discourses, apparatuses of data collection and patient management, accounting procedures, and so on.

Crucially, Foucault's version of the gaze changes the problematic of vision from individuals to collectives (see also Cardullo and Stevens in this volume). For example, surrounding the medical gaze is an apparatus (*dispositif*), which Foucault describes as a complex ensemble of discourses, and agencies of implementation: 'a thoroughly heterogeneous ensemble consisting of discourses, institutions, architectural forms, regulatory decisions, laws, administrative measures, scientific statements, philosophical, moral and philanthropic propositions ... the said as much as the unsaid ... the elements of the apparatus' (1977: 194). Thus for example, parts of the public health *dispositif* that developed in the nineteenth century were accounting practices inasmuch as a major condition of possibility for a medicine applied to populations was the development of probability theory. To articulate accounting practices with medical services, non-medical personages were added to the health *dispositif*, supplementing other new agents, for example, policing authorities whose roles became important once the control of contagion had become an issue.

Similarly, what has occurred in the evolution of the military's war *dispositif* – its network of decision-making and implementing agencies, along with the discourses and technologies of militarization that sustain them – is the addition of a complex array of 'contactors' who operate on the fringes of the military's *dispositif*. (The writer Don DeLillo anticipated that complexity in his novel *White Noise* (1985) when he invented characters he designated as 'food stylists for NASA').

Both the Lacanian and Foucauldian accounts of the gaze – treating the disruption from the returned gaze and the collective resonances that result within the military *dispositif* through which the gaze is articulated respectively – apply to contemporary security practices, most notably as those practices are reflected in the 'manhunts' (Chamayou 2012) that characterize the current mobile topography of US warfare. To articulate the two, I begin with an analysis of the first episode in Season Four of the Showtime television series *Homeland* (2014), 'The Drone Queen'. Promoted to the level of 'Station Chief' in Kabul, Carrie Mathison (Claire Danes) gets a call from Sandy Bachman (Corey Stoll), her Islamabad counterpart, that a 'high value target', a leading Taliban insurgent, has been seen in the tribal area of Pakistan. Being assured that the 'intel' is solid, she directs a couple of F-15 fighter jets to bomb the target. As Carrie, her colleagues in the control room, and the viewers, are watching through the feed of a drone, the targeted building is destroyed. Shortly thereafter, the 'intel' turns out to have been flawed. Carrie and her staff learn from a news report that she has called in bombs on a wedding party and killed forty civilians.

When they send the drone back to give them a view of the site of the bombing, they see a lone survivor, a young medical student, Aayan Ibrahim (Suraj Sharma), looking up at the drone, returning their gaze. After they fret about who he might be and the implications of his having witnessed the atrocity, things get worse. His smart phone camera has footage of the wedding party, which goes viral when Aayan's politically zealous roommate sends the footage (which includes the bride and little girls dancing) to YouTube. To make matters worse for the 'Drone Queen' and the violence-delivering *dispositif* within which she works, Sandy, who sent the 'intel', is grabbed from a car he's riding in with Carrie and her assistant, the Black Ops specialist, Peter Quinn (Rupert Friend). Having been identified by an angry mob seeking revenge for the atrocity – informed and choreographed by undercover personnel in Pakistan's intelligence service (ISI) – he's kicked to death by the mob. Quinn prevents Carrie from trying to intervene and drives away to escape a similar fate. The consequences of the rash decision to blow up a building with civilians, and the inability to save Sandy, shakes up the extended security apparatus (*dispositif*) within which 'antiterrorist' weapons function.

As I have noted elsewhere,

> a weapon, aside from its operation as part of the killing operations of a fighting force, is a complex design and commodity that emerges from extensive interactions among political, commercial and knowledge agencies, all involved in the larger (media-propagated) motivations associated with

global structures of enmity and national structures of career advancement and prestige.

(Shapiro 2015: 81)

After the bombing fiasco it becomes evident that there is a crucial temporality structuring the weapons *dispositif*, taking it beyond its emergence to the vagaries of its use. Those who are part of the decision process through which the weapons are used are always already in the future, justifying the decisions.

An appreciation of that aspect of decision complexes was rendered effectively in the methodological investigations of Harold Garfinkel. In the inquiries in his *Studies in Ethnomethodology*, Garfinkel's ethnographic subjects (e.g. jurors deciding guilt or innocence and bureaucrats classifying suicides) are always already in a future scene of justification. In his words, 'Decisions [have] an unavoidable futurity' (Garfinkel 1991: 16).

The presence of the witness, Aayan, bears on the CIA personnel's 'futurity.' What he has seen is threatening to the careers, and in some cases, the sheer survival of people in all the levels of the US security *dispositif*, as well as those in oppositional apparatuses (Pakistan's ISI and the Taliban insurgent structure). Aayan is attacked and threatened by hired thugs from the ISI who warn him to no longer speak about the incident (he had been cornered and interviewed on television); he's taken in by Carrie and lured into sexual intimacy so she can extract information about the CIA's target, Aayan's uncle, Haissam Haqqani (Numar Acar), who turns out to be still alive; and when he goes into the mountains to bring medicine to his uncle, his uncle kisses his cheek and then shoots him because the drone circling overhead is there because Aayan has led it there, having been gulled into admitting that his uncle is alive. As it turns out, Aayan's return of the gaze incites all the relevant apparatuses to respond, giving us a view of all the networks involved in the post 9/11 'War on Terror', articulated especially as what sociologists have deemed 'moral careers'.

Added to the complex agencies surrounding the incident is the situation of Saul Berenson (Mandy Patinkin), the former station chief who now works for a private security firm. While helping Carrie, he's abducted by ISI agents and turned over to Haqqani, where he effectively serves as a human shield. Although Carrie wants to 'take the shot' from the drone to eliminate Haqqani, Quinn intervenes and prevents it because Saul would perish as well. Inasmuch as it has been well publicized that Saul, the former agency head, is a captive, the entire security *dispositif* is roiled. Added to the mistaken destruction of civilians is the inability of 'The Company' to protect its staff.

From the drone queen to the drone *dispositif*

Although *Homeland*'s Aayan is an aesthetic subject, operating in a fictional story, the complex reactions he attracts as a result of his return of the militarized security-oriented gaze serves as a stand-in for much of the blowback that the US's drone warfare has experienced. Among the functional equivalents of the return of the gaze is the Stanford-NYU investigation of the use of drones in Pakistan, which summarizes the situation as follows:

> In the United States, the dominant narrative about the use in Pakistan is of a surgically precise and effective tool that makes the US safer by enabling 'targeted killing' of terrorists with minimal downsides or collateral impacts.
> (Stanford *et al.* 2012)

Countering that dominant narrative, the investigation disclosed an alarming level of atrocity visited on innocent civilians: 'From June 2004 through mid-September 2012, available data indicate that drone strikes killed 2,562–3,325 people in Pakistan, of whom 474–881 were civilians, including 176 children' (ibid.). Those disclosures, imitated effectively in Showtime's *Homeland*, bid to effect political and bureaucratic careers (the primary concern expressed by the fictional CIA head in *Homeland*, Andrew Lockhart (Tracy Lett). The precarity for him and the rest of the anti-terrorist drone warfare apparatus has been played out in the hearings for appointment of William Brennan, Obama's 'Drone Warrior' as CIA director (Brennan 2013). There, as before, he has been called to account as civilian deaths have mounted in both Pakistan and Yemen. Moreover, others who serve on the periphery of the drone *dispositif* are being questioned for their role in the thanatopolitical decision process that determines who gets targeted by the drones.

At the outset of the executive-level decision process, the planned targets were 'militants', who were marked for assassination (extra-judicial killing) by a decision-making chain that frequently ran all the way up to the 'Commander-in-Chief' and White House staff. The identity of the 'militant' blurs the boundary (which historically is always already 'blurred' (Kinsella 2011: 2–3)), between combatants and non-combatants, while at the same time making the ethics or morality of war an issue that various media have begun raising anew. Among other things, the roles of peripheral knowledge agents have become an issue. For example, the targeting 'intelligence' has been aided and abetted by a CIA security-oriented anthropology as the warrants for killing have turned from 'personality' targeting to 'signature' targeting (where the latter strikes are against 'men believed to be militants associated with terrorist groups, but whose identities aren't always known' (Ackerman 2011)).

The cultural 'knowledge' soliticited by the CIA has come from a suborned social science that has been recruited and/or has recruited itself into the security *dispositif*. The military and security agency designation for the cultural aspects of war zones is the 'Human Terrain System'. That 'system's' representatives have been recruiting knowledge agents at meetings of the American Anthropological Association (Commentary: Do No Harm 2012). Strongly criticized by that Association, undeterred uniformed anthropologists have been embedded in both combat and intelligence operations. As Marshall Sahlins puts it:

> The principal role of academics in the service of counterinsurgency is to develop the human intelligence (HUMANINT) that will allow a triage

between those elements of the population to be attacked (or assassinated) and those it would be better not to – in brief, sophisticated targeting.

(Sahlins 2009: vi)

Gregoire Chamayou raises a relevant question: 'What authorizes someone to engage in manhunting?' (2012: 6). As I have suggested, the 'what' is a complex set of interacting agencies and legitimations in which justifications and careers are colliding. And as regards the ethics of violence, there has been a step toward anonymous killing through a process in which the killers and those who authorize them (knowledge agents, intelligence agencies, and weapons operators) are epistemologically, physically, and perceptually remote. Prior to the advent of such remote killing,

> a soldier's right to kill his or her opponents depend[ed] on the condition of mutual risk [so that those] piloting weaponized drones from the other side of the globe [are engaged in] riskless war ... [thus creating a] deep challenge [to what has been called 'the *morality* of warfare'].
>
> (Sauer and Schörnig 2012: 373)

In addition to the ambiguity of what a riskless 'warrior' flying a drone from a remote location can see is the change in the temporal structure of the targeting decision. The possible interval for sensitivity to civilian casualties (and mistaken 'signatures') has been radically altered. In the case of drones,

> ... the sensor (formerly the UAV [non-weaponized drone]) and the shooter (formerly a manned airplane, an artillery unit, etc.) no longer have to be coordinated but are now two-in-one, unmanned combat air vehicles (UCAVs) [that] reduce the sensor-to-shooter gap from hours to minutes or seconds.
>
> (Ibid.: 370)

The ethics of the gaze

It has become clear that inasmuch as the security gaze is articulated through weapons and targeting decisions operate with very little time for inter-agency deliberation, the weapons themselves are increasingly making preprogrammed decisions about who will be targeted. As a result, self-appointed 'ethicists' are weighing in with suggestions. For example, P. W. Singer offers protocols for what he calls an '"ethical" killing machine' (2009). He imagines an internal software 'checklist' for the rules of engagement built into autonomous robotic weapons that he suggests might ethicize the robots:

> Is the target a Soviet made T-80 tank? Identification confirmed. Is the target located in an authorized free-fire zone? Location confirmed. Are there any friendly units within a 200-meter radius? No friendlies detected. Are there

any civilians within a 200-meter radius? No civilians detected. Weapons release authorized. No human command authority required.

(Ibid.)

In response to Singer's 'ethical killing machine' fantasy, I have evoked Immanuel Kant's prescient answer of more than two centuries ago. 'Asking himself about the implications of "man's" direct access to the noumenal realm, specifically to an apodictic set of moral protocols, he surmised that in effect, the human would become a lifeless automaton (read robot!)' (Shapiro 2015):

> The moral worth of actions, on which alone the worth of the person and even the world depends in the eyes of the supreme wisdom, would not exist at all. The conduct of man, so long as his nature remained as it is now, would be changed into mere mechanism, where as in a puppet show, everything would gesticulate well but no life would be found in the figures.
>
> (Kant 1956: 152–153)

To conclude with this brief reflection, I want to return to the epistemological support rendered to targeting by professional anthropologists and treat what I will call the return of the anthropological gaze. As I noted in my treatment of war crimes:

> The primary discursive condition of possibility for the Nuremberg war crimes trials was a new collective subject, 'humanity'. Inasmuch as the Nazi death apparatuses included extensive anthropological concepts, which constituted hierarchical versions of human nature (for example Alfred Hoche's notorious gloss on 'life unworthy of life'), a juridical response required a counter anthropology as part of the Nuremberg justice *dispositif*. For that, 'the conceptual development of a notion of "crimes against humanity"' was crucial, even though that new collective subject, 'humanity as a whole', as an object of a crime fit uneasily within established legal discourse.
>
> (Shapiro 2015: 15)

Recently, a counter-anthropology has been asserted against the anthropological supports of the droning *dispositif*. Robert Greenwald's documentary, *Unmanned: America's Drone War* provides a powerful, evidence and concept-heavy challenge to the US's drone decision process. Along with the testimony of many who knew the victims of drone targeting is a sequence on an important cultural practice. The documentary shows a jirga assemblage, a peaceful meeting in which cultural conflicts are mediated in Pakistan. That assemblage was hit by a hellfire missile, shot from a drone, killing most of those assembled. While anonymous US officials are quoted to the effect that the assemblage was a terror-planning meeting (it wasn't the planning of a 'Bake sale', according to one), the documentary goes into the details of the jirga, providing information from cultural authorities about what was taking place.

As has been the case for many aspects of the abuses involved in the US's 'War on Terror', documentary film continues to return the official gaze with artistic texts that (in Deleuze's terms) counter-actualize the events that have terrorized populations in (among other places) Pakistan and Yemen. The documentary genre-as-critique responds to the official 'truth weapons' that Foucault has elaborated: posing the question, 'What is the principle that explains history [and right]?', Foucault's answer is that it is to be found in 'a series of brute facts' such as 'physical strength, force, energy', in short in 'a series of accidents, or at least contingencies'. 'However, governments dissimulate the events of global violence by interpolating the use of raw force into implementations of rationality and right.' In a passage that captures the sense of how the two governments use their truth weapon, he adds,

> The rationality of calculations, strategies and ruses; the rationality of technical procedures that are used to perpetuate the victory, to silence ... the war ... [and he adds that] given that the relationship of dominance works to their advantage, it is certainly not in their [the government's] interest to call any of this into question.

The counter to the truth weapon is 'critique ... the movement by which the subject gives himself the right to question truth on its effects of power and question power on its discourses of truth' (Foucault 2007: 47).

Biographies and counter-biographies

Among the 'truth weapons' that legitimate drone targeting is what Gregoire Chamayou refers to as a 'necro-ethics' – a designation of the drone as 'the humanitarian weapon par excellence – articulated to support 'the right to "targeted assassination"' (2015: 17). Here I want to inflect that legitimation to treat the temporality of that targeting, which articulates itself as what I will call necro-biographies. As Chamayou points out, the anti-terrorist manhunts follow a 'principle of creating an archive or film of everyone's life' (a brief biopic!), because as he notes, 'Optical surveillance is not limited to the present time. It also assumes the important function of recording and archiving.' As a director of the surveillance contractor, Logos Technologies, puts it, 'The idea behind persistent surveillance is to make a movie of a city-size area, with the goal of tracking all the moving vehicles and people' (Chamayou 2015: 39).

> To locate [the] anonymous militants [whom they assassinate], targeters 'rely on what officials describe as "pattern of life analysis", using evidence collected by surveillance cameras on the unmanned aircraft and from other sources about individuals and locations [which they use] to target suspected militants, even when their full identities are not known.'
>
> (Chamayou 2015: 47)

What the US counterterrorism operatives regard as 'obvious' determines who gets targeted: once the necro-biographies/biopics are produced, 'those who end up being killed,' says a US counterterrorism official, ' "are people whose actions over time have made it obvious that they are a threat" ' (ibid.: 49). Of course biographies always have to be understood in the context of the ontologies and practices for interpreting and managing lives that are contemporaneous with their production. Thus, the contemporary War on Terror and the *dispositif* it has spawned provide the context for the necro-biographies that legitimate extra judicial killing. A challenge to those necro-biographies requires a critique of the presumed objectivity on which they are based. The history of biography is among other things a history of the ontologies within which life has been understood and consequently a history of the loci of power over life. Without going into a lengthy chronology of the ontological and power-invested frames within which lives have been understood, I want, for purposes of illustration, to jump directly into medieval culture in which 'the individual was seen as a symbol of the general' (Gurevich 1985: 294) and biographical writing, practiced as a didactic representation of exemplary lives, served to affirm the ontologies and power structures of theocratic societies involved in the 'spiritual appropriations of reality' (ibid.).

If we leap ahead a few centuries and land in the middle of the nineteenth, we discover a juridical biographical practice – another historical episode of the will to truth described by Foucault in his gloss on the problem of the 'dangerous individual in 19th-century legal psychiatry' (Foucault 1978). Foucault refers to 'the gradual emergence in the course of the nineteenth century of [an] additional character, "the criminal" '. Whereas in previous centuries, there were merely crimes and penalties, the nineteenth century witnessed the emergence of a new subject, which, having become an object of knowledge, was to be professionally interrogated and asked to provide an account of her/his thoughts and impulses. As a result, conversations about the criminal/subject began taking place between doctors and jurists. Psychiatry had entered the courtroom because it was part of a new medical *dispositif*, focused on 'a sort of public hygiene' applied to a new target of governance, the social order.

The modern courtroom is of course a mere annex with respect to the contemporary governmentality within which governance, as Foucault points out, turned from a focus on the continuous reactivation of sovereign power – the power 'to take life or let live' – to biopower, the management of life which involves the power, 'to "make" live or "let" die' (Foucault 2003: 241). Because the health and wellbeing of a new collective entity, the population, had become a focus of governance, the subjects of governance had become objects of knowledge rather than merely targets of procedures to ensure obedience. The development of public hygiene was, among other things, a concern with recruiting useful bodies, those able to serve in citizen armies, a concern that produced correlative calculating agencies. Accordingly, a medicine directed by the state is a medicine of cases. No longer a healer, the physician's gaze is deflected from the individual to the collective, and the health *dispositif* becomes radically entangled with the security *dispositif*.

With that as background, we can assess the new object of knowledge, the terrorist whose habitus is surveilled and whose movements are tracked. As Chamayou puts it,

> The tools of human geography and the sociology of social networks are now enlisted in the service of a policy of eradication in which 'persistent surveillance' makes it possible to pick out [the new] *dangerous individuals* [my emphasis]. The painstaking work of establishing an archive of lives progressively gathers together the elements of a file that, once it becomes thick enough, will constitute a death warrant.
>
> (Chamayou 2015: 49)

Thus the contemporary security state has re-inflected biopower. It now makes die rather than lets live. And to do so it mobilizes a thanatopolitical *dispositif* composed of political leaders and intelligence agency leaders, bureaucratic functionaries, knowledge disciplines, and technologies to assemble necro-biographies and eradicate the biographical subjects. What then is the medium within which one can mount a critique of the 'War on Terror's' necro-biographies? As I have suggested, the HBO's television series, *Homeland*, is one. However there is a much more compelling alternative. The contemporary equivalent of Foucault's genealogical critique of governance's concern with 'life' is a documentary, which provides a series of counter-biographies that effectively return the CIA's anthropological gaze – Robert Greenwald's above-noted *Unmanned: America's Drone Wars*.

Conclusion: a documentary challenge to the US drone *dispositif*

Greenwald's *Unmanned* begins with a brief autobiography by Brandon Bryant, shown in close-up on screen (Figure 3.1) as he recounts details of an unremarkable childhood, his decision to enter the Air Force (he wanted a reprieve from mounting student loans), and his position as a drone warfare sensor, directing missiles against those designated as terrorists (the job involves 'killing people' he's told). Remorseful by the time he has left the Air Force, he testifies to the arbitrariness of the targeting in which he was involved. Returning to the documentary after Pakistani victims are shown and their relatives and friends testify on screen to the misapprehensions that led to their targeting, Bryant recounts an episode of firing on and killing three men whose eligibility for eradication consisted only in the fact that they were walking around, carrying rifles. Bryant notes that as a resident of Montana, it was not unusual to see men walking around with rifles and wonders why the same scenario in Pakistan warrants killing them.

The other most significant bio is of a sixteen-year-old high school student, Tariq Assiz (Figure 3.2), who is targeted and killed while in a car with his brother and cousins, on the way to a soccer team recruitment. It becomes apparent that Tariq's CIA bio had thickened to the point that he was eligible for eradication. What data was available to constitute Tariq as a terrorist? As visuals of his

Figure 3.1 Brandon Bryant.
Source: courtesy of Brave New Films.

Figure 3.2 Tariq.
Source: courtesy of Brave New Films.

movements and local testimony indicate, he attended a large public meeting in Islamabad in which tribal elders, Pakistani officials, other civic leaders, political candidates, and interested members of the public were present, primarily to share information about the drone killing of innocent civilians (for example, one of Tariq's cousins) and to protest the drone programme.

As testimony indicates, it is likely that an 'informant' turned over Tariq's name to the CIA (for pay, as is the case with the CIA's informant practice). That information, along with the CIA's anthropological conceits, made a sixteen-year-old high school student, whose 'crime' was the political activism of attending a

The gaze and the drone dispositif   49

public meeting, a victim of extra judicial killing, i.e. summary execution without a chance to testify about his intentions and behaviour. Unlike what was available to the CIA and the rest of the targeting *dispositif* involved in the targeting decision, viewers of the documentary get to know this innocent high school student – a soccer player with good defensive talent, a youngster with a good sense of humour, a high school student admired by his teacher, Mr Wali, and a politically energized citizen, prompted to get involved after a cousin dies in a drone attack.

Much of what the documentary conveys is done with images. In one scene, the camera closes in on a soccer ball, an important cultural object that functions in both Pakistani culture in general and specifically in Tariq's filmed biography. The shot is wide-angled enough to show at the same time a large plane flying overhead (Figure 3.3). On the one hand, there is extensive ethnographic information one can discern with interviews of people who knew the victims of drone attacks and can testify to the cultural practices on the ground (where the soccer ball sits). On the other is the distant anthropology of the CIA-Military gaze, represented by a plane flying thousands of feet over the scene.

In Tariq's case, as in the case of the documentary's other notable coverage of the drone attack on a jirga (a democratic assemblage in which tribal elders gather with townspeople to settle local disputes; Figure 3.4) in the North Pakistan town of Datta Khel, the intelligence was misguided. As testimony and images show, within forty minutes of the start of the meeting, drone attacks kill most of the participants, and subsequent interviews with Pakistani officials (for example the former Ambassador to the US) and the relatives of the victims indicate that a major cultural event was interpreted as a terrorist plot.

Interspersed with the testimonies about the nature of the cultural event and the loss experienced by the relatives (mostly sons of tribal elders whose bodies were in fragments to the point where one son could not distinguish his father's feet from his hands), are onscreen remarks by US officials who dispense the

Figure 3.3 Soccer ball and plane.
Source: courtesy of Brave New Films.

Figure 3.4 Jirga in Datta Khel.
Source: courtesy of Brave New Films.

administration's 'truth weapons' to legitimate the murders – e.g. 'There's every indication that this was a group of terrorists, not a charity car wash in the Pakistani hinterlands.' (Tellingly, the anonymous official spokespersons are screening Pakistani culture through their own cultural practices.)

Subjecting America's drone warfare to 'a philosophical investigation', Chamayou refers to 'a crisis of intelligibility' because drone warfare defies the 'established categories' that have hitherto been applied to warfare (Chamayou, 2015: 14). Chamayou's emphasis is on the way the new militarized gaze has constituted parts of the world as a hostile environment viewed through the lens of CIA anthropology and the resultant apparatuses constructed to implement their perspective. Robert Greenwald's documentary constitutes a return of that gaze. As the documentary shows, the implementation of that gaze has created precarious lives and the deaths of many innocents, while what the US public hears are official lies – for example, CIA head William Brennan at a press conference: 'In the last year there hasn't been a single collateral death.' Here is the documentary's main juxtaposition. On the day Tariq Assiz was murdered, an innocent sixteen-year-old high school student was murdered (as his high school teacher, Wali, points out on screen). Cut to the *Washington Post*'s reporter Karen de Young: 'I asked the CIA about the strike and they said no child was killed.' The truth weapon remains a major part of the US's arsenal.

Note

1 The chapter is a much abbreviated version of a chapter in Michael J. Shapiro, *Politics and Time* (2016).

References

Ackerman, S. (2011). CIA Drones Kill Large Groups Without Knowing Who They Are. *Wired* on the web at: www.wired.com/dangerroom/2011/11/cia-drones-marked-for-death/ [Accessed 5 April 2017].
Bigelow, K. (2008). *The Hurt Locker*. Film produced by Warner Bros.
Brennen, P. (2013). John Brennan, Obama's Drone Warrior. CNN on the web at: www.cnn.com/2013/01/07/opinion/bergen-brennan-drones/index.html
Chamayou, G. (2012). *Manhunts: A Philosophical History*. Princeton, NJ: Princeton University Press.
Chamayou, G. (2015). *A Theory of the Drone*. New York: New Press.
Commentary: Do No Harm (2012), *C4!SA Journal* 4/25/2012. On the web at: www.defensenews.com/article/20120425/C4ISR02/304250001/Commentary-8216-Do-No-Harm-8217-html [Accessed 5 April 2017].
DeLillo, D. (1985). *White Noise*. New York: Penguin.
Foucault, M. (1973). *The Birth of the Clinic: An Archaeology of Medical Perception*. Trans. A. Sheridan. New York: Pantheon.
Foucault, M. (1977). The Confession of the Flesh. In: C. Gordon, ed., *Power/Knowledge: Selected Interviews & Other Writings 1972–1977*. Trans. C. Gordon, L. Marshall, J. Mepham. and K. Soper. New York: Pantheon.
Foucault, M. (1978). On the Concept of the 'Dangerous Individual' in Nineteenth Century Legal Psychiatry. *International Journal of Law and Psychiatry* 1, pp. 1–18.
Foucault, M. (2003). *Society Must Be Defended*, trans. D. Macey. New York: Picador.
Foucault, M. (2007). What is Critique? In: L. Hochroth and C. Porter, trans., *The Politics of Truth*. New York: Semiotext(e).
Garfinkel, H. (1991). *Studies in Ethnomethodology*. Cambridge, UK: Polity.
Gurevich, A. J. (1985). *Patterns of Medieval Culture*. Princeton, NJ: Princeton University Press.
Kant, I. (1956). *Critique of Practical Reason*, trans. W. S. Pluhar. New York: Macmillan.
Kinsella, H. M. (2011). *The Image Before the Weapon: A Critical History of the Distinction between Combatant and Civilian*. Ithaca, NY: Cornell University Press.
Lacan, J. (1979). The Eye and the Gaze. In: A. Sheridan, trans., *The Four Fundamental Concepts of Psycho-Analysis*. London: Penguin.
Sahlins. M. (2009). *The Counter-Counterinsurgency Manual*. Chicago, IL: Prickly Paradigm Press.
Sauer, F. and Schörnig, N. (2012). Killer Drones: The 'Silver Bullet' of Democratic Warfare? *Security Dialogue* 43(4), pp. 43–51.
Shapiro, M. J. (2015). *War Crimes, Atrocity, and Justice*. Cambridge, UK: Polity.
Shapiro, M. J. (2016). *Politics and Time: Documenting the Event*. Cambridge, UK: Polity.
Singer, P. W. (2009). *Wired for War*. New York: Penguin.
Stanford *et al.* (2012). Living Under Drones: Death, Injury, and Trauma to Civilians from US Drone Practices in Pakistan. The International Human Rights and Conflict Resolution Clinic of the Stanford Law School and the Global Justice Clinic of the NYU Law School, on the web at: http://livingunderdrones.org/ [Accessed 5 April 2017].

4 CCTV oddity
On the archaeology and aesthetics of video surveillance

Paolo Cardullo and James Stevens

Setting the field: surveillance and artistic interventions

In the present chapter we reflect on two hacktivist art projects that sought to exploit ubiquitous CCTV cameras in the streets and academic campuses of London. We aim to explore three trajectories. First, we want to open up the video surveillance *dispositif* and expose its controlling gaze. By describing and critically engaging with our art interventions, we begin unpacking the 'normal' functioning of CCTV cameras in a specific surveillance context. In so doing, and second, we want to rethink the crucial relations that make CCTV a technology of surveillance: the coupling of representations – a 'suspicious' event but also a specific aesthetics – and instances of identity – categories, classifications, and databases (see Fuller 2005). Since our projects remix such a relationship, they expose the contingency and indeterminacy through which surveillance is made meaningful.

From a methodological perspective, and third, we invite a consideration of the productive work art projects do in engaging with the field, rather than just investigating it. In this sense, art projects can be critical interventions that expose the 'normal' functioning of social relationships. Because they perform the experience of surveillance, the projects below can be considered also as an 'inventive' form of methodology (Lury and Wakeford 2012). An important disclaimer therefore needs to be made from the very beginning: as a performance, our interventions – but this can be extended to most practice-based research – can only be partially translated on paper. These projects were played 'live' and their liveliness is also the materialist energy that characterizes them (see Back 2012). In other words, readers should be mindful that the art is *in* the performance and installations, the unpacking of the surveillance apparatus *in* the experience it provokes, rather than *through* the pages of this chapter. The intervention is the 'data', so to speak. The best we can offer here is a thorough description, a few images, and links to clips or webpages. The rest has to be imagined by an active reader, who will always be in a space other than the space of participants.

Video surveillance theoretical frameworks reproduce a dense theoretical debate around the notions of ontology, what effectively constitute the technology of 'surveillance', and of epistemology, what the study of surveillance output, videos and stills, can reveal. Little attention has been given to the space of surveillance and the performative experience of being in that space (see McGrath 2004).

Drawing on the Foucauldian tradition, we can imagine surveillance as a more or less coherent *dispositif*, that is, a network of ordering and discipline, a system of rules, guidelines, and norms (Bussolini 2010; Legg 2011). For Foucault, a *dispositif* is 'an absolutely heterogeneous assembly which involves discourses, institutions, architectural structures, regulatory decisions, laws, administrative measures, scientific enunciations, philosophical, moral, and philanthropic propositions; in short: as much the said as the unsaid' (in Bussolini 2010). The disciplinary society it fosters finds its sublimation in institutional places such as the school, the hospital, the army, and of course the prison. Its most productive and infamous determinant is the catching architectural space of the Panopticon: a system of transparent openness of the 'other' to the gaze of a central but remote watch tower (or CCTV control room). The imagined disciplinary gaze ultimately reconnects to an always remote viewer, a sort of anonymous and unaccountable Big Brother, who oversees and masters camera feeds. This is thought of as a one-way relationship where the gaze cannot be returned to the watchers (Koskela 2003; see also Shapiro in this volume). Watchers are therefore imagined (also physically) at the centre of the disciplinary society.

Although Foucault does not equate power to the surveillant gaze, he reworks the concept of the Panopticon in his research on modern power: 'the tendency in Bentham's thought is archaic in the importance it gives to the gaze; but it is very modern in the general importance it assigns to the techniques of power' (cited in Levin *et al.* 2002). The surveillant gaze is eventually interiorized 'to the point that each individual exercises this surveillance over and against himself [*sic*]' (ibid.). As a consequence of this process, people's behaviours and their bodies are eventually modified, regulated, and administered: disciplinary societies express a moral and philosophical programme that changes people's bodies and souls from within.

However, Foucault had an architectural conceptualization of space: the metaphor of the Panopticon emphasizes the spatialization of power rather than the effect of power on space (Wood 2007). Therefore, it appears important to us to address the link between surveillance and people's acting *as if* they were under surveillance. This connection shifts the focus on the production of surveillance space itself, as the lived and constructed space where surveillance is experienced (see Lefebvre 1996; McGrath 2004). Rather than 'ideological' positions on visual surveillance, McGrath (2004) invites us to take a pragmatic approach to what he calls the 'surveillance space', by looking at the experience of surveillance and the performativity that it induces.

According to Kittler (cited in Fuller 2005: 61), Foucault's work was mostly concerned with textual material and therefore it leaves unquestioned the complications brought by digital technologies and computation. The second model of surveillance refers to a Deleuzian philosophical tradition in which computational power and circulation are crucial elements of media systems. Life is here rendered meaningful to the extent that is revealed by streams of data. In this sense, 'surveillance applies very little to the act of seeing', the event here and now. Rather, 'surveillance is a socioalgorithmic process' and a dynamic composition occurring not so much in the present, at the time of the observation, but in history, backwards, through a process of reordering, associating, and reconstructing the life of an 'event', and how this connects to a specific 'identity'. Ultimately, what surveillance sees is this backward association, the combination of 'event' and 'flecks of identity' captured in a database: number plates, faces, DNA, names, etc. (Fuller 2005). Modern surveillance suggests a process of 'sorting' and prediction, or calculation and risk-assessment (Lyon 1994; Amoore 2009).

This second model frames surveillance as a more complex, messy, and undetermined sociotechnological assemblage in which connections, linking, and accountability of its diverse parts become essential. While the first model of surveillance maintains the one-way-ness of the gaze – 'capturing and ordering with omniscient foresight' (Legg 2011) – in the sense of a control society, CCTV cameras are other than a technical, impartial, and objective recording device. We would further suggest with the present chapter that the social construction of the surveillance gaze articulates sociotechnical and ethical relationships within generative surveillance ecologies and technological visions of security.

In the following two case studies, the controlling surveillant gaze is dissected and rebuilt in hybrid forms of -veillance. New gazes emerge with new agencies and ethical accountabilities are dispersed through the determinants of this new ecology. This means that our interventions played with different systems of video surveillance, changing production, accountability, and destination of the CCTV visual output. This also means that we resist a straightforward and definitive analysis of these surveillance systems, since they have been exposed, opened to changes, and repackaged in other discourses – of the arts, alternative media, or hacktivism.[1] The visual technology of the CCTV is part of our method here.

In the first part of this chapter, we look at the *making* of a sociotechnical assemblage of video surveillance by describing an art installation done in 2013 at Goldsmiths, University of London, during the International Visual Sociology Association conference called 'The Public Image'. *#OCTV* consisted of six surveillance cameras streaming live from selected conference rooms to video displays positioned in each of the six rooms. Each camera feed was then linked to a webpage, made visible as a QR-code to scan, that is, as a composition of black and white pixels in the characteristic square shape (see Figure 4.1; for an analysis of QR codes see Gómez Cruz 2016). Phones with the required software were therefore able to connect to the 'control room' page and then switch to the desired camera.[2] The stream of still images, however, presented some unexpected findings, which we discuss below.

In the second part of the chapter, we open vernacular forms of video surveillance for scrutiny by presenting *CCTV Sniffing*. This project was hosted by Deptford.TV and consisted of workshops and urban walk performance.[3] Thanks to commonly available digital receivers, participants were able to hack into the digital feed of lower-end CCTV cameras in the streets of Deptford, inner-city London. The acquired raw clips were then recorded onto a memory card for later editing. The workshops managed to redirect the apparently seamless flow of security images into different discourses – those of urban research, art intervention, and hacktivist media.

There is a long tradition of arts engagement with the surveillance gaze, its transmission through technological devices, and its reception from a more or less participant audience. We want to position our work along the intersection between art and surveillance studies. At the crossroad of various disciplines, 'art-veillance' has produced numerous models of interpretation, dissection, and re-assemblage of the *dispositif* of video surveillance (see Brighenti 2009 and McGrath 2012, for an overview). In 2001 the massive exhibition 'CTRL [SPACE]'[4] explored a wide range of practices from more traditional imaging and tracking technologies to the largely invisible practices of what is referred to as data-veillance. The exhibition and voluminous publication that followed recall a trend in art practices that puts technologies at the centre of this exploration: from TV monitors and cables to wireless digital creations (Levin *et al.* 2002). The other strand of creativity around video surveillance is the direct intervention and disturbance: from theatrical performance to the use of 'pranks' or *détournement* – diverting bland or oppressive materials for subversive purposes. These art practices draw from the Situationist International and their project of turning to the streets and to everyday life. The Surveillance Camera Players (1996–2006) performed theatrical plays in front of CCTV around the world, especially in the subway in New York City, in order to redeem the watchers from their own surveillance system: 'How boring it must be for law enforcement officers to watch the video images constantly being displayed on the closed-circuit television surveillance systems?'[5] McGrath's book (2004), *Loving Big Brother*, a key work in this field, takes up the notion of art and performance as a productive way to think through and critique surveillance. 'Surveillance space', here, is co-produced by the technological apparatus and through practices of its occupants; it is a lived and experienced space crossed by power relationships as well as by performativity.

While our first project falls into experiments with technologies of surveillance, the second one is decisively hinged on the tradition of play and disruption. Both projects produced CCTV images. These are deemed as 'authentic' images when they assume a self-evident place in our perceptual repertoire, made of a distinct aesthetics of CCTV-based films and stills (Brighenti 2009; Leblanc 2009; McGrath and Sweeny 2009): 'Lo-Fi' and low resolution, lack of continuity and time-code bars, flickering images and silent stillness. Surveillance images are poor images, compressed for space and velocity of circulation (see Steyerl 2009).

#OCTV: making video surveillance

In conversation with media artist James Steven from the collective SPC,[6] we realized an installation with CCTV cameras at Goldsmiths, University of London. This complemented a panel discussion on video surveillance that we organized at the International Visual Sociology Association annual conference, 'The Public Image', in July 2013. The aim was to raise awareness of the complexities of CCTV systems and to open a debate beyond the discourse of power and control, with which CCTV is usually associated. In order to start unpacking a dialogic, although unequal, process of gazing the 'other' via CCTV, we wanted to create a sort of playful and democratic control room. We invited participants to reflect on the possibilities offered by open networks: *To what extent are bystanders involved in a performance, returning the gaze to the cameras?* We worked with a literature on surveillance that, although with different shades, frames video surveillance within the determinants of the Panopticon. In particular, our installation worked with the concept of a 'mutual gaze', which Koskela summarizes well in an early article:

> A camera represents total one-way-ness of the gaze by making it impossible to look back. One may see the cameras but an eye-contact with it is impossible. There is no 'mutual' gaze. It would feel ridiculous to try to flirt with a surveillance camera. Its objects are constantly seen but with no possibility to 'respond' or 'oppose' the gaze.
>
> (Koskela 2003: 298)

This view reflects the 'normal' functioning of the controlling gaze – the one-way, top-down view. We would contend that, in order to grasp the opportunities and complexities of visual surveillance, we would need to leave behind the technological determinism implicit in the disciplinary gaze. This refashions a linear equation: production of images, transmission, and their reception as meaningful 'event' (Fuller 2005: 23–24). This is what the *dispositif* of surveillance eventually sees, the final stage of a wholesale process.

#OCTV consisted of six CCTV cameras[7] positioned in six different conference rooms over two buildings on campus. These used the college network and were linked to a set of large computer screens positioned in the same rooms where the cameras happened to be. Conference delegates saw a poster about the installation featuring a QR-code (see Figure 4.1). This would link to a 'control room' page offering camera switch options. De facto we managed to enable a digital system of switches connected to participating individuals' mobile phone, which somehow fed into the public internet. In other words, the *#OCTV* project created a simple open circuit that gave viewers control of its 'control room': 'Whoever gets there first pushes the button', one of the hackers who worked on the project explains with a large smile.

An under-the-hood feature of our CCTV cameras allowed a random snapshot to be sent to a Twitter feed called @octvivsa.[8] The algorithm governing this

Figure 4.1 #OCTV stills, #OCTV composite.

exchange uses a simple affordance of the digital cameras: a sensor that triggers a photograph whenever a movement in the room is detected. We can think of this algorithm as another element in a set, which forms contemporary ecologies of surveillance: '[algorithm] can never be understood as a simply technical, objective, impartial form of knowledge or mode of operation' (Kitchin 2014: 10). As a result, the surveillance assemblage moves out from its enclosure, into a new and generative ecology of images as well as ethical entanglements. The snapshot from our CCTV would eventually appear as a link in the microblogging feed, which we then collected and analysed.

We want to show three sets of findings deriving from our experimental method. First, the ludic element of play and surprise, which we briefly cover in the next paragraph: people started experiencing the surveillance space and performing, even by returning the gaze to the cameras (see McGrath 2004, 2012). Second, experimental methods are often ethically troubling: we address this below, talking of the process that made the installation possible, our curatorial 'hack'. Third, we reflect on experimental methodologies as critical and reflexive performance: these might generate unexpected results that disrupt or reinforce our understanding of how video surveillance works.

1. The event had to be played live during the unfolding of the conference; it became a performance. Camera feeds are intrusive: once escaping the normality of being a fact in people's everyday life, especially in London, surveillance becomes visible and exposing. Seeing themselves watching someone speaking in an IVSA panel can be annoying and can distract from the talk. Sometimes CCTV needed to be switched off. Questions were asked, especially on the first day when delegates were not familiar with the workings of the device. Towards the end of the three-day conference, though, we noticed a sharp increase in interest: people started appearing closer to the cameras, selecting options, broadcasting their own appearance, even asking for stills. Some expressed their disappointment for not being able to broadcast themselves over the internet to their loved ones and colleagues in other parts of the world, Brazil, US, and Canada, among others. The installation started producing its own debate, becoming 'a mode of research' in itself (see Back and Puwar 2012). It created a performative space for re-enacting surveillance while, at the same time, opening to the technological proneness of creating and sharing our own image – taking a 'selfie' with a CCTV system, basically.

2. Surveillance is a process and a sociotechnological assemblage. In order to make the CCTV system work this way, meetings had to be arranged, numerous requests to college staff had to be initiated and followed, bureaucratic entanglements had to be tweaked. This intense process of negotiation is important because it shows how many people, protocols, and competencies went into the making of this new or altered surveillance system. Our aim to experiment with surveillance technology, code, and images was already producing contention. Or rather, it was reproducing the specific habitat on which the sociotechnical assemblage of video surveillance would eventually sit, a new ecology in fact.

We would argue that two distinct and interrelated 'hacks' were eventually put in place in order to produce this installation, and these are very much a transdisciplinary outcome:[9] the first one is the 'proper' technological hack, implying the writing of a code that linked networked cameras to screens, to a webpage, and eventually to Twitter. The second hack involved the process of acquiring permissions, of presenting the project to various bystanders and stakeholders in acceptable terms, and finally of remixing results in a critical way.[10] This 'curatorial hack' is also about knowing who to speak to, about moving into different areas of competence, and about conquering the hearts and minds of a few people whose everyday work is to make things happen: technicians, IT personnel, second and third grade decision-makers, security, and cleaners. Without a precise plan of action – which would have implied, for instance, a precise inventory of the technology available at college and a prior knowledge of our experiment's outcome (we were actually asked those questions!) – everyone had to add some degree of improvisation.

Latour suggests that scholars are limited by 'the modes of cultural critiques they are schooled in' (Back and Puwar 2012: 10). Scientists collect proper data with a proper ethical protocol. Scientists design their protocols. They stick to it, or so it seems. This is imperative in order to maintain the status of 'science'. The 'hack', then, is also about knowing that by framing the installation as another art project in an art-based college – by wearing the artist's apron rather than the scientist's hat – it might allow you to get away with things that traditional sociology would not, such as data collection, operationalization, consent forms, ethical approval, solid evidence, statistical relevance, wordy publications. To what extent is #OCTV a sociological project rather than an art installation? Are the two things interchangeable? Les Back writes in his 'Live Sociology' manifesto:

> We need to move from the arrogant convention in sociology to assimilate other practices on its own terms and within its own image (i.e. a 'sociology *of* art' or a 'sociology *of* computing') to a more collaborative practice that is mutually transformative (i.e. sociology *with* art or sociology *with* computing).
>
> (Back and Puwar 2012: 33 emphasis in the original)

It is our contention that, in the mutual exchange between art practice and social science research, a methodology that is inventive, creative, and lively has to maintain its radical contextualization. The context in this case remains that of an academic conference in which visual-oriented scholars from different parts of the world gather to discuss, among many other things, visualization of security and surveillance, mostly funded by their universities or foundations. We pulled a sociotechnical assemblage (video surveillance) out of its original context of being *just* a CCTV-operated system. In this apparent contradiction, the friction between disciplines can be reworked.

3. In this final part, we want to focus on very few instances of our CCTV visual output, teasing out 'flecks of identity' that started to appear (see Fuller

2005). Simply filtering our CCTV stills by day/night, we noticed that the output would feature two very distinct sets of people: academics and manual workers that make the college function every day. Hacking into the semiotics of identification from a video surveillance system, we can forge a new procedure of observation, which brings working-class work alive. We are able to see the night-shift manual labour of maintenance, room cleaning, and safeguarding of equipment – that included our hard-working CCTV cameras too. This can be framed in terms of rhythm-analysis (Lefebvre 1996). Attuning our senses to the very different noises, smells, visions, and dynamics of the city at night, we become aware of the ebbs and flows of the city, its economic and social dimensions, and its ontological layers that become invisible during everyday routines. The space these forces produce, the city during the day and at night, is a dynamic temporal and spatial process.

There is another side of this unexpected result, which prompted a serious discussion among the scholars who gathered to contribute to the present edited collection. Night shift, manual workers remained unaware of the recording CCTV cameras and therefore excluded from the playful performance (see Figure 4.2). At night, in fact, the same security staff we involuntarily filmed while patrolling college facilities had to switch computer screens off. Therefore, they were not able to watch themselves but were still watched. They were somehow excluded from the 'right to look' (Mirzoeff 2011), to return the gaze or play with it as daytime participants. They remained potentially subjugated to the authority of a remote gaze.

A complementary point here is that cameras are devices that maintain a drive to power, a will to record: they are persistent in the function they were made for in the first place (Flusser, cited in Fuller 2005). Because images are polysemic, that is they carry a reservoir of meanings, they also invite the audience's productive interpretative work (Harper 2012; Andersen *et al.* 2015). For this reason, images invoke a process of radical contextualization, in both the formation of academic knowledge and political action (Keith 1995). Contemporary surveillance becomes meaningful when we combine, in a productive (for surveillance purposes) way, what we think happens with some 'traits' of identity (see Fuller 2005). What we see here is arguably the 'performativity' of manual work at unsociable hours in a very mixed inner-city London borough, and this is set in

Figure 4.2 #OCTV by night, OCTV stills.

juxtaposition to predominantly white and middle-class academics. Another way of seeing this is to work with images intertextuality: how they produce meanings when compared, juxtaposed, or used in conjunction with other (predominant) sets of images or discourses (Rose 2007: 135–187). Cardullo (2014) argues that our CCTV images can be valuable when set against a predominant discourse around the end of manual work or, rather, around the disappearance of manual work from representation (see also Stallabrass 1997). Either way, it is rather clear that, in this case, a mutual gaze with the CCTV camera did not fully happen. The unexpected results, however, gave us a chance to reflect on different aspects of visibility of work, social division of labour in inner-city London, and finally on the limits offered by an open surveillance system and of the public sphere associated to it.

'CCTV Sniffing': unmaking video surveillance

We briefly analyse a second hacktivist project, in order to show the *unmaking* of a video surveillance system. This second example draws on a series of practice-based workshops on collaborative filming and 'CCTV sniffing' with the aim 'to store, share and re-edit the documentation of the urban change of South East London'.[11]

We first describe the functioning of this unusual video surveillance assemblage. We then discuss this in relation to dynamics of the surveillance gaze that this new ecology generated. In particular, we look at the possibility of an inversion in the control gaze, from the watchers to the watched: the so-called 'sous-veillance'. This 'gaze from below' has recently attracted some interest, mostly from artists and activists, and it can be summarized with a mix of: open source protocols, shareable content, human-centred affordable technology – recorded at eye level, possibly with a wearable recording technology (Mann and Ferenbok 2013).

We maintain that sous-veillance too is a peculiar assemblage, which in terms of surveillance has to refer to a chain of associations of meaningful 'events' and meaningful 'identities' to link to. Again, these can be up for grabs. Our workshop ethos was, for instance, to look at the process of urban change in Deptford, an area of inner-city London undergoing sustained material and cultural gentrification.[12] Cardullo (2014) has discussed the gentrification milieu in which the workshops took place as well as the symbolic strengths of the hacked videos.

Most of the considerations made with regard to our first installation, *#OCTV*, are applicable to the *CCTV Sniffing* performance (see Figure 4.3) and we will partly repeat them here – ecologies and spaces of surveillance, distributed agency, and ethical issues. Particularly, we want to reflect on the technology that determined these images. This is because this technology, a vernacular and almost redundant surveillance system, is constitutive of the surveillance ecology and space it creates. Small 'corner' shops usually deploy the cheapest digital systems available, with a low level of protection that hackers were quick to exploit. The digital receivers used for the workshops are also widely available from electronic stores at a very reasonable price. Cameras' bad positioning,

Figure 4.3 Sniffing devices, Deptford.tv.

overflowing of light or darkness, and lack of maintenance (e.g. dirty lens) contribute to the bad quality of images we managed to reproduce. The 'poor images' (see Steyerl 2009) that CCTV cameras transmit, however, fully convey the aesthetics we wanted to achieve: low resolution for speed of data over wireless connections and everydayness of their subjects and scenes, with the unmissable time code on one corner of the image. In addition, one can imagine the CCTV digital card being re-flashed every time it fills up, maybe by default every day, and its content relentlessly recorded and deleted by the software operating the cameras. These images are probably unusable for surveillance purposes.

This does not mean that the images are less 'real'. When disconnected from the linear connection that makes them useful for common understanding of surveillance, CCTV images can be productive in their own terms. They partake to the huge, almost impossible-to-be-accounted-for, pile of digital waste: 'The poor image is no longer about the real thing, the originary original' (Steyerl 2009). The poor image is, as Steyerl elegantly puts it, 'a lumpen proletarian in the class society of appearances, ranked and valued according to its resolution'.

The predominance of family-run shops in the hackers' reach provides our film clips their peculiar flavour. The scenes captured from CCTV cameras give texture to this changing urban landscape. Working-class Deptford started to appear: the clips reveal inner-city London's incredible diversity and some of its manual work practices in mundane places of encounters: the 'local', the familiar place of everyday dwelling, the corner shop, the halal butcher and the African hairdresser, the East Asian nail parlour and the Chinese take-away (see Figure 4.4). The surveillance feeds from these places, normally not linked, become involuntary actors in an unpretentious surveillance system, which was opened – at least temporarily – by the inventiveness of a few hackers and urban researchers.

Our experimental approach puts emphasis on ordinary practices of video surveillance, affordable security, and involuntary participation of shopkeepers and

Figure 4.4 CCTV Sniffing, 2011.

customers. These were sometimes co-opted in the project by showing them the feed from their own CCTV being recorded live on the remote screen of our digital cameras. But was shopkeepers' occasional involvement in our performance a way of making a collaborative video? And who is watching whom here? Can we perhaps suggest that urban researchers and hackers enacted a form of surveillance on 'corner' shops attendants, who are also the owners or keepers of those vulnerable security devices? Our replies are temptingly negative: it is hard to frame this intervention as a participative effort or to neatly distinguish between watchers and watched. By reshuffling the role of author and audience, watched and watchers, social categories and cultural practices, we however opened up a private surveillance assemblage to a new configuration, a generative ecology with a new set of ethics concerns and potential forms of agency.

Concluding remarks

The experimental visual research practice we describe here reflects upon the ever-changing technology of visual recording, in this case two video surveillance systems. These are similar in using CCTV cameras, but they are different with regard to all the other determinants and variables that make their ecology. Our projects exposed and explored the singularities of each video surveillance system – its composition, layers, technological affordance and agency, aesthetics, ethical contexts, and the discursive deployment of its visual output. Decoupling social practices from the suspicion of surveillance, we were able to envision forms of representations that were played live in urban walks and during an international academic conference. Naively, these performances exposed manual work as being at the heart of inner-city London's social reproduction process, through maintenance of education facilities and provisions for everyday shopping. Such work, and the populations undertaking it, emerged as central to the gaze of the cameras in both of our experimental performances.

We created new ecologies of video surveillance and complicated, at least momentarily, the social construction of the surveillance gaze. The notion of ecology denotes a multiple and complex bricolage, 'a massive and dynamic interrelation of processes and objects, beings and things, patterns and matter'

(Fuller 2005: 2). The term 'ecology', then, has higher potentials than the term 'assemblage', since it is broader in scope. While assemblage points towards sociotechnological complexities, an ecology would also need to take into account institutional constraints and regulations, ethics concerns, political contexts, materialities of production, and circulation of visual output and technologies – that is, their critical geographies – as well as the context, milieu, or habitat, on which an assemblage nests. While assemblage might start from 'elements that have been selected from a milieu, organised and stratified' (Anderson and McFarlane 2011), an ecology incorporates the shifting milieu on which each assemblage seems to hold: arrangements, temporary ethics configurations, and institutional improvisations. Ecology emphasizes multiplicity, emergence, heterogeneity, provisionality, and indeterminacy (Swyngedouw and Heynen 2003; Gandy 2005). Ecology points to a sense of futurity, of generative becoming, in which the experimental ethos of our research is all too evident.

Thus, in order to investigate the opportunities and complexities of surveillance ecologies, we need to leave behind the technological determinism implicit in the controlling gaze. This seems to foster a linear equation: production of CCTV images, their transmission and eventual reception as meaningful 'events' (see Fuller 2005). Taken together, the elements of this equation make the ontology of visual surveillance. Dissected, they can give scope to a myriad of different ecologies. Understanding video surveillance as an indeterminate ecology unlocks the potential configurations the system might take at any stage. We showed how these elements are part of complex and, at the same time, specific processes.

In this sense, our methodology is also 'inventive', because it detects and actively contributes to the happening of interrelations, events, and debates in a specific space and within technological, institutional, and ethical arrangements that constitute the ecology of surveillance images. Because of their experimental nature, artistic interventions can sometimes lead to unpredictable outcomes (they are intrinsically and poetically 'serendipitous'). Once removed from the specific context of security, in fact, the CCTV gaze can reveal places, people, and practices that often remain invisible. Or, it can recontexualize them in a completely different scenario.

From the perspective of whether the gaze was returned to the cameras, we would need to ask also to whom, if ever, such a gaze would be returned? The totalitarian will of the CCTV camera to see the whole from above, here and now, is at odds with the way in which visual scholars construct the workings of the gaze. Bell, for instance, thinks the surveillance gaze in terms of its positionality in space (2006), and the power relationships implicit in the exchange with the camera, something also highlighted in the relationship a visual ethnographer builds over a period of time with her subjects (Back 2007).

Since digital devices are so ubiquitous and easy to use, the boundaries of the surveillance gaze are getting blurry, to the extent that 'the differentiation between watchers and watched has disappeared' (Koskela 2008: 163). The everydayness of surveillance has, in Koskela's view, moved away from the critical counter-surveillance of 'vigilant individuals, NGOs and artists': ordinary people's surveillance does not form 'any critical or other statement' since it has 'no agenda'. It 'is not used for political aims, it presents no claims, has no objectives and there is no organizational structure behind it' (Koskela 2008: 162–163). At the opposite end, we find Mann's determinism: the proliferation of digital devices implies a 'critical mass' of sous-veillance, which becomes a 'political force' (Mann and Ferenbok 2013). Importantly, sous-veillance is, for Mann, not the opposite of surveillance, does not counteract the authority of the remote watcher, as our installations tried to do. Rather, sous-veillance co-exists with surveillance, 'creating a feedback loop for different forms of looking', a Panopticon from below.

The argument of our chapter is rather that ecologies of video surveillance can give space to unpredictable manifestation of the visual, actively partaking in the social construction of surveillance images – their aesthetics, 'meaningful' associations, and significance. We argue that sous-veillance, too, is a peculiar ecology. Technology, gaze or 'right to look', interconnections with other media systems (e.g. the internet), everyday overflowing of images, and ubiquitous presence of digital devices, are all loose elements of (dis)assembling ecologies. The outcome of complex and evolving ecologies of surveillance is therefore unpredictable too. It is difficult to assert a priori whether and how such a production can be meaningful for surveillance purposes. To the extent that it created reflexivity and awareness of the functioning of visual surveillance, we would argue, our intervention started a process of disruption and appropriation. Among the productive achievements of our experimental interventions were, then, a sense of confusion between watchers and watched, as well as the destabilization of the outcome from CCTV feeds.

The final consideration to be made is with regards to the methodology we used. This is obviously experimental, as already suggested. It is also critical to the extent that it makes an intervention. It becomes a political stance by bringing the 'field' alive (Back and Puwar 2012; Lury and Wakeford 2012; Aradau and Huysmans 2014). We contributed to opening particular CCTV systems to scrutiny and showed how contingent, diversified, and ephemeral video surveillance is, once its inbuilt assumptions are stripped away. Consequently, we also attempted to reclaim the non-linearity of the surveillance gaze in relation to the social construction of surveillance images

Notes

1. A similar consideration can be made with regard to the different (sub)disciplines this paper has been in dialogue with: security studies, visual sociology, critical media, technology studies.
2. At any time while reading this piece it is possible to scan the QR-code on Figure 4.1 and be taken to a reconstruction of the #octvivsa original webpage.
3. In collaboration with CUCR and SPC.org, 2007–2010.
4. http://ctrlspace.zkm.de/e/
5. www.notbored.org/the-scp.html
6. http://SPC.org

7 We would like to thank IVSA for the small grant that made the installation possible.
8 all #OCTV images can be seen at https://osf.io/a68u7/
9 In the sense that certain competences and skills remain separated: for instance, writing lines of code and writing this paper.
10 'Curating sociology' is about moving research questions into different fields of creative practices, in which the researcher-curator has an active role as producer (Puwar, in Back and Puwar 2012: 41).
11 For further information on Deptford TV projects and platform, see this interview to Adnan Hadzi: http://tinyurl.com/ccwt3zj
12 Three sets of workshops were organized by Deptford.TV, the Centre for Urban and Community Research, and SPC.org in 2007–2010.

References

Amoore, L. (2009). Algorithmic War: Everyday Geographies of the War on Terror. *Antipode*, 41(1), pp. 49–69.
Andersen, R. S., Vuori, J. A., and Mutlu, C. E. (2015). Visuality. In: C. Aradau, J. Huysmans, A. Neal, and N. Voelkner, eds., *Critical Security Methods: New Frameworks for Analysis*. London and New York: Routledge, pp. 85–117.
Anderson, B. and McFarlane, C. (2011). Assemblage and Geography. *Area*, 43(2), pp. 124–127.
Aradau, C. and Huysmans, J. (2014). Critical Methods in International Relations: The Politics of Techniques, Devices and Acts. *European Journal of International Relations*, 20(3), pp. 596–619.
Back, L. (2007). *The Art of Listening*. Oxford & New York: Berg.
Back, L. (2012). Live Sociology: Social Research and Its Futures. *The Sociological Review*, 60, pp. 18–39.
Back, L. and Puwar, N. (2012). *Live Methods*. Oxford: Wiley-Blackwell.
Bell, V. (2006). Performative Knowledge. *Theory, Culture & Society*, 23(2–3), pp. 214–217.
Brighenti, A. M., (2009). Artveillance: At the Crossroads of Art and Surveillance. *Surveillance & Society*, 7(2), 175–186.
Bussolini, J. (2010). What is a Dispositive? *Foucault Studies*, 10, pp. 85–107.
Cardullo, P. (2014). Sniffing the City: Issues of Sousveillance in Inner City London. *Visual Studies*, 29(3), pp. 285–293.
Fuller, M. (2005). *Media Ecologies: Materialist Energies in Art and Technoculture*. Cambridge, MA: MIT Press.
Gandy, M. (2005). Cyborg Urbanization: Complexity and Monstrosity in the Contemporary City. *International Journal of Urban and Regional Research*, 29(1), pp. 26–49.
Gómez Cruz, E. (2016). Photo-genic Assemblages: Photography as a Connective Interface. In: E. Gómez Cruz and A. Lehmuskallio, eds., *Digital Photography and Everyday Life: Empirical Studies on Material Visual Practices*. Routledge Studies in European Communication Research and Education. London and New York: Routledge, pp. 228–242.
Harper, D. (2012). *Visual Sociology*. London: Routledge.
Keith, M. (1995). Shouts of the Street: Identity and the Spaces of Authenticity. *Social Identities*, 1(2), pp. 297–315.
Kitchin, R. (2014). *Thinking Critically About and Researching Algorithms*. Rochester, NY: Social Science Research Network. Available at: http://papers.ssrn.com/abstract=2515786 [Accessed 17 November 2014].

Koskela, H. (2003). Cam Era – the Contemporary Urban Panopticon. *Surveillance & Society*, 1(3), pp. 292–313.
Koskela, H. (2008). Hijacking Surveillance? The New Moral Landscapes of Amateur Photographing. In: K. F. Aas, H. O. Gundhus, and H. M. Lomell, eds., *Technologies of InSecurity: The Surveillance of Everyday Life*. London: Routledge
Leblanc, P. B., 2009. From Closed-Circuit Television to the Open Network of Live Cinema. *Surveillance & Society*, 7 (2), 102–114.
Lefebvre, H. (1996). *Writings on Cities*. Cambridge, MA: Blackwell.
Legg, S. (2011). Assemblage/apparatus: Using Deleuze and Foucault. *Area*, 43(2), pp. 128–133.
Levin, T. Y., Frohne, U., and Weibel, P. eds. (2002). *Ctrl [space]: Rhetorics of Surveillance from Bentham to Big Brother*. Karlsruhe, Germany/Cambridge, MA: ZKM Center for Art and Media/MIT Press.
Lury, C. and Wakeford, N. eds. (2012). *Inventive Methods: The Happening of the Social*. London and New York: Routledge.
Lyon, D. (1994). *The Electronic Eye: The Rise of Surveillance Society*. Cambridge: Polity Press.
Mann, S. and Ferenbok, J. (2013). New Media and the Power Politics of Sousveillance in a Surveillance-dominated World. *Surveillance & Society*, 11(1/2), pp. 18–34.
McGrath, J. (2004). *Loving Big Brother: Performance, Privacy and Surveillance Space*. London: Routledge.
McGrath, J. (2012). Performing Surveillance. In: K. Ball, K. Haggerty, and D. Lyon, eds., *Routledge Handbook of Surveillance Studies*. London: Routledge.
McGrath, J. and Sweeny, R. J. (2009). Editorial: Surveillance, Performance and New Media. *Surveillance & Society*, 7 (2), 90–93.
Mirzoeff, B. N. (2011). The Right to Look. *Critical Inquiry*, 37(3), pp. 473–496.
Rose, G. (2007). *Visual Methodologies: An Introduction to the Interpretation of Visual Materials* 2nd edn. Los Angeles, CA: SAGE.
Stallabrass, J. (1997). Sebastiao Salgado and Fine Art Photojournalism. *New Left Review*. Available at: http://newleftreview.org/A1909 [Accessed 9 March 2010].
Steyerl, H. (2009). In Defense of the Poor Image. *e-flux* (10). Available at: www.e-flux.com/journal/in-defense-of-the-poor-image/ [Accessed 16 March 2015].
Swyngedouw, E. and Heynen, N. (2003). Urban Political Ecology, Justice and the Politics of Scale. *Antipode*, 35(5), pp. 898–918.
Wood, D. (2007). Beyond the Panopticon? In: J. W. Crampton and S. Elden, eds., *Space, Knowledge and Power: Foucault and Geography*. Aldershot: Ashgate Publishing Ltd.

Part II
Security spectacles and spectatorship

5 The humanity of war
Iconic photojournalism of the battlefield, 1914–2012[1]

Lilie Chouliaraki

Introduction

In her acclaimed book, *The Cruel Radiance: Photography and Political Violence* (2010), Susan Linfield argues that the photojournalism of war has changed in time, moving from less to more explicit visualizations of violence – a historical trend that she attributes to the fact that 'since the end of the cold war ... violence has become less tethered to political aims, which is to say it has become more nihilistic and more "autonomous"' (2010: 133). In a relevant interview, she contrasts the photojournalism of the Spanish Civil War, which inspired unprecedented acts of international solidarity, with contemporary photojournalism, where '... that kind of solidarity and political clarity is very, very hard to come by. So I think', Linfield concludes, 'what we're presented with visually is the bodily disfigurement, the tortured bodies, but without any kind of political context in which to understand it'.[2]

Whereas I agree with Linfield that the visualizations of war have indeed become more explicit, my argument in the present chapter shifts the empirical focus from her, primarily, non-Western towards Western contexts of war so as to nuance and complicate her claim in two important ways[3]: first, I demonstrate that visual explicitness is today primarily about the psychological trauma of war, rather than 'bodily disfigurement', and second, I claim that, even though we are indeed far from the international solidarity of 1936–1939, we are now presented with an intensely moralistic context for understanding war as humanitarian benevolence, rather than the nihilistic context of autonomous violence.

My argument centres upon war photojournalism as a practice of visual representation that mundanely confronts us with the realities of the battlefield. Together with other public genres of story-telling, like television news, films, novels, or computer games, photojournalism constitutes what I call a 'war imaginary' – a configuration of popular practices of representation through which war is imagined as a constitutive dimension of our public morality. This is because, whilst war is denounced as a cause of extreme suffering, it is always also fought in the name of moral principle and, therefore, simultaneously carries specific visions of humanity that we are all called to endorse – what Howard calls 'the liberal paradox of war' (1978).

Starting from this tenuous articulation of deliberate inflictions of suffering with moral visions of humanity that defines the war imaginary, I explore how photojournalism has historically sought to resolve this paradox and how, in so doing, it has participated in changing visions of humanity, at two crucial moments in time: the first half of the twentieth century and the early twenty-first century. I start with a review of the major paradigms of war communication studies, propaganda and memory studies, to argue that, despite their contributions, neither focuses on historical change in the ethics of war. After introducing the war imaginary as a theoretical concept with important analytical implications, I proceed with a discussion of Anglo-American and Australian, iconic images of World Wars I (1914–1918) and II (1939–1945) as well as the War on Terror (2001–2012) in terms of how they portray the battlefield. *Pace* Linfield, I conclude, the increasingly explicit visualization of war centres on the *emotional*, rather than physical, impact of the battlefield upon both soldiers and civilians, whilst the political context of this photography of trauma, far from absent, is one of *humanitarian wars* fought with a view to 'alleviating the immediate images of death and suffering', rather than wars over national sovereignty (Coker 2001: 130; see Möller in this volume on obscure visualization in photography).[4]

Paradigms of war communication studies

Two strands define the literature on war communication: war as propaganda and war as cultural memory. Whereas the former is about how photojournalism manipulates war communication with a view to legitimizing it in people's 'hearts and minds', the latter focuses on how war images contribute to working through the traumatic memories of those subject to its suffering.

War as propaganda, largely concerned with visual persuasion (e.g. Roeder 1993), is part of the broader field of strategic communication, which it has largely helped to shape. Its usefulness lies in scrutinizing invisible relationships of complicity between governments, the military, and the media and, thus, explicating the formidable mechanisms that nation-states mobilize to guarantee loyalty among publics and allies in wartime. Seminal pieces of propaganda research include Harold Lasswell's *Propaganda Technique in World War I* (1971), which offers the first systematic conceptualization of propaganda in terms of the promotion of 'war aims' as 'the catalysts of transnational political action' and 'the management of public expectations' as 'the illusion of victory' (1971: xxiii–xxiv), but also, more recently, Herman and Chomsky's *Manufacturing Consent* (1988), which discusses Vietnam as a paradigmatic case of how war propaganda can fail when political elites disagree. Their contributions granted, propaganda studies suffer from two limitations: despite their emphasis on communication, they ignore the performative work that representations, that is, the images and language of propaganda, do in constituting the subjects of national loyalty (Butler 2006) and, as a result, they under-theorize the role of such acts of representation in forming public dispositions – assuming instead that propaganda messages can have a uniform effect of brainwashing upon their publics (Corner 2003).

War as memory, born out of a (revised) tradition of psychoanalytic trauma studies, draws attention to the ways in which war images participate in processes of collective remembering (Alexander 2004). Unlike propaganda, which is marked by instrumentality, memory studies view war communication as a therapeutic form of communication that addresses the disruptive experience of violence, by articulating it with fantasy and, thereby, contributing to the narrative healing of traumatized publics. Central to this process are the popular genres of representation through which memory is fashioned: 'cultural memory', as Sturken puts it, 'is produced through representation – in contemporary culture, often through photographic images, cinema and television' (1997: 8). This centrality of representation, lacking in propaganda studies, has led to important research that explores the role of popular culture in working through twentieth-century traumas, such as Paul Fussell's seminal *The Great War and Modern Memory* (1975), which examines how popular genres have established dominant ways of remembering WWI, Jay Winter's *Sites of Memory, Sites of Mourning* (1995), which uniquely illustrates the European experience of grief after WWI, and Barbie Zelizer's *Remembering to Forget* (1998), which shows how our over-familiarization with Holocaust images may be weakening our response to contemporary atrocities. Far from adopting a deterministic view on publics as uniformly shaped by war messages, as propaganda does, this strand emphasizes instead the multiple ways in which images may cumulatively shape collective memory in our culture. The critical analysis that informs these studies also informs my own work in the communication of war, but, ultimately I engage neither with trauma and the restorative effects of popular narratives nor with cultural memory and the ways in which atrocity photography may 'help us make sense of the past and the future' (Zelizer 1998).

The war imaginary

My starting point is the communication of war as an imaginary: a structured configuration of representational practices, which produces specific performances of the battlefield at specific moments in time, with a view not only to informing and persuading us, as per the instrumental aspect of propaganda, but also to cultivating longer-term dispositions towards the visions of humanity that each war comes to defend. Even though the intellectual trajectory of the term 'imaginary' passes through Lacanian psychoanalysis and Castoriadis' (1975/1987) political theory, my own use draws on Charles Taylor's conception of social imaginaries as spaces of popular communication consisting precisely of 'those images, stories and legends' through which '... people imagine their social existence, how they fit together with others, ... and the deeper normative notions and images that underlie these expectations' (2002: 106).

The war imaginary, in this sense, partly encompasses and partly transcends cultural memory assumptions, in that its focus on popular representations entails a strong normative dimension, implicit in memory studies. In communicating war, this approach has it, the war imaginary does not simply seek to shape the present or heal the past, but simultaneously enables us to imagine who we should be and how we should act as citizens – in Frazer and Hutchings' words, the imaginary acts as a resource for 'the distinction and relation between civic and military virtue' (2011: 58). This virtue-oriented normativity of the imaginary, as performative practices that mobilize image and language in order to sustain the collective self-description of communities of virtue, points to the fact that such practices, rather than simply persuading or healing their publics, in fact, habitually constitute these publics as moral subjects at the moment that they claim to address them.[5] The force of habituation is, in this sense, not a simple corrective to a pre-existing public morality but bears a *constitutive* force on this morality, as it routinely uses the pictorial performances of war so as to call an ethics of humanity into existence.

From the multiple performances of war, the battlefield, where mass killing takes place at an unimaginable scale, is the most poignant site of the war imaginary. Here, the ambivalence of the imaginary, summed up as it is in the incongruous coexistence of inhumane violence with visions of humanity, is most dramatically enacted. Under the pressure of this tension, the force of habituation that marks the war imaginary as a performative mechanism of moral dispositions can never be a purely mindless repetition of moral norms. It requires, instead, a reflexive re-engagement with the particular contexts of its emergence and, hence, entails an always renewed performance that may subvert these norms in the act of reproducing them. It is this iterative process, whereby the imaginary is transformed through the very representational practices that reproduce it, that bears the potential for a historical account of change in war photojournalism. Explaining such transformations, I argue, tells us something important about changing moral visions of humanity in the past hundred years.

Analysing the war imaginary: Drawing on iconic photojournalism from the first half of the twentieth century (World Wars I and II) and the first decade of the twenty-first (War on Terror), I discuss how the visual configuration of *bodies in battle* has shifted in time. Despite the wealth of pictorial material on these wars, my choice of, specifically, iconic imagery of the battlefield draws attention to the enduring, ubiquitous, and recurring presence of particular photographs that have, in time, acted as 'symbols of cultural and national myth' and so shaped the war imaginary of the West (Griffin 1999: 123).[6]

The claim to objectivity in professional journalism granted, let us remember that the spectacle of war always emerges within specific 'spaces of appearance' – institutionalized sites of spectatorship, where the regulation of visual performance is absolutely crucial in the production of a unified moral imagination (Butler 2006). In the case of war propaganda, Butler argues, such regulation applies 'not only on content – certain images of dead bodies in Iraq, for instance, are considered unacceptable for public visual consumption – but on what "can" be heard, read, seen, felt and known' (2006: xx). Breaking from conceptions of aesthetics as apolitical, this approach points to war photojournalism as an aesthetic practice of power, through which the spectacle of battlefield is institutionally regulated so as to represent 'what "can" be heard … seen … felt' in a legitimate and persuasive manner.

I, therefore, approach my first analytical category, the *aesthetic quality* of war photography, as evidence of this visual regulation along the two key representational dimensions of the battlefield: the organization of *human bodies* and their technologies within specific spatial zones of activity, or *landscapes*. It is this focus on the aesthetic strategies through which certain compositions of combative action become intelligible to us that allows me, in a second move, to reflect upon the moral agency that these images make possible. The analytical category of *moral agency*, then, opens up to critical scrutiny the question of how war images operate as a resource of collective moralization – how, that is, they propose specific conceptions of humanity as legitimate and desirable for all, at any point in time. I begin with the early twentieth-century battlefields of WWI and WWII and proceed to address the contemporary battlefields of the War on Terror.

World Wars of the twentieth century

WWI was the first to become immediately visible to civilians: 'During the First World War', Carmichael says, 'it was for the first time possible for people to see and read about a major conflict more or less as it happened' (1989: 4). This new visibility of the war was, however, shaped by two factors: the large scale of military operations, which defied 'spectacularization' by the technical apparatus of the time, and the strict state regulation of war information (Carruthers 2000: 57–58). As a result, WWI photojournalism was defined, on the one hand, by the photographers' continuous efforts to capture the huge scale of events on the battlefield and, on the other, by a visual production that rarely challenged official interpretations of the war. The bulk of WWI pictures was consequently 'antiseptic', consisting mostly of 'archaic images of individual suffering and heroism' (Farish 2001: 279).

Despite the enormity of its war operations, far exceeding those of WWI, WWII photojournalism became more dynamic, both because technical equipment was now more powerful and mobile and because the information strategy of the Allies changed from rigid control to 'regulated truth telling' (Roeder 1993). Rather than correcting the wrongs of WWI propaganda, however, this turn to the truth was accepted as a pragmatic move in the face of the fact that 'war on this scale couldn't simply be hidden, however much states might seek to obscure their losses' (Carruthers 2000: 93). A more humane and tragic imagery of the battlefield now emerged, though one that shares with WWI a similar ethics of heroism (Winter 1995). Let me summarize the key aesthetic features of WWI and II photography in terms of their visual configuration of *bodies in battle*.

i Aesthetic quality

Bodies: The majority of WWI photographs is about soldiers posing with or using technology in the battlefield – primarily artillery, such as guns and cannons, but also objects and vehicles, such as gas masks (from 1915) and tanks (from 1916).

This recurring connection between soldier and technology, always articulated in productive relationships of complementarity (soldiers in control of machines) or extension (soldiers protected by machines), operated within a prosthetic imagination, characteristic of the early twentieth century – an imagination that celebrated the synergies between man and machine in discourses of heroic virtue and technological utopia: 'War is beautiful' as futurist Marinetti put it, 'because it initiates the dreamt-of metalization of the human body' (1930 in Der Derian 2005: 27). It did so, however, at a cost. It ignored the contradictory relationship between body and technology that, in the context of the first industrialized war, span this relationship out of control and gave rise to the mass phenomenon of war neurosis or shell shock. Far from a pure fear of death, Leed argued, the unprecedented rise of war neurosis on the Western Front was a direct consequence of the new relationship of bodies-in-battle stuck in immobilized warfare and the new, long-distance calculations of risk that this warfare entailed. Long-range artillery, machine guns, and barbed wire had, in other words, imposed new rules for the conduct of war, making war neurosis 'the direct product of the increasingly alienated relationship of the combatant to the modes of destruction' (Leed 1979: 164).

Beyond ignoring the complex emotionality of combative agency in favour of a romantic celebration of the soldier as machine, WWI photojournalism also largely ignored the dead body in the battlefield (Carruthers 2000). It is not so much that pictures of the dead were unavailable, but rather that such imagery was heavily regulated to portray the dead enemy rather than friend (Carmichael 1989; but see Winter 1995 for a rare exception). Building upon the American Civil War documentary style, the representation of these dead took place through an objectivist aesthetic that emphasized the mass nature of war killing. They did so by portraying the body as part of 'regularized compositional wholes', such as landscapes of barbed wire or trench lines, and were often accompanied by captions, such as 'The Dawn of Passchendaele' or 'Death the Reaper' (see Figure 5.1), that contextualize the scene in broader narratives of the 'picturesque' (Griffin 1999: 136–137).

By WWII, the status of the body is both similar and different. On the one hand, it continues to be defined by discourses of technological militarism, particularly in the celebration of new war machinery, such as aircraft carriers and armoured vehicles that made the war more mobile. On the other, the body also begins to appear dissociated from technology and, after President Roosevelt's recommendation to show more 'blood and gore' (1943, in Roeder 1993: 28), a different imagery started to appear – one that, whilst coexisting with the heroic, acknowledged the traumatic impact of battle upon soldiers, both physical and emotional: 'a grittier perspective now emerged', Carruthers says, in which 'fear, boredom and courage all found a place' (2000: 94). Even though this new discourse served the purposes of hardening public morale, it also introduced a new legitimacy for the wounded body and, with it, a new conception of heroism not as the negation but as the conquest of fear: 'the legend that soldiers don't cry', as war photographer Dickey Chapelle put it, 'robs them of their personal victories over fear and pain'.

Figure 5.1 Frank Hurley, 'Death the Reaper' (combined negatives), 1917.[7]

This new photographic sensibility is perhaps best reflected in Robert Capa's 'magnificent eleven', his eleven surviving photos from the D-Day landing, which were published in *Life* magazine. These placed the configuration of bodies in battle within concrete narratives of dramatic action – showing allied soldiers with rifle and equipment, drifting or crawling in shallow water, just before they stepped onto Omaha Beach.

New shooting techniques (wide-angle lens), which put the viewer in the scene of action, but also a new professional ethics, the 'concerned photographer', gave rise to a moral imagination that inserted the body in discourses not only of heroic sacrifice but also human agony and grief (Griffin 1999). Whilst still operating within the realm of objective representation, Capa's aesthetic, with its bold emphasis on black-and-white and the out-of-focus frame, invited a more intense relationship to combative agency than WWI pictures did – one that was mediated by 'an artist who can transfigure human suffering and a spectator who can redeem this suffering, ... by grasping important moral insights' (Friday 2000: 375).

In summary, the move from WWI to WWII marked a shift from the body-as-machine to the body-as-fragile, both physically, through the acknowledgement of injury and death, and psychologically, through a recognition of the intense emotionality involved in battle. Despite this 'new frankness', in Fussell's words, however, both World Wars were dominated by a romantic conception of combative agency that celebrated soldierly suffering as heroic and sustained a largely cleansed photojournalistic depiction of the battlefield – one that, ultimately, only 'showed intact bodies and revealed little of the agonies of death' (Roeder 1993: 9).

Landscapes: Its multiple theatres of action granted, the most iconic imagery of WWI photojournalistic landscape is the Western Front's No Man's Land – a scape characterized by a 'total negation of habitual perception', ravaged as it was by an amorphous mass of battlefield waste (Huppauf 1996). Far from simply destroying the topological order of pre-war life, this imagery of No Man's Land came to replace modernist conceptions of rural landscape as a zone of natural beauty with a new imagination of nature as a zone of technological destruction: 'the war explodes the landscape back into a state of wilderness', says Huppauf, 'which is, at the same time, the landscape of modern technology' (1996: 46). Unable to capture action-as-it-happened, these photojournalistic images were static, concentrating on the aftermath of war, where fusions of mud, crater marks, bomb debris, and human bodies construed the battlefield as a liminal space between here and there, us and enemy, life and death (Leed 1979: 14). This was a 'sublime' aesthetic register that, according to Boltanski (1999), grasps this scary liminality through a double move: framed as it was by an aesthetic of the aftermath, the initial horror of the spectacle of death-in-battle was quickly replaced by a sense of safe distance from the scene and offered itself to spectators as an object of reflexive contemplation.

Out of the multiple landscapes of WWII photojournalism, the most iconic ones involve city bombings: the Blitz of London and the atomic attacks on Japan. Unlike Western Front images, which separated combative from non-combative landscapes, the photojournalism of WWII blurred the two in a new conception of the battlefield, which now included civilians into the sphere of legitimate killing. As acts of expressive violence, prioritizing a symbolics of destruction over material military gains, these bombings operated less as strategic operations and more as horror spectacles that had 'to be seen and to strike fear in the hearts of the observer, the real target of an act of terror' (Bousquet 2006: 744). The characteristic of such spectacular photojournalism is, therefore, the long distance shots of cityscapes in flames or in ruins (see Figure 5.2).

Distance abstracts from the details of human injury in order to focus upon the magnitude of the battlefield in a God's-eye view of hyper-destruction. What emerges is again a sublime aesthetic that locates this battlefield in a hybrid register of 'ecstatic destructiveness' (Bousquet 2006). At the heart of such aesthetic lies a war imaginary that recognizes extreme violence as the most effective means for securing peace: Hiroshima, the most radical instance of the imaginary, signals precisely this shift towards a Cold War morality, where the stability of the new world order now rests upon the constant threat of nuclear annihilation (Huppauf 1996: 9).

The representation of landscapes is the clearest manifestation of the paradox of the war imaginary, in the early twentieth century. In different ways, No Man's Land and the WWII ruins reflected a predominantly dystopian vision of technology. Either as a liminal zone of waste that defies rationalization or as the apocalyptic

The humanity of war 79

Figure 5.2 US National Archives, Hiroshima, 1945.

horizon of burning hell, these sublime landscapes undermined both the romantic optimism of technology and the heroic celebration of soldiers that, in various degrees, defined the representation of bodies-in-battle in the two World Wars.

ii Moral agency

The category of moral agency examines the role of photojournalism in addressing the existential question of war: which conceptions of humanity, of self and other, does photojournalism come to legitimize?

The conception of humanity emerging out of the photojournalism of the battlefield, in twentieth-century wars, is radically ambivalent. It is, as we saw, a humanity suspended between discourses of technological perfectibility, glorified in the prosthetic imagination of bodies-as-weapons or the suppression of emotion, and discourses of corporeal fragility, testified in the acknowledgment of suffering and the recognition of fear in combat. Whilst the self gradually opens up to discourses of imperfectability, however, the enemy continues to be construed as a radical other. It is only enemy soldiers that are shown in a state of absolute fragility, death, whilst the mass suffering inflicted upon the Hiroshima civilians is prohibited from view. Both voyeurism and invisibility operated here as strategies of dehumanization that sustained a phantasy of enemy lives as inhuman or simply irrelevant (Fussell 1975).

Even if the otherness of the enemy is a persistent theme of war, the ambivalence of the self reflects a historical shift in conceptions of humanity during the first half of the twentieth century. It marks a departure from chivalric genres of moral agency as aristocratic valour towards a new discourse of agency as military servitude – one that recognizes heroic virtue not in the artful dexterity of the distinguished warrior but in the disciplined skill of the nationalized soldier, thrown as he is into industrialized battlefields of mass killing. These soldiers of the first half of the twentieth century, what Walzer calls 'soldiers as instruments', are not 'members of a fellowship of warriors; they are "poor sods just like me" trapped in a war they did not like' (2006: 36). Evident in the dystopian vision of battlefield landscapes as liminal zones of destruction, this humble agency of the soldier does not, however, mark the end of heroism.

Rather, this humanity redefines heroism within a new moral imagination, informed by what I call an aesthetic of the sublime – an 'emotionally detached and amoral representation of mass environmental destruction and death' that turns the battlefield into an object of reflexive contemplation (Huppauf 1997: 138–139). Far from a purely stylistic decision, the sublime is the consequence of institutional restrictions on war correspondents as well as of the technological norm of total visibility that journalists sought to capture in the battlefield (Farish 2001). Yet, at the same time, the distanced objectivity of the sublime is also a key aesthetic response to a deeper crisis of representation in early twentieth-century war, namely the lack of an appropriate language to capture the experience of battlefield through conventional visual practices. This is evident, for instance, in WWI techniques of image manipulation to capture the simultaneity of full-scale violence; or in the rhetoric used by X. Lawrence, the only military photographer to fly above Hiroshima, who described the spectacle through epic language: 'awe-struck, we watched it shoot upward like a meteor coming from the earth instead of from outer space ... it was a living thing, a new species of being, born right before our incredulous eyes' (quoted in Dower 2010: 275).

The 'poor sods', in these sublimated battlefields, were thus heroes not because they possessed a masterful combative agency but precisely because they were all too aware of themselves as both agents and victims of killing on a mass scale: 'however profound the despair of the individual', as correspondent Philip Gibbs described the advance of the Somme, 'the mass moved as it was directed' (1920: 359–360). And even though other public genres, such as poetry and painting, addressed this crisis of representation through the modernist registers of irony and the surreal, which emphasized bitter knowingness or the irrationality of futile sacrifice (Fussell 1975), photojournalism operated as a gate-keeping genre that sustained more conventional narratives of war. Even Capa's concern with human suffering worked, in fact, to individualize and authenticate, rather than break with, the discourse of heroic sacrifice (Coker 2001).

In summary, early twentieth-century photojournalism attempted the impossible task of renewing the promise of humanity under inhumane conditions through a sublimation of the battlefield. In the process, it maintained the traditional conception of the enemy as dehumanized other but did not, ultimately, manage to keep intact the conception of the self; its humanity, earlier celebrated in the invincible soldier as machine, is increasingly problematized as a precarious condition that war tragically disintegrates.

Wars of the twenty-first century

If WWI introduced a new visibility of the battlefield, the War on Terror is marked by a thoroughgoing technologization of combat – a tight articulation of war with technology that goes beyond reporting from the battlefield and refers to the very constitution of war through a media logic, as 'mediatised conflict' (Cottle 2006). Whilst this articulation emerged as early as the Vietnam War, the first 'televised war', mediatization gradually became a military strategy throughout the 1980s, culminating with the first Gulf War in 1991. Despite its celebration as the first real-time war, offering battlefield access from cameras adjusted on aircraft cockpits, this war's imagery was largely confined to 'night vision' visuals that 'fictionalized' the battlefield and maximized, rather than diminished, distance from it (Der Derian 2005). The 'virtual' Gulf war thus anticipated the digital nature of the War on Terror, in its use of ICTs both as propaganda mechanisms and as logistical systems of combat. In this ever-evolving media ecology, photojournalism remains important but, given the proliferation of real-time distribution platforms such as the internet, and digital cameras and phones, its scope becomes increasingly differentiated (Hoskins and O'Loughlin 2010).

i Aesthetic quality

Bodies: Similarly to the prosthetic imagination of the early twentieth century, technology continues to be celebrated in twenty-first-century photojournalism. Now, however, the articulation of the mechanical with the corporeal is further intensified. State-of-the-art sensory devices, high-tech weapon systems, and uniform fabrics are only some of the ways in which the twenty-first-century imaginary construes a new kind of body – the cyborg soldier (Masters 2005). Constituted in technoscientific discourses of military action, which further locate this body in virtual reality-simulated exercises and digitized battlefields, the cyborg soldier is no longer defined by the ways in which his/her body is complemented by weapons but by a whole new 'juncture of ... metals, chemicals, and people that makes weapons of computers and computers of weapons and soldiers' (Gray 1997: 8). Yet, even if this technological imagination renders the soldier 'post-human', in that technologies now perfect the biological senses, this imagination is simultaneously associated with a new emphasis on human vulnerability.

Indeed, controversies ensuing from the rare depictions of death in the War on Terror, in Julia Stevenson's 2009 *New York Times* image of a US Marine lethally wounded on the legs or in the 2005 AP imagery of a series of US flag-draped coffins on their way out of Iraq (see Figure 5.3), testify to the deep anxieties that traverse the cyborg soldier. What these contested visualities suggest is that,

Figure 5.3 Flag-draped US soldiers' coffins, 2005, Department of Defense.[8]

whilst constructed as a perfected version of the biological body, the cyborg is simultaneously unable to overcome its corporeal vulnerability and remains dramatically open to mortal threat in the battlefield (Lenoir 2000).

This ambivalent humanity is further combined with a thorough psychologization of the soldier. Going far beyond the recognition of fear, there is today an intense focus on the visualization of his/her tortured psyche that replaces earlier masculinist conceptions of humanity with a new fascination of agony-in-battle (Coker 2001). Evident in the proliferation of a subjectivist aesthetic in war images, including David Tumbler's grieving soldier (World Press Photo of the Year, 1991) and Craig Walker's Iraq War veteran suffering from acute post-traumatic stress disorder (Pulitzer, 2012), the depiction of soldiers in sorrow not only recast the battlefield as a space of individual trauma but also reposition photojournalism as itself an intimate practice of witnessing personal pain.

A century away from WWI pictures of the soldier-as-machine, these images may project a moral agency of emotional fragility, but cannot ultimately resolve earlier tensions of the soldier as a killing machine. Despite their hyper-emotionalization, twenty-first-century imageries of the cyborg ultimately approximate the WWI soldier, in that both are torn between technological fantasy and bodily mortality: 'military technologies have been "techno-masculinized", as Master says, 'while human soldiers ... have been "feminized" and reconstituted within the realm of those needing "protection"' (2005: 114).

Landscapes: Similarly to bodies, the landscapes of twenty-first-century war are less sites of battle and more sites of humanitarian action. From aid packages

The humanity of war 83

to medical equipment and from mechanical tools to children's toys, the representation of combative space moves away from the infliction of suffering and towards assisting vulnerable others (see Figure 5.4).

'We are', as Coker puts it, 'increasingly interested in reducing the material and human destructiveness of the battlefield' so as 'to reduce the incidents in which our own soldiers are traumatised or maimed or in danger of being killed, as it is to mitigate our own inhumanity to our enemies' (2001: 20–12). 'Embedded' forms of reporting, which bring together journalists and the military in close relationships of collaboration, further contribute to this humanitarian imagination of the army and, in so doing, establish a new sensibility of benevolence at the heart of the War on Terror. Seeking to legitimize the peacekeeping and nation-building NATO operations in Afghanistan and Iraq, such images cannot, however, break free from the constitutive contradiction of the war imaginary: military humanitarianism is, in fact, a war operation that, in the name of peace, costs hundreds of lives every year. If anything, as Der Derian argues, the War on Terror has reversed the mortality rates between soldiers, now safer, and civilians, now more vulnerable: 'war-related fatalities have been reversed in modern times, from 100 years ago when one civilian was killed per eight soldiers, to the current ratio of eight civilians per soldier killed' (2005: 26).

Simultaneously, the imagery of twenty-first-century landscapes has radically blurred the boundaries between battlefield and civilian sites that we encountered in WWII. Rather than aerial warfare, though, it is now terror attacks in city centres that redefine the battlefield. Whilst, therefore, the fields of Afghanistan and Iraq continue to be key theatres of combative action, the battlefield has come

Figure 5.4 US Department of Defense, Bagram Air Base, Afghanistan, 2005.[9]

to include the close-up suffering of civilians in Kabul and Basra but also in New York, London, and Madrid. Characterized by an aesthetic of the aftermath, these images represent sites of atrocity where emergency services, pools of blood, bodies, and scattered personal items come to stand for the horrors of urban killing. Even though the aftermath is a historical trope of atrocity, dominant, as we saw, in the sublime register of WWI battlefields, this aesthetic now re-emerges invested with a new emotionality. This is evident in professional photo-journalistic imagery, such as Massoud Hosseini's picture of an Afghan girl screaming after a suicide attack (Pulitzer, 2012), but also in the practice of amateur photojournalism, as reflected in the shaky 9/11 videos of the WTC plane crashes and the grainy mobile camera pictures from the 7/7 London attacks.

What these images share is, again, a register of 'ordinary witnessing', which prioritizes not a plenary view of the landscape-after-combat but an intimate view of human suffering from the perspective of those subject to it (Chouliaraki 2010). A new authenticity of photojournalism emerges, as a result – one that rejects the objectivism of the 'total gaze' and embraces the testimonial truth of the person-in-the street (Allan 2003). Drawing upon a subjectivist aesthetic of unreconstructed (non-edited) and embodied (randomly framed and erratically moving) mediations (Andén-Papadopoulos and Pantti 2011), the landscapes of the War of Terror inscribe any territory within ever-expanding violent cartographies and, in so doing, establish an emotionality of perpetual threat at the heart of today's war imaginary (Furedi 2007).

ii Moral agency

Twenty-first-century war photojournalism has redefined the relationship between self and other in ways that both evoke and surpass older tensions between human and machine. Even though the body still remains the focus of military performance, it is now embedded in broader calculations of life and death, where technology is not only a means of killing but primarily a means of maximizing survival – of soldiers and local others. This distinction between an early authoritative or 'disciplinary' and a contemporary empathetic or, more accurately, 'biopolitical' form of humanity (Foucault 1987), points, in turn, to a new moral imagination that moves away from a single focus on exterminating enemies towards 'the targeting of whole populations for political support' but also away from the soldier as killing machine and towards the soldier as 'a medium of communication' with such populations – what Bell refers to as the 'civilianisation of warfare' (2011: 310). This move of the war imaginary away from extreme violence and around the biopolitical imperative of managing lives is visually expressed in an aesthetic of trauma, where war is represented both as an intimate experience of sorrow and a public act of peacemaking. Let me summarize each.

Reflected in a series of prize-winning images on the intimate emotions of the soldier, the moral agency of civilianized war, I argued, is imagined through subjectivist registers, which abandon the objectivity of the 'total gaze' or the sublime, in favour of an intense affective expressivity. Even though the problematization of the soldier-machine had started as early as WWII, the contemporary dominance of an aesthetic of trauma over the sublime challenges the traditional morality of war in important ways. Celebrated as a triumph of the modernist 'culture of sympathy', this 'increasing respect for humanism and human life' is informed by the humanitarian vision of avoiding cruelty, which has now replaced the grand narratives of imperialism or nationalism that drove earlier wars (Coker 2008: 457).

This revaluation of humanity as biological life, however, may simultaneously be seen as an intensification, rather than relaxation, of the power relations of twenty-first-century warfare. The biopolitical force of these relations lies, according to Dillon and Reid (2009), in transforming the battlefield from an antagonistic confrontation with the enemy into a site for the micromanagement of individual lives without, simultaneously, being able to escape the nature of war as a practice of killing and being killed: 'Even though many recent military operations have been characterized as peace-keeping missions or stability operations', an important study, funded by the Iraq Afghanistan Deployment Impact Fund, claims, 'many of these efforts may share the same risks and stressors inherent in combat – exposure to hostile forces, injured civilians, mass graves, and land mines, for example'. Indicative of this dramatic ambivalence of humanitarian war is the unprecedented rise of suicide rates among Afghanistan-based US soldiers, in 2012.[10] Similarly expressive of this ambivalence, albeit in different ways, is the depiction of US atrocities in Iraq and Afghanistan, which further complicates the aesthetic of trauma with disturbing insights of the self as perpetrator – for instance, in the infamous Abu Ghraib amateur snapshots, which portrayed Iraqi prisoners as sub-human (see Figure 5.5).

The Abu Ghraib atrocities granted, however, the conception of the other in humanitarian war is primarily defined by massively proliferating images of empathetic exchanges between local populations and soldiers (see Figure 5.4 above). This is, again, a photojournalism of subjectivism that places a deeply asymmetrical relationship within what Boltanski (1999) calls, the 'topic of sentiment' – a mode of representing human suffering that evokes gratitude towards the benefactors and tender-heartedness towards the beneficiaries of the exchange. Part of the military communication strategy to 'win hearts and minds', the topic of sentiment may manage to give visibility to local others, but does so at a cost, insofar as their visualization as vulnerable recipients of aid construes these others as subordinate to the Western soldier. Suspended thus between subordination and dehumanization, this visual sentimentalization of war forges, according to Holmqvist, encounters of 'non-recognition' that, rather than acknowledging the cultural and political difference of local populations, subjects them to a double violence – symbolic, in that it humanizes 'them' only as subordinate to 'us', and physical, in that it abuses or kills 'them' unless they desire the same as 'us': 'the "other" of this present-day war', she argues, 'is not thought of as an Other but rather a different version of the self' (2014).

86 *Lilie Chouliaraki*

Figure 5.5 Abu Ghraib prison, 2004.[11]

In summary, the Anglo-American and Australian photojournalism of the twenty-first century has taken a turn towards a subjectivist aesthetic, which places a moral imagination of expressive sentimentality at the heart of war. This aesthetic of trauma attempts to resolve the paradox of the war imaginary, by construing war as primarily humanitarian and by psychologizing the power relations of the battlefield. Grounded on a photojournalism of embedded reporting and ordinary testimony, both of which, in different ways, favour intimate descriptions of the battlefield, this aesthetic breaks with the sublime and its proposal for an objective contemplation of the war in order to tell more personal stories of benevolent action. Despite its ambition to rescue the humanity of the battlefield, however, affective expressivity seems to accentuate the split between war as protecting and war as killing. It may intend to break from early portrayals of soldiers as human machines, yet inserts them into a more inhumane regulation of human lives in contexts of deliberate suffering. Similarly, this expressivity may attempt to acknowledge the humanity of others, yet it ultimately manages to either collapse this humanity to a Western vision of the self or to demonize it as impenetrable otherness. The new aesthetic of trauma, in conclusion, may be celebrated as humanizing war, but only manages to throw into dramatic relief the injured subjectivities that emerge in its course.

Conclusion: the ethics of war

Linfield's investigation on changing war images has been driven, similarly (but not identically) to mine, by the question of: 'how has the photography of political trauma and political witness responded to the radical changes in how war is made, and what it is made for, in the course of the past eight decades?' (2010: xvi). Whilst her response has been informed by images of civilian suffering within and beyond the West, my own response has been informed by iconic Western (Anglo-American) photojournalism of major battlefields. Consequently, our conclusions as to the political context of contemporary war photojournalism also differ. For Linfield, war photojournalism demonstrates a historical shift from the twentieth-century ideological battles to contemporary 'pure' violence, thereby giving rise to 'new kinds of images, because the atrocities they so nakedly depict are almost completely divorced from religious, political, or historical redemption' (2010: 205).

The idea of humanity, as Linfield argues, may no longer matter in non-Western conflict zones, yet, as I have shown, conflicts of the West continue to be informed by a moral imagination of humanity – one that wages war in the name of humanitarian benevolence. Far from new, I have also shown, this paradox is embedded in the centennial trajectory of the war imaginary, where the idea of humanity is constantly torn between a utopia of invincibility and a dystopia of destruction. In the wars of the early twentieth century, this ambivalence is expressed through objectivist aesthetic registers, notably a sublimation of the battlefield that invites a reflexive engagement with the spectacle of warfare in two of its most important manifestations – as heroic, in imageries of 'our' technological might and steely bravery, or as horrific, in imageries of 'their' dead bodies and the ravaged landscapes of combat. In the wars of the twenty-first century, the ambivalence of humanity is articulated through increasingly subjectivist aesthetic registers that now focus on war as an intensely psychological experience in two of its most prominent manifestations – the humanitarian battlefield, in imageries of benevolent encounters between troops and locals, and the traumatized individual, in imageries of victims in the civilianized landscapes of war. Rather than a move towards benevolence, I have finally cautioned, this transformation intensifies the power relations of war and the traumatic impact of the battlefield upon soldiers and civilians alike. War is becoming more humanitarian but less humane.

Even if photojournalism is a conservative genre of the war imaginary, echoing the values of the military, its aesthetic variations are indicative of broader societal changes: cultural ones, in the pervasive emotionalization of the public sphere (Coker 2001); institutional ones, in the technologies, ethics, and professional styles of reporting (Allan 2013); and geopolitical ones, in the global order and the conduct of war (Der Derian 2005). Insofar, however, as such changes are also about *communication* – the representational resources that nurture our public morality – it remains an urgent task of critical scholarship in this field to reflect upon the practices, past and present, through which the spectacle of the battlefield invites us to imagine the humanity of ourselves and that of the others who happen to be 'our' enemies. For, as Der Derian reminds us, it is ultimately the sight of the dead, the absolute sufferers, that, censored as it always is, comes to provide 'the corporeal gravitas of war' (2005: 30). And it is precisely this irreducible corporeal gravitas, in its sublimated or hyperemotional forms, that, by speaking about war, it also speaks of us – of who we are and how we should feel as witnesses of its horrors.

Notes

1 This chapter has been previously published in *Visual Communication*, Vol. 12(3) (2013). We thank the author and publisher for the permission to reuse the text here.
2 'Ethics, War and Photography' interview (2010): http://cisac.stanford.edu/news/cultural_critic_susie_linfield_discusses_the_ethics_of_seeing_20101029
3 Whilst Linfield focuses on the Holocaust or the Chinese Cultural Revolution and contemporary contexts of violence, such as Sierra Leone, Sudan, or Afghanistan, I focus on major WWI and WWII battlefields as well as major War on Terror sites, in Afghanistan and Iraq but also Western cities, such as New York and London. This variation drives our different claims about photojournalistic visualizations of suffering as well as different assumptions about the political contexts of such visualizations.
4 Whilst Linfield acknowledges this, in 'The hubris and despair of war journalism' (*Guernica*, June 2012), she does not pursue its implications for the changing visualities of photojournalism.
5 Butler (2006) for 'performativity'; Chouliaraki (2012) for 'performativity' and 'virtue ethics'; and Chouliaraki (2006) for the analytical approach on performativity introduced below.
6 Due to its temporal proximity, War on Terror photojournalism does not yet enjoy the universal recognisability of earlier visualizations. In this case, I define iconic photojournalism as award-winning (Pulitzer and World Press Awards) or globally influential photojournalism.
7 Available at http://picturesofworldwar1.com/photographer-frank-hurley/death-the-reaper
8 Available at: defense.gov or www.sfgate.com/news/article/Flag-draped-coffin-photos-released-Pentagon-had-2676780.php
9 Available at: www.defense.gov/photos/newsphoto.aspx?newsphotoid=7340
10 For instance, www.guardian.co.uk/world/2012/jun/08/suicide-rise-us-military
11 Available at: https://commons.wikimedia.org/wiki/Abu_Ghraib_prisoner_abuse. These images are in the public domain because they are ineligible for copyright. Pictures taken by US military personnel as part of that person's official duties are ineligible for copyright.

References

Alexander, J. (2004). *Cultural Trauma and Collective Identity*. Berkeley, CA: University of California Press.
Allan, S. (2013). *Citizen Witnessing: Revisioning Journalism in Times of Crisis*. Cambridge: Polity.

Andén-Papadopoulos K. and Pantti M. (eds.) (2011) *Amateur Images and Global News*. Bristol: Intellect Books.
Bell, C. (2011). Civilianising Warfare: Ways of War and Peace in Modern Counterinsurgency. *Journal of International Relations and Development*, 14(3), pp. 309–332.
Boltanski, L. (1999). *Distant Suffering: Politics, Morality and the Media*. Cambridge: Cambridge University Press.
Bousquet, A. (2006). Time Zero: Hiroshima, September 11 and Apocalyptic Revelations in Historical Consciousness. *Millennium – Journal of International Studies*, 34(3), pp. 739–765.
Butler, J. (2006). *Precarious Life: The Powers of Mourning and Violence*. London: Verso.
Carmichael, J. (1989). *First World War Photographers*. London: Routledge.
Carruthers, S. (2000). *The Media at War: Communication and Conflict in the 20th Century*. New York: St Martin's Press.
Castoriadis C. (1975/1987). *The Imaginary Institution of Society*. Cambridge: Polity.
Chouliaraki, L. (2006). *The Spectatorship of Suffering*. London: Sage.
Chouliaraki, L. (2010). Ordinary Witnessing in Post-television News. *Critical Discourse Studies*, 7(4), pp. 305–319.
Chouliaraki, L. (2012). *The Ironic Spectator: Solidarity in the Age of Posthumanitarianism*. Cambridge: Polity.
Coker, C. (2001). *Humane Warfare: The New Ethics of Postmodern War*. London: Routledge.
Coker, C. (2008). *Ethics and War in the 21st Century*. London: Routledge.
Corner, J. (2003). Debate: The Model in Question: A Response to Klaehn on Herman and Chomsky. *European Journal of Communication*, 18(3), pp. 367–375.
Cottle, S. (2006). *Mediatized Conflict: Developments in Media and Conflict Studies*. Maidenhead: Oxford University Press.
Der Derian, J. (2005). Imaging Terror: Logos, Pathos and Ethos. *Third World Quarterly*, 26(1), pp. 23–37.
Dillon, M. and Reid, J. (2009). *The Liberal Way of War: Killing to Make Life Live*. London: Routledge.
Dower, J. (2010). *Cultures of War: Pearl Harbor, Hiroshima, 9–11, Iraq*. New York: Norton.
Farish, M. (2001). Modern Witnesses. Foreign Correspondents, Geopolitical Vision and the First World War. *Transactions of the Institute of British Geographers*, 26(3), pp. 273–287.
Foucault, M. (1987). The Subject and Power. *Critical Inquiry*, 8(4), pp. 777–789.
Frazer, E. and Hutchings, K. (2011). Virtuous Violence and the Politics of Statecraft in Machiavelli, Clausewitz and Weber. *Political Studies*, 59(1), pp. 56–73.
Friday, J. (2000). Demonic Curiosity and the Aesthetics of Documentary Photography. *British Journal of Aesthetics*, 40(3), pp. 356–375.
Furedi, F. (2007). *Invitation to Terror: The Expanding Empire of the Unknown*. London/New York: Continuum.
Fussell, P. (1975). *The Great War and Modern Memory*. London: Stirling Press.
Gibbs, P. (1920/2009). *Now It Can Be Told*. Cabin John, MD: Wildside Press.
Gray, C. H. (1997). *Postmodern War: The New Politics of Conflict*. New York: The Guilford Press.
Griffin, M. (1999). The Great War Photographs: Constructing Myths of History and Photojournalism. In: B. Brennen and H. Hardt, eds., *Picturing the Past. Media, History and Photography*. Chicago, IL: University of Illinois Press.

Herman, E. and Chomsky, N. (1988). *Manufacturing Consent: The Political Economy of the Mass Media.* New York: Pantheon.

Holmqvist, C. (2014). *Policing Wars: On Military Intervention in the Twenty-First Century (Rethinking Political Violence).* Basingstoke: Palgrave Macmillan.

Hoskins, A. and McLoughlin, B. (2010). *War and Media: The Emergence of Diffused War.* Cambridge: Polity.

Howard, M. (1978/2008). *War and the Liberal Conscience.* New York: Columbia University Press.

Huppauf, B. (1996). Walter Benjamin's Imaginary Landscape. In: G. Fischer, ed., *With the Sharpened Axe of Reason: Approaches to Walter Benjamin.* Oxford: Berg, pp. 33–54.

Huppauf, B. (1997). Modernity and Violence. Observations on a Contradictory Relationship. In: B. Huppauf, ed., *War, Violence and the Modern Condition.* Berlin: de Gruyter.

Lasswell, H. (1971). *Propaganda Technique in WWI.* Cambridge, MA: MIT Press.

Leed, E. (1979). *No Man's Land: Combat and Identity in World War I.* Cambridge: Cambridge University Press.

Lenoir, T. (2000). All but War is Simulation: The Military-Entertainment Complex. *Configurations*, 8(3), pp. 289–335.

Linfield, S. (2010). *The Cruel Radiance: Photography and Political Violence.* Chicago, IL: Cambridge University Press.

Masters, C. (2005). Bodies of Technology. Cyborg Soldiers and Militarised Masculinities. *International Feminist Journal of Politics*, 7(1), pp. 112–132

Roeder, G. (1993). *The Censored War: Experience during World War II.* Boston, MA: Yale University Press.

Sturken, M. (1997). *Tangled Memories: The Vietnam War, the AIDS epidemic, and the Politics of Remembering.* Berkeley, CA: University of California Press.

Taylor, C. (2002). *Modern Social Imaginaries.* Durham, NC: Duke University Press.

Walzer, M. (2006). *Just and Unjust Wars: A Moral Argument with Historical Illustrations.* New York: Basic Books.

Winter, J. (1995). *Sites of Memory, Sites of Mourning: The Great War in European Memory.* Cambridge: Cambridge University Press.

Zelizer, B. (1998). *Remembering to Forget.* Chicago, IL: Cambridge University Press.

6 World Drug Day and visual rituals of security in West Africa

Adam Sandor

Introduction

Since the 1990s, observers of politics in Africa have shown that the continent has become a significant transit route for drug trafficking flows destined for European consumption (see Klein 1994; Allen 1999; Bayart *et al.* 1999). The increased scope of this trend became evident in the early to mid-2000s, when a slew of multi-ton seizures of cocaine occurred in several West African countries, leading some to be dubbed the world's first 'narco-states' (Ellis 2009; Carrier and Klantsching 2012; Shaw 2015). For international actors, the infiltration of drug trafficking and other criminal networks into the governance structures of West Africa poses an immediate global threat, notably if this merges with armed Islamist groups in a nebulous drugs-terror nexus (Lacher 2013; Raineri and Strazzari 2015).

This chapter analyses the relationship between visuality and security and the social construction of the drug threat in West Africa. I make the argument that in addition to the power of images to speak threat, public ritual spectacles also compose an important genre of visual security practice, especially in environments that rely heavily on forms of political communication other than through televised media, such as via public gatherings. In West Africa, security actors instrumentalize visual practices associated with ritual and spectatorship by staging displays of power in the performance of securitizing moves. This is done in order to better fix the security understandings of targeted audiences who participate in security rituals through their spectatorship. These visual practices of ritual occur through government ceremonies, rallies, concerts, parades, and other staged performances. At these events, multiple forms of media are utilized, but heavy stock is placed on visual modalities in order to 'draw in' audience spectators. These events are often highly choreographed, steeped in symbolic content, and informed by historical context that audiences require for a securitization move to be successful, and wherein audience participants interiorize the meaning of the security rituals performed.

The chapter proceeds in three sections. First, I outline what the disparate literatures on the process of threat construction within securitization theory (Buzan *et al.* 1998; see also Fish in this volume) can learn from an emphasis on ritual performance. Ritual action is the meaningful use of symbols on a repetitive basis meant for public viewing and consumption. The second section argues that ritual performance has a special reference point for African politics. By drawing on literature from political anthropology in West Africa, the second section discusses the importance of ritual performance in the maintenance of power. African security and political elites use the visual structure of ritual performance in their security efforts. Governments in Africa, for example, routinely use live performance events to remind citizens of their coercive abilities, to make visible displays of accumulation and distribution of material resources, one's ethnic or 'traditional' pedigrees, and ultimately their invented political legitimacy (see Miles 1989; Schatzberg 2001). State officials' attempts to have individuals witness live ritual performances is a tactic they use to inculcate dispositions of subservience in citizen participants to the powers of the state by coaxing participation in visual spectacles and performances, thereby linking visual and affective registers.

The third section uses these insights to analyse the visual rituals of security of West African governments on 26 June, World Drug Day. On this day, West African security agents charged with administering the 'fight against drugs' perform rituals of security through grandiose visual spectacle. They perform securitizing moves by drawing on repertoires of globally perceived weaknesses and locally perceived strengths and power (Bayart 2000). Through the ritual of burning annually seized narcotics, such securitizing agents are playing to multiple audiences simultaneously: first, state agents signal to local civil society visual displays of the power of the state in the fight against drug use, narco-trafficking, and transnational crime more broadly; second, through this visual performance, state agents signal to the international community of donors and security-advisers present at World Drug Day activities of West African state agents' lack of resources but simultaneous operational will to tackle transnational criminality in the expectation that these international spectators will provide them with various security rents.

Securitization: the visual, and the ritual

One of the most fruitful insights of what is now referred to as 'the broadening debate' within Security Studies concerns how threats are socially constructed. Securitization theory has been extremely influential in its demonstration of how this occurs: threats are defined and responded to through intersubjective processes amongst securitizing agents and audiences (Buzan *et al.* 1998: 31). Refinements of securitization theory have drawn on two principal methodological avenues (Balzacq 2011): one refines the discursive foundations of securitization and the central role of language and its social performance, derived from debates in the philosophy of language (Stritzel 2007; Wæver 1995, 2011); the second, inspired by sociological methodologies, highlights the role of practices, technologies, and competitions that together call up security politics (Bigo 2000; Huysmans 2006, 2011). While seemingly very stark, the divide between the philosophical and sociological variants of securitization theory need not reduce the possibility for analytical combinations and eclectic thinking. This is especially the case when empirical challenges and contexts limit ideal type formulations, and require analytical tools able to excavate the problem/questions at hand. Instead of adhering to methodological or philosophical orthodoxies, combining analytical tools and research approaches may help us answer different types of questions in distinct sociopolitical contexts.

Analysing the relationship that images have with security provides a prominent example. Given the 'media-saturated' characteristics of political communication in industrialized countries (Williams 2003: 526), examining how iconic images can 'speak security' and facilitate the social construction of threats has been an important addition to the discursive emphasis in securitization's original framework (Hansen 2011: 54–55; 2015). As Heck and Schlag (2013: 896) and others demonstrate, particular visual artefacts like photographs, drawn images like cartoons, memes, or clips of video can and do facilitate acts of 'showing and seeing' threats, which are made visible to wider audiences to justify security or military action (see also Möller 2013). Analyses of images have laid bare the symbolic representations of threat construction that guide security discourse towards the implementation of extraordinary measures beyond political debate, and the power of images to create multiple meanings of (in)security.

The emphasis on analysing specific instances of visual representation – images – however, can overshadow how visuality more generally is central in informing and constituting security knowledges and practices. Visuality constitutes a relation of knowledge by which things are rendered socially visible, invisible, or visible to some and not others (Andersen *et al.* 2015). While images can play a significant role in the construction of threats, they do not exhaust the potential for other visual mediums, modalities, and practices of threat communication and production. For example, when audiences witness the security functions of urban spaces and architectures such as fences, ramparts around embassies, or one-way corridors of international airports, they are coaxed to follow practices that visibly signal acquiescence and discipline to aspects of that particular *dispositif* (see Coaffee *et al.* 2009). The connected act of seeing and surveilling particular groups is a political relation whereby targets of vision are ascribed threatening characteristics (see Mitchell 2014), a process whereby other structures of power and violence are rendered invisible (Dixit 2014). Seeing an event unfold before one's eyes as a live audience participant, as I argue below, involves visual techniques and practices that make security and insecurity possible. Thus, the act of seeing forms a key element of the politics and governance of security. When it comes to the social construction of threats, therefore, 'seeing, knowing and power are interrelated' (Hooper-Greenhill 2000: 14). This implies the need to understand those diverse practices and context-dependent 'visual security economies' that enable ways in which political subjects see, are seen, and then come to interpret this social relation in their own political actions (Amoore 2007; Campbell 2007). A broader conceptualization of visuality shifts our focus away from specific forms and artefacts of vision towards other genres of visual practice and performance.

Ritual performances form a potent, routinized visual modality by which threats are called into being, represented, and legitimized by diverse audiences in contemporary security politics. While it is impossible to do justice to what is now an enormous literature in Anthropology, Sociology, and Religious Studies, ritual performances are understood here as socially conventionalized symbolic behaviour that is expressive, repetitive, and public.[1] Taking a cue from Cohen, power relations are 'expressed ... [and]... camouflaged by means of symbolic forms and patterns of symbolic action' with ritual performances constituting vehicles for their public consumption and spectatorship (1979: 89). Rituals perform social and political orders by connecting disparate events and symbols to construct a definitive and anchored reality through competent performances consumed and spectated by audiences (Giesen 2006: 349; Kertzer 1988).

Ritual performances are a universal modality of political action common to governance the world over, and contribute directly to the social construction of threats (see Alexander 2011: 159–194). The ritual performance of the US 'State of the Union' address sets the scene for several securitizing moves to be made to the audience of members of US Congress and a wider viewing national population; the opening of Canadian parliamentary debates begins only after the introduction of a ceremonial mace to the chamber of parliament, symbolizing the authority of the head of state and witnessed by members of parliament; the public issuing of national medals to soldiers following periods of violent combat, the erection of grand monuments to those fallen, and other ceremonial rites that aggrandize the nation-state, are all ritual performances that require being seen in order to establish a context for the legitimate delivery of appropriate forms of security discourse. The symbolic content of these rituals, couched in the visual, delineates how or when security actors can present arguments in favour of securitization or desecuritization.

Analysing security rituals, how they are simultaneously meant for communicating visions of the world, and spectating and consuming, bridges the visual/linguistic and sociological variants of securitization theory. Few researchers engaging with securitization theory (of either variant) have analysed the practice of ritual performance as a component of the securitization process (cf. Balzacq 2014). Nevertheless, the theoretical fount from which sociologically inspired securitization analysts draw highlights the centrality of ritual in the constitution of social universes.

Goffman, for whom ritual performance was key to understanding routine social interactions (1967/2005), inspires Salter's (2008) dramaturgical approach to securitization. Salter argues that different settings will influence the types of security claims made by security actors. Security actors adopt specific roles within particular settings as technicians, scientists, consultants, bureaucrats, elected officials, military officials, intelligence officers, which 'structures the speaker–audience relationship of knowledge and authority, the weight of social context, and the success of the securitizing move' (2008: 328–330). This insight dovetails with Stritzel's (2007) claim that security actors must craft their securitizing moves by taking discursive contexts seriously in order to tap into security's performative power on an audience (see also Balzacq 2011).

Context-sensitive discourses, attuned to social settings and the roles that security actors play, however, also incorporate ritual action that is more often than not couched in visual practices of displaying and witnessing. Staging and performance in the orchestration of political events makes clear the importance of ritual action and its visual aspects in the creation of successful securitization. Security rituals are competently executed expressive performances that enact threats that are meaningful to specific, intersubjective relationships premised in a range of shared to contested understandings of danger, and socially consumed by diverse audiences. As such, these rituals are performed to condition participant response and adherence to the call for security when they are observed.

The practice of international diplomacy found in bilateral security and peace summits gives a potent example. Receiving visiting dignitaries and foreign heads of state is a routine occurrence meant to visually communicate the commencement of official relations between sovereign representatives. This practice is an intensely meaningful political enactment, where seemingly minute missteps like (not) denouncing an act of violence, displaying national flags, not announcing formal titles or full names, or not arriving to a red carpet upon leaving a presidential aircraft may immediately set a tense tone to the diplomatic proceedings. Like the pronouncement of security truth-claims or 'securitizing moves', diplomatic performances are often meant for public consumption, spectatorship, and witnessing, to signal a depiction of a political order and to elicit an acknowledgment of the authenticity of the events' performers (like security agents) by targeted audiences (see Stritzel 2011: 350–352; Côté 2016: 547).

Like power, security 'must be clothed in effective means of displaying it, and will have different effects depending upon how it is dramatized' (Goffman 1959: 241). Scientists and experts, for example, are paraded before government committees and the media to publicly articulate their authoritative security claims, as in the case of the lead-up to the US war in Iraq, or more recently and regularly with regard to climate change and refugee and migrant flows (O'Reilly 2008; Methmann and Rothe 2014). When expressing the dangers associated with a given threat, ritual performances are visually displayed and spectated to convey the symbolic and coercive potential of security actors, and the legitimacy of their plans, techniques, and practices to counter threats.

While they range in terms of their formality, rituals induce communication through visual symbols, participation in the performance, and affective or emotional response (Parkin 1996: xxii–xxiii; Apter 2006: 233; see Lewis 1980). Alexander explains that socio-political actors take the elements of visual performance into account to have the audiences

> take this script as real, to experience it, not as a 'script' – nor as symbolic or contrived – but as completely real, as having an ontological status.... If they are to identify with you and to connect emotionally to your script, then they must believe you. They must accept your symbolic projection.
>
> (2011: 83)

For example, moments of silence, or the ceremonial folding of national flags, as observed to commemorate Armistice Day, or the 11 September 2001 attacks in the United States, are often highly formalized, stylized, and communicative of sacrifices and dangers experienced in the past by political communities, such that the threat of mass war or terrorism achieve an ontological status made visible through ritual performance and ceremony.

Elites hold an important place in the enactment and production of security rituals (see Smith 2014). Such ritual managers choreograph visual performances through crafted content and by staging displays of spectacle to trigger emotional responses from its witnesses, to inspire fear, or wonder (Cohen 1974; Kertzer 1988: 99–101; Kong and Yeoh 1997: 216–219). To make the presentation of a message resonate with an audience in hopes of shrinking the space between spectator and the spectacle itself, rituals require careful preparation and resources. Such performances also take into account an understanding of the performance setting and the power relations between sets of ritual performers and audience members. This is precisely why entire teams of diplomatic officials incorporate measured, and symbolically fine-tuned textual and visual scripts that draw from cultural and historical tropes – to properly set the stage for the social drama to unfold, and to envelop audience members in it by 'selling' their vision of diplomacy, alliances, threats, and proposed responses in an authentic way. When audiences identify actors that transgress the choreography and settings of security actors performing securitizing moves, or which deviate from their roles in this process by 'going off script', the result is often the latter's delegitimization, and a loss of their capital in the security field.

Of course, not all such security theatrics are equally meaningful or resonant to all audiences and settings. Indeed, ritual performance requires adaptation by securitizing actors in terms of which aspects of technical design will best convey the prepared message. This may include coupling multiple sensory modalities such as use of images, the display of statistics and graphs, playing background music, even the demonstration of touchable objects, all in attempts to coax the acceptance of an audience to sediment their political understandings, values, and behaviours. When these elements are combined through captivating spectacle, ritual performances form an indispensable element not only for the construction and recognition of an actor's authority, which is so crucial to the success of any securitizing move, but for its continual (re)creation (see Cohen 1974; Geertz 1980; Williams 2007: 64–68).

The acceptance of the securitizing move by an audience will depend on the performance of symbolic action through the inclusion of visual practices meant for spectating and shocking audience members into becoming actively engaged in it, and coaxing them to rally to the meanings conveyed in and through the security ritual.

Ritual, power, and politics in West Africa

While the ritualistic characteristics of politics are pervasive regardless of geographical location (rituals are part and parcel of politics in Western states, as much as they are for the politics in 'the postcolony') (see Comaroff and Comaroff 2006), the place of visual ritual performances in the politics of African states is especially prominent for two important reasons. First, politicians in West Africa recognize the need to hold public forums wherein they use 'traditional' oral litanies and tropes that will be legitimized by targeted audiences. Being present at religious ceremonies, public rallies and speeches, and other presentations is a common and flashy occurrence in West Africa that is extensively mediatized, and intended for wide public viewing to envelop audience members in the performance of the state (see Schatzberg 2001: 78–80; Lentz 2001). Ritualized, public 'ceremonies of political hospitality' can at times also provide local groups an avenue to communicate their values and concerns to political elites through the intermediary of local chieftaincies, social associations, and other institutions, thereby highlighting the familiarity of visual ritual performance as an important element of the negotiated nature of African statehood (Karlström 2003: 66; see Barnes 1996; Hagmann and Péclard 2010).

Second, staging ritual performances allows state officials to demonstrate the ostentatious nature of their power, framed as eminent importance, luxurious generosity, or as an overt capacity to exert coercive force. Mbembe (1992: 7–10) argues that visual, ritualistic performances like ceremonies and other public events are central mechanisms for the postcolonial African '*commandement*' to express and 'dramatize its magnificence and prodigality'. It is precisely through the demonstration of high levels of opulence performed in public settings and in ritualistic fashion that political elites in Africa seek to render political resistance less likely. They stage and manipulate public rituals of visual performance to remind subordinate groups present of the state's simultaneous benefaction and coercive abilities, coaxing at least the presence of citizen participation in body if not in spirit. When audience members do not sufficiently demonstrate their subjection to this networked apparatus of power, by enacting '"spontaneous" obedience, or evidence of "gratitude"', the resort to striking levels of arbitrary coercion by state agencies is often the result (Mbembe 2001: 42).

Political rallies and annual festivals are examples of such visual ritual performances. Sitting governments and political parties use them to drum up support in electoral contests, or to amplify the citizenry's support for specific state policies (see Miles 1989; Lentz 2001). Singing, drumming, and the performance of customary dance are often included in the performance repertoire, used as familiar symbolic devices for audience members. Loudspeakers play party songs or national anthems. Bright coloured t-shirts, scarves, and bumper stickers marked by party slogans, or that denote the specific theme of the rally or ceremony, are regularly given, and are nearly always immediately worn. Providing these small gifts is considered a banal but symbolically significant practice for audience participants, as these theatrical 'acts of generosity' fetishize the power of African political elites (Mbembe 1992: 9). Not giving out small offerings at a political rally could prove disastrous to less well-financed political challengers, since West African publics often interpret not providing gifts as 'stinginess'. Demonstrating ostentation through ritual performance can, therefore, increase the perceived legitimacy of political elites when seen providing material inducements in public ceremony.

Who ends up attending the rally is just as important as the types of theatrical elements performed, meaning that visible opulence is optimally coupled with being seen with the 'right people' and in 'the right places'. These include local chiefs, notables, businessmen, or international partners in influential towns of religious or political significance, where elites can mobilize networks that support government efforts (Schatzberg 2001: 62–82). Government officials use these occasions to visibly demonstrate their political connections and social power or status, combined with the coercive abilities and material resources at their disposal. The presence of notable figures such as local chief authorities, prominent local businessmen, and ministerial officials or advisers are strategized in order to convey the legitimacy of the proceedings.

Lastly, African political elites increasingly capitalize on visual performances of ritual in their interactions with the international. As explained by Bayart's concept of extraversion (2000), African political elites use the relations of asymmetry with international actors in order to acquire resources that are then used to consolidate strategies of rule domestically. Representatives of international organizations, diplomatic actors, and other potential donors are invited to attend public ceremonies in order to demonstrate the political will to tackle issues of concern such as development, and peace and security. Through these public demonstrations, African political elites perform their partnerships with international actors and thereby depict adherence of 'their end' of the unstated bargain, in expectations of reciprocal patterns of acknowledgment and material reward.

Thus, political elites in Africa play at multiple audiences, through multiple simultaneous visual tactics, and for purposes that may run at counter purposes. The performance of visual rituals on World Drug Day is a potent example. By demonstrating to national citizens that the coercive apparatuses of the state are capable, effective, and wield the potential for overwhelming violence, political elites remind local groups to acquiesce to an established political order. By inviting foreign dignitaries, officials from international organizations, and global security experts and partners, African political elites also visually demonstrate their gatekeeper status and political backing to national media outlets covering these events and to their citizens present, or individuals subsequently observing the ritual performance on the nightly news. Likewise, African political elites use World Drug Day events and performances in hopes of convincing international actors of the need to provide material and symbolic resources to tackle complicated security issues while insisting on their lack of capacity to do so. In this way, African political elites pursue grandiose, choreographed visual performances of security in ritualized fashion, the end game of which is to legitimize their social positions and global relationships, while also rendering banal the state's inaccessibility for local populations.

World Drug Day: ritual performances of security spectacle[2]

African government elites make a space of policy manoeuvrability in their relations with the international donor community through their very weakness and dependence on the international. This includes presenting security frames of reference that occupy international actors' concerns, and attempts to visually display their own authenticity regarding shared threats. In the post-9/11 context, West African governments have successfully manipulated the development of the subregion's infiltration by transnational organized crime networks and terrorist groups to their advantage by using the international donor community's policy consensus regarding the transversal nature of these threats, and by framing themselves as willing and capable partners of Western actors (Sandor 2016: 501; see also Bayart 2010). This hierarchical relationship, therefore, is premised in West African governments rendering visible their vulnerability to cross-border threats, being seen by members of the international donor community to be in need of technical and financial assistance, and willing to pursue international mandates. World Drug Day is one opportunity to perform such a set of visual security practices.

While there has been a proliferation of activity and concern around the question of drug trafficking in the subregion since the early 2000s (see WACD 2014), agreement about the threat of drug trafficking to West Africans is far from universal. Both West African political officials and ordinary citizens often question the importance of countering narcotics flows in the region. Many citizens do not believe that there is a problem with drug use in West Africa since the local market for narcotics is so limited. The general perception in both official and unofficial circles in the subregion is that narcotics use is a European problem first, and only partially a West African one. Furthermore, the stockpiling and storing of narcotics in the subregion for eventual transfer to Europe provides lucrative opportunities to make quick and substantial sums of money in a region that has been so negatively affected by international economic policies (Ellis 2009: 178–179). As a result, international organizations like the UNODC, UNDP, and the EU have used the allure of donor contributions to incentivize West African governments to be more actively engaged in counter-trafficking efforts.

The inflow of government representatives from Western states, international organizations delegations, private consultancies, and second-party NGOs that administer development projects specifically targeting the social and economic effects of drug trafficking and drug use has been a boon to the governments of the subregion. International responses to counter transnational criminal activity into West Africa has been to provide capacity-building initiatives to the subregion's law enforcement and security institutions. Western governments have stationed police liaisons and technical experts in most West African capitals, who have developed relationships and interact on a regular basis with the subregion's security actors. For example, international policing experts have supported the organizational development of specialized, inter-agency counter-trafficking units in many ECOWAS[3] states. The majority of governments of the subregion have also developed inter-ministerial committees dedicated to countering drug trafficking in their states. In general, these committees are represented by at least one official from each government ministry, so as to better involve all aspects of government and to develop comprehensive solutions to better fight the war on drugs. Inter-ministerial drug committees, and specialized transnational crime units (dubbed TCU by most international donors supporting them) are the main securitizing actors in the social construction of the drug threat in West Africa.

Twenty-six June, World Drug Day, has become the date whereon West African security actors have attempted to make themselves and their efforts visible as efficient partners in the war on drugs to their international counterparts. The day is marked by sophisticated demonstrations orchestrated by government inter-ministerial committees against drugs, along with workshops, radio interviews, and meetings with civil society groups to explain the dangers of drug use and trafficking. It has simultaneously become a day associated with ritual performances of the power of West African states for its citizenries, and a picture of weakness, lack of government capacity, and the urgent need for international help to counter the threat of drug-trafficking presented to the donor community.

World Drug Day ceremonies in the subregion are meticulously planned and choreographed to create a spectacle in attempts to perform the securitization of the drug issue.[4] The spaces of World Drug Day activities are structured so as to prime the vision of participants to see and understand the risks involved in drug trafficking. For ceremonies held in Accra, Ghana in 2012, audience participants entered into the conference centre where World Drug Day activities were held, and were corralled through rope-cordoned queues directing them towards roughly fifteen feet of billboards filled with photographs of arrested traffickers before entering the auditorium.[5] Even the distance between where participants stood in line and the billboards of images were planned, to create an optimal distance for either focusing on the large-scale set of images, or for direct focus on specific images.[6] The billboards outlined 'Methods Used in Trafficking', where images of arrested traffickers are permanently caught on display. While the images of arrested traffickers were taken prior to the judicial proceedings associated with these infractions, this did not deter national drug policing officials from highlighting the culpability of the criminals, and the multiple ways in which they were caught moving product through airports, seaports, and across the subregion's land borders.[7] The photographs showed how product is hidden in women's wigs and weaves, embedded into hollowed-out soles of platform shoes, taped around the bodies of women to give the impression of mature pregnancy, in secret compartments in luggage, or in stash compartments of automobiles.[8]

Corralling an audience of citizens and directing their movements past the images is a choreographed visual practice meant to symbolically recall understandings of political compliance and order in West African polities. Due to the lack of trust that most West African citizens have for agents of their states, audience participants tend to comply with their assigned choreographic roles, and pay their due attention to the images of the arrested traffickers, often for fear that not looking would draw the attention of state agents in the crowd of informants in the crowd.[9] This view was born out in discussions with interlocutors that had previously attended World Drug Day activities over the assumed role of the state in providing security for ordinary citizens in West Africa. The comment '*L'état, c'est l'uniforme!*' (The State is the uniform) was indicative of the view that the state is synonymous with coercive institutions, meaning distrust and fear of the state and its predatory nature, instantiated by police officers in uniform (see also Guillaume *et al.* in this volume). By organizing the corral in such a way as to direct the vision of the audience, World Drug Day organizers ritualize the performance of citizen subservience to state authority, with citizens shying away from not participating when present to mitigate the possibility of offence. Such a choreographed presentation of visual spectatorship, and the discipline of being seen by state agents symbolically performs an understanding of citizenship in West Africa from the hierarchical view of the state, where respect for individual rights-holding/exercising citizens takes the second position behind displays of public violence and surveillance (Mbembe 2001: 35–36, 42).

The images of the arrested traffickers, and the use of billboards are more than simply objects or artefacts of visions. They constitute the visual structuration of the security encounter between ritual managers and audience participants by symbolically stressing and consolidating visions of the determination, will, and power of the state's coercive institutions. These images display proof that state agents have outsmarted non-state criminal actors, thereby conveying to spectators the need to discipline their political behaviour or suffer the consequences. Poster advertisements of previous World Drug Day ceremonies depict the use of these corralled lines of citizens viewing the billboard images, donned with serious expressions, with headlines that include 'Don't be fooled', and 'It's not worth it!' Not only do the images presented display criminals caught, and therefore the efficacy of Ghana's security apparatuses, but also failed attempts at trafficking that have resulted in death, and the risks associated with criminal action. In Accra, several sections of the billboards were littered with images of dead African bodies, cut open presumably during an autopsy after a trafficking mishap and drug overdose. Contrary to arguments of a widespread presence of rule via techniques of liberal governmentality in Africa, such visual images of gore on open display render visible the state's mechanics of social and political control through sovereign power over these criminalized bodies (see Mbembe 2006; Joseph 2010).

World Drug Day activities are only partially organized and performed with West African citizens in mind. The day is also an opportunity to leverage international discourses of the drug threat in theatrically performing securitizing moves. In Senegal, for example, the Inter-Ministerial Committee in the Fight Against Drugs (CILD) conducts World Drug Day ceremonial planning.[10] In the past, the CILD has been understood by the country's police officers to be a place where obstreperous police lieutenants were sent to keep them out of the senior police leadership's affairs.[11] However, during the late 2000s, following some spectacular seizures of cocaine off the country's coast in 2005–2008, the CILD became an important centre of diplomatic activity centred around World Drug Day ceremonies.[12] The annual activities take months of planning, in particular to identify what types of activities should be showcased, and which international actors and media outlets to invite for attendance. Activities normally include weeklong awareness activities and workshops with live demonstrations where participants can observe specimens of seized drugs, and speak with police and health officials. To ensure a strong international attendance, CILD officials have created contact lists of regional and international diplomatic actors to inform regarding the activities they have planned, and insist that well-performed World Drug Day ceremonies should catalyse their activities with international actors for future months.

The pinnacle performance of World Drug Day is the public incineration ceremony. In official discourse, the entirety of the year's national drug seizures are saved for the event, unless the seized goods are currently used for legal proceedings as evidence.[13] In Senegal, the event is conducted with much official fanfare and national symbolism. The event occurs in the neighbourhood of Mammelles, on the plateau of one of two hills. From multiple conversations with local Dakarois, it seems that all know the location well due to its annual occurrence, even if they have never attended the ceremony. In 2010, Ministry of Interior officials strategically selected the site since it overlooks the Senegalese national monument of African Renaissance – a governmental symbol of pride and national sovereignty, but a local symbol of misuse of public funds. When I attended the 2016 ceremony, a circular pile of drugs lay in a twenty- to thirty- metre circumference consisting of hundreds of kilograms of cannabis, some ten to twenty kilos of cocaine, methamphetamines, fake pharmaceuticals, khat, and heroin, smelling of diesel fuel laid on the plateau, guarded by a dozen Senegalese police officers, dressed in white hazmat suits.[14]

Twenty metres in front of the intended pyre, a tent was erected to provide shade for invited guests. In 2016's ceremony, those guests included officials from the US embassy, French diplomats, UNODC officials, some Nigerien counterparts, a host of Senegalese dignitaries, and local and international media. The most numerous cohorts among the attendees, however, were Senegalese law enforcement actors: the higher-ranking officials in their ceremonial suits, pinned with medals and lapels indicating institutional rank, and the remainder in heavily militarized uniforms.

World Drug Day incineration ceremonies, like the commencement of international summits and conferences, do not begin until the senior national authorities are present to officially commence the event, in this case the Minister of the Interior. Upon the minister's arrival, he immediately approached representatives from the UN and EU, shaking their hands and thanking them for their attendance, making sure to be seen by photographers present who took copious pictures. A senior customs official noted to me that the French and American ambassadors were not present; otherwise they would have been seen to receive the first greetings from the minister. Once this diplomatic practice was accomplished, an aide of the Minister communicated to a member of the CILD to begin the ceremony.

The Minister's act of approaching international partners upon arrival at the event site is only one display of symbolic communication to international audience members of Senegal's relations of asymmetrical partnership through participation in World Drug Day activities. In fact, the incineration ceremony is strategically directed in excessive minutiae at international partners that had been invited weeks before, which includes police and customs liaisons and other security experts. Liaisons and capacity-builders constitute a crucial audience to which Senegal's security and political elites perform in the day's activities in order to consolidate working security relationships forged over the post-Cold War period through law enforcement operations and mentoring.[15] Indeed, some of Senegal's security institutions' relationships with international partners, notably with their French counterparts, have been tense, as the latter often find that Senegalese drug police could do more to combat trafficking in the country. Through the World Drug Day activities, Senegalese drug law enforcement agents present visual evidence of their operational capacity through the seized drugs to be destroyed, and their acts of outreach to civil society organizations to explain the social harms associated with drugs and organized criminality.

Part of the planning of the performance includes orders from the National Police leadership for the dress and comportment of the country's law enforcement and military actors in attendance. The donning of uniforms symbolizes the rank and order of those present, and therefore an order of importance amongst the corps of national security actors. Importantly, this display also has an intended visual effect for the audience of international actors present. Senegalese security actors stress the need to be seen as sovereign, capable, professional, law enforcement agents (Sandor 2016: 500). This sets them apart from other regional security forces in the subregion, which are often viewed as vectors of insecurity by international actors. Of course, law enforcement officials the world over wear uniforms to make them easily identifiable to citizens. Nevertheless, even Senegalese drug police, who for operational reasons never wear uniforms due to the nature of their work, don uniforms in settings where international actors are present in order to maintain an already well-established view that they form the region's most stable public security force. In other words, this is a visible display of being seen by international partners, and reminding them of Senegalese agents' capacity and professionalism.[16] Upon asking one of the lower-ranked gendarmes donning his militarized uniform why so many security actors present were dressed in operational uniforms, weapons at their sides and boots polished, he stressed that it was a command for the day's activities, probably to display gratitude for foreign partners present who had provided them with the equipment, and to convey the officialdom of the state security institutions.[17] These visual practices signal to international actors the trustworthiness of Senegalese partners in their asymmetrical relations of power with global security actors. (See Figure 6.1.)

Figure 6.1 Officers in uniform light up the seized drugs.

Prior to the incineration itself, the Chief of Senegal's National Drug Police commenced his introductory remarks, urging the visiting international dignitaries to sit in the front row of seats under the tent, or to move closer to the pyre for a better view. He then commanded that the pile be set ablaze, when the spectators were only a metre away from its edge. Fire spread so quickly that the crowd needed to quickly push back due to the intense heat, and the noxious smell of the burning materials soaked in accelerant. Journalists' cameras next to the blaze caught on fire, causing a commotion between law enforcement actors shouting for the crowd to move back, and cameramen, rushing to save burning tripods (see Figure 6.2). A Western official beside me chortled, 'They know how to put on a show', and then left to his car to return to the embassy.[18]

While most likely stated sarcastically, and to emphasize the irresponsibility of the security agents for not providing safe distance from the fire, this global security expert's comments play directly into the intended and desired interpretation that the ceremony's organizers were hoping for. The visual display of the scale of seized drugs was substantial, and was acknowledged by several IO experts and police liaisons present. However, these individuals subsequently stressed that the seized drugs used in the incineration were only indicative of a fraction of the narcotics that must be passing through Senegal. One official reminded me that in 2013, a tanker arrived in a port in the United Kingdom

Figure 6.2 The spectacle gets out of hand.

having just left the Port of Dakar, filled with hundreds of kilograms of cocaine, proving that the vulnerability of Senegal to drug trafficking is certain.[19] Working with Senegalese law enforcement agents, therefore, was necessary since they demonstrated their capability to seize narcotics, but equally were seen as being simultaneously vulnerable to this cross-border threat. In this way, while the actual ritual performance of incinerating the drugs went slightly pear-shaped, it nevertheless was visually felicitous in symbolically articulating the authority of Senegalese security actors to a targeted international audience (see Figure 6.3).

The asymmetrical nature of Senegalese security actors' relations with international counterparts is premised in being seen as weak and under-resourced, but capable and trustworthy security partners against the subregion's cross-border threats. Trust between global security experts, the majority of which are Western, and their African counterparts more often than not runs quite thin. International security and diplomatic partners do not hold operational trust and regard for local West African officials in equal measure, since many governments and security institutions are known to be dangerously corrupt. At the drug incineration ceremonies held in neighbouring Guinea in May 2008, for example, the US Ambassador requested to see a sample of some of the reported 390 kilograms of cocaine that was seized a month before, set to be burned. The Ministers of the Interior, and of Justice denied the Ambassador's request, had the pile of material

Figure 6.3 The bonfire.

doused in gasoline, and quickly set ablaze (US Embassy Conakry 2008). Despite previous visual activities, which included similar performance trappings as those used in Ghana and Senegal, such as having the ministers pose for photos with the Ambassador, and giving a speech on the dangers of transnational criminality in the form of drug trafficking, the Ambassador's request was an indictment of Guinea's political elites being directly linked to criminal activity. US support of Guinean officials promptly degraded when it came to support in the war on drugs, since the Guinean authorities were not viewed as credible partners – only weak and incapable ones too corrupt to work with.[20]

In Senegal, however, through the performance of World Drug Day ceremonies, this visual representation of simultaneous capability and vulnerability is successfully accomplished by carefully orchestrating participation by an audience of international actors in the day's ritual, spectacular activities. Discussions with Senegalese and Ghanaian security officials with regard to the fight against drugs confirm this. In nearly every interview and conversation held, these officials explained how necessary it was for their services to be seen making 'big seizures' by international actors. The presence of international actors, they insisted, at World Drug Day activities, especially to witness the incineration ceremony, was a way of visually displaying their force's efficiency. They hope to demonstrate operational capacity through collecting seized drugs from the previous year and placing these together, in bulk, on one specific day to ceremonially burn. Such a display, in their minds, illustrates the scale of the phenomenon of drug trafficking as a threat to their states, and their recognized authority over contemporary security matters like transnational organized crime. In the region, Senegalese and Ghanaian security actors have arguably been the most successful in demonstrating a vision of their capabilities, symbolized on World Drug Day by the size of drugs seized, ready to burn. For Senegalese political and security elites, the spectacular height and depth of the flames that are the national annual seizures' material and caloric outcome, burning in full view of Senegal's most visible national monument, constitutes a felicitous visual performance of their security status to international donors.

Burning the seized narcotics is an attempt to provide a physical manifestation of a symbolic discourse that resonates with both local and international audiences as spectators on emotional and affective registers. While the World Drug Day events have been banalized through annual repetition, which would indicate a weaker attachment to the ritual ceremony, there was nonetheless an element of reverence for the proceedings in Dakar. The incineration itself was impressive, with flames reaching high into the air and flashing in front of the country's controversial national monument and symbol of sovereignty, obscured by dense smoke.[21] From twenty metres away from the pyre, the heat of the burning products radiated towards the seated area. Once participants were at a safe distance from the flames, a noticeable feeling of catharsis, and expressions of fascination and satisfaction overtook several audience members' faces, both local and international audience participants. Crucially for the act of spectatorship of this ritual action, audience participants discussed together how the ritual act itself could be improved to reach larger groups in Senegal, demonstrating their participation in this performance of security diplomacy. After recording the statements made by the head of the national drug police, Senegalese journalists and reporters approached several international audience members for comment regarding the threat of drug trafficking to the country, and the nature of their partnerships and bilateral initiatives with Senegal's security authorities. The ritual performance of incinerating seized narcotics, therefore, provides a staged setting in which audience spectators and participants are given the chance to 'fuse' their understandings of the drug threat with those displayed by ritual performers, by articulating the dangers of this form of criminality to West Africa, and their will to partner with willing security actors on the national scene (see Alexander 2004).

Finally, publically incinerating the narcotics is a practice that is visually and symbolically meaningful for African publics. While several international actors view the public ceremony as a quaint oddity for West Africa, and something that would never be replicated in Europe, publically burning objects deemed threatening in Africa for visual consumption is decidedly context sensitive. Of course, the use of fire as an element associated with ritual action is far from a solely African affair, but is found in rituals across the globe, as the 'Burning Man' festival attests; it is nevertheless a common occurrence on the continent (see Turner 1967, 1969; Gilmore 2010). After the signing of peace agreements with armed rebel movements, for example, burning guns and ammunition to symbolize the destruction of tools of war in exchange for peace is routine. Public vigilante justice in Africa, notably against migrants caught in acts of petty criminality, often uses the horrific practice of 'necklacing', where fuel-soaked tires, which are set ablaze, are donned about the necks of individuals (see Grätz 2011; Hammerstad 2012). The use of fire, and its purpose in ritual performance in West Africa, therefore, is familiar to local participants. The fact that incineration is the method used in destroying the narcotics, guns, and other objects of harm performs a symbolic, metonymic display of sovereign power in Africa (see Reed 2006: 153–154). Not only does setting ablaze seized drugs visually symbolize the violent mastery over crime and the mobility of illicit flows in the subregion's embattled states, but it also expresses to those spectating the ritual the normalization of exceptional coercion and mastery over life and death that is a recurrent feature of African politics (Mbembe 2006).

Conclusion

The security ritual of World Drug Day in West Africa is an attempt to pin down and fix security understandings, to acquire an acceptance by audiences of the roles that securitizing actors allocate for them, and to communicate the powers of state coercion. By so doing, West African security actors hope to (re)produce their authority in security matters and to remind international actors of the need to support their governments, presumed to be assailed by the threat of narcotraffickers and other related threats. Simultaneously, citizens are urged to participate in the fight by cooperating with West African security forces, and to fear and comply with the coercive capabilities of the state. Each group experiences the visual ritual, and therein learns and, it is hoped, comes to understand its place within this security context.

Seeing and being seen is central to this public, visual spectacle of security ritual. West African political and security elites, aware of their relations of hierarchical dependence with the international system, visually perform their sovereign responsibilities in the fight against drug trafficking and its criminalization to garner both material and symbolic diplomatic support from the international donor community. Through the ritualized visual spectacle of World Drug Day proceedings, they also make themselves seen as sovereigns capable of wielding extraordinary means in the capture and control of citizens who contravene the law. Thus, the visual practices and theatrics, like the structuring of space to highlight images of captured traffickers, the display of the Minister welcoming international actors to the ceremonies, and the incineration of drugs themselves, play on the spectacle and spectatorship of multiple simultaneous audiences, who are drawn into the ritual's participative arithmetic and rhythm.

Whether or not such visual spectacles are felicitous, of course, is an empirical matter. While ritual managers may craft and choreograph their visual displays of (in)security, they often still fail to garner the type of audience 'fusion' or adoption of the reality being portrayed in the ritual performance, as Guinean officials failed to do with their American guests. Given the alleged involvement of high-ranking political officials in West Africa in criminal affairs, many citizens in the subregion do not accept the securitizing moves made against drug trafficking that visual spectacles like World Drug Day activities are supposed to convey. There are definitive ambiguities surrounding the larger context of criminality and politics in West Africa that such grandiose spectacles do not calm or clarify. This means that additional work is required to master the visual choreography of public displays of (in)security in the subregion. What is certain is that African political and security actors enact their place of dependence and their sovereignty (both diplomatic and exceptional) by visually performing their (in)security to others, and need to be seen doing so. Their ritualized theatrics are a routine and necessary component of symbolically communicating and reproducing an order of security that ultimately enables the recognition of their place in the international system, and the legitimization of some African political and security actors over others.

Notes

1 For some classic sociological and anthropological works on ritual, see Durkheim 1915; Turner 1969; Cohen 1974; Geertz 1980; Kertzer 1988; Bell 1992; Alexander 2003; Collins 2004.
2 The following section relies heavily on interviews and participant observation conducted in July through September 2012, January and February 2013, and June and July 2016, in multiple West African capitals.
3 Economic Community of West African States.
4 Interview, two Guinean drug law enforcement officials, Ouagadougou, 2 August 2012.
5 Participant observation, Accra, 26 June 2016. While the conference centre where these activities took place also served to host that year's United Nations Head of National Drug Law Enforcement Agencies (HONLEA), Ghanaian officials confirmed that alternate sites for World Drug Day activities were also spatially oriented in this fashion.
6 Interview with Ghanaian official, Accra, 26 June 2016.
7 Interview with Ghanaian drug police official, Accra, 28 June 2016.
8 Participant observation, Accra, 25–29 June 2012.
9 Interview with Journalist, Dakar, 12 August 2012; interview with local civil society organization representative, Dakar, 15 January 2013.
10 Le Comité Interministérielle de Lutte contre la Drogue (CILD).
11 Interview, senior Senegalese Drug Police official, Dakar, 18 January 2013.
12 Interview, UNODC official, Dakar, 7 August 2012; interview, CILD official, Dakar, 27 August 2012.
13 Interview, Senegalese CILD official, Dakar, 22 January 2013.
14 Participant observation, Dakar, 27 June 2016. In 2016, the incineration ceremony was held on Monday.
15 Interview, Senegalese CILD official, Dakar, 23 June 2016.
16 Interview, Head of Senegalese National drug police, 16 January 2013.
17 Conversation, Senegalese gendarme, Dakar, 27 June 2016.
18 Conversation, Western security official, Dakar, 27 June 2016.
19 Conversation, UNODC official, 5 July 2016.
20 Interview, two Guinean drug law enforcement officials, Ouagadougou, 2 August 2012.
21 Conversation with three IO officials, Dakar, 27 June 2016.

References

Alexander, J. C. (2003). *The Meaning of Social Life: A Cultural Sociology*. Oxford: Oxford University Press.

Alexander, J. C. (2004). Cultural Pragmatics: Social Performance Between Ritual and Strategy. *Sociological Theory*, 22(4), pp. 527–573.

Alexander, J. C. (2011). *Performance and Power*. Cambridge: Polity Press.

Allen, C. (1999). Africa and the Drugs Trade. *Review of African Political Economy*, 26(79), pp. 5–11.

Amoore, L. (2007). Vigilant Visualities: The Watchful Politics of the War on Terror. *Security Dialogue*, 38(2), pp. 139–156.

Andersen, R. S., Vuori, J. A., and Mutlu, C. E. (2015). Visuality. In: C. Aradau, J. Huysmans, A. Neal, and N. Voelkner, eds., *Critical Security Methods: New Frameworks for Analysis*. London: Routledge.

Apter, D. E. (2006). Politics as Theatre: An Alternative View of the Rationalities of Power. In: J. C. Alexander, B. Giesen, and J. L. Mast, eds., *Social Performance: Symbolic Action, Cultural Pragmatics, and Ritual*. Cambridge: Cambridge University Press, pp. 218–256.

Balzacq, T. (2011). A Theory of Securitization: Origins, Core Assumptions, and Variants. In: T. Balzacq, ed., *Securitization Theory: How Security Problems Emerge and Dissolve*. London: Routledge.

Balzacq, T. (2014). Théorie de la Performance Rituelle. Paper Presentation, University of Ottawa, 24 March.

Barnes, S. T. (1996). Political Ritual and the Public Sphere in Contemporary West Africa. In: D. Parkin, L. Caplan, and H. Fisher, eds., *The Politics of Cultural Performance*. Oxford: Berghahn Books.

Bayart, J.-F. (2000). Africa in the World: A History of Extraversion. *African Affairs*, 99(395), pp. 217–267.

Bayart, J.-F. (2010). Le piège de la lutte antiterroriste en Afrique de l'Ouest. Médiapart. 28 June. https://blogs.mediapart.fr/jean-francois-bayart/blog/280710/le-piege-de-la-lutte-anti-terroriste-en-afrique-de-louest [Accessed 5 April 2017].

Bayart, J.-F., Ellis, S., and Hibou, B. (1999). *The Criminalization of the State in Africa*. Oxford: James Currey.

Bell, C. (1992). *Ritual Theory, Ritual Practice*. Oxford: Oxford University Press.

Bigo, D. (2000). When Two Become One: Internal and External Securitizations in Europe. In: M. Kelstrup and M. C. Williams, eds., *International Relations Theory and the Politics of European Integration*. London: Routledge.

Buzan, B., Wæver, O., and Wilde, J. de. (1998). *Security: A New Framework for Analysis*. London: Lynne Rienner.

Campbell, D. (2007). Geopolitics and Visuality: Sighting the Darfur Conflict. *Political Geography*, 26(4), pp. 357–382.

Carrier, N. and Klantsching, G. (2012). *Africa and the War on Drugs*. London: Zed Books.

Coaffee, J., O'Hare, P., and Hawkesworth, M. (2009). The Visibility of (In)security: The Aesthetics of Planning Urban Defences Against Terrorism. *Security Dialogue*, 40(4–5), pp. 489–511.

Cohen, A. (1974). *Two-Dimensional Man: An Essay on the Anthropology of Power and Symbolism in Complex Society*. Berkeley, CA: University of California Press.

Cohen, A. (1979). Political Symbolism. *Annual Review of Anthropology*, 8, pp. 87–113.

Collins, R. (2004). *Interaction Ritual Chains*. Princeton, NJ: Princeton University Press.
Comaroff, J. and Comaroff, J. eds. (2006). *Law and Disorder in the Postcolony*. Chicago: University of Chicago Press.
Côté, A. (2016). Agents without Agency: Assessing the Role of the Audience in Securitization Theory. *Security Dialogue*, 47(6), pp. 541–558.
Dixit, P. (2014). Decolonizing Visuality in Security Studies: Reflections on the Death of Osama bin Laden. *Critical Studies on Security*, 2(3), pp. 337–351.
Durkheim, E. (1915/1974). *The Elementary Forms of Religious Life*. Translated by Joseph Swain. Glencoe: Free Press.
Ellis, S. (2009). West Africa's International Drug Trade. *African Affairs*, 108(431), pp. 171–196.
Geertz, C. (1980). *Negara: The Theatre State in Nineteenth-Century Bali*. Princeton, NJ: Princeton University Press.
Giesen, B. (2006). Performing the Sacred: a Durkheimian Perspective on the Performative Turn in the Social Sciences. In: J. C. Alexander, B. Giesen, and J. L. Mast, eds., *Social Performance: Symbolic Action, Cultural Pragmatics, and Ritual*. Cambridge: Cambridge University Press, pp. 325–367.
Gilmore, L. (2010). *Theatre in a Crowded Fire: Ritual and Spirituality at Burning Man*. Berkeley, CA: University of California Press.
Goffman, E. (1959). *The Presentation of the Self in Everyday Life*. New York: Doubleday.
Goffman, E. (1967/2005). *Interaction Ritual: Essays in Face-to-Face Behaviour*. New Brunswick: Transaction Publishers.
Grätz, T. (2011). Vigilantism in Africa: Benin and Beyond. In: M. Berg and S. Wendt, eds., *Globalizing Lynching History: Vigilantism and Extralegal Punishment from an International Perspective*. Basingstoke: Palgrave Macmillan, pp. 207–223.
Hagmann, T. and Péclard, D. (2010). Negotiating Statehood: Dynamics of Power and Domination in Africa. *Development and Change*, 41(4), pp. 539–562.
Hammerstad, A. (2012). Securitisation from below: The Relationship between Immigration and Foreign Policy in South Africa's Approach to the Zimbabwe Crisis. *Conflict, Security & Development*, 12(1), pp. 1–30.
Hansen, L. (2011). Theorizing the Image for Security Studies: Visual Securitization and the Muhammad Cartoon Crisis. *European Journal of International Relations*, 17(1), pp. 51–74.
Hansen, L. (2015). How Images Make World Politics: International Icons and the Case of Abu Ghraib. *Review of International Studies*, 41(2), pp. 263–288.
Heck, A. and Schlag, G. (2013). Securitizing Images: The Female Body and the War in Afghanistan. *European Journal of International Relations*, 19(4), pp. 891–913.
Hooper-Greenhill, E. (2000). *Museums and the Interpretation of Visual Culture*. London: Routledge.
Huysmans, J. (2006). *The Politics of Insecurity: Fear, Migration and Asylum in the EU*. London: Routledge.
Huysmans, J. (2011). What's in an Act?: On Security Speech and Little Security Nothings. *Security Dialogue*, 42(4–5), pp. 371–383.
Joseph, J. (2010). The Limits of Governmentality: Social Theory and the International. *European Journal of International Relations*, 16(2), pp. 223–246.
Karlström, M. (2003). On the Aesthetics and Dialogics of Power in the Postcolony. *Africa*, 73(1), pp. 57–76.
Kertzer, D. I. (1988). *Ritual, Politics, and Power*. New Haven, CT: Yale University Press.

Klein, A. (1994). Trapped in the Traffick: Growing Problems of Drug Consumption in Lagos. *Journal of Modern African Studies*, 32(4), pp. 657–677.

Kong, L. and Yeoh, B. (1997). The Construction of National Identity through the Production of Ritual and Spectacle: An Analysis of National Day Parades in Singapore. *Political Geography*, 16(3), pp. 213–239.

Lacher, W. (2013). Challenging the Myth of the Drug-Terror Nexus in the Sahel. WACD Background Paper. 4 August. www.wacommissionondrugs.org/wp-content/uploads/2013/08/Challenging-the-Myth-of-the-Drug-Terror-Nexus-in-the-Sahel-2013–08–19.pdf [Accessed 5 April 2017].

Lentz, C. (2001). Local Culture in the National Arena: The Politics of Cultural Festivals in Ghana. *African Studies Review*, 44(3), pp. 47–72.

Lewis, G. (1980). *Day of Shining Red: An Essay on Understanding Ritual*. Cambridge: Cambridge University Press.

Mbembe, A. (1992). Provisional Notes on the Postcolony. *Africa*, 62(1), pp. 3–37.

Mbembe, A. (2001). *On the Postcolony*. Berkeley, CA: University of California Press.

Mbembe Achille. 2006. On Politics as a Form of Expenditure. In: J. Comaroff and J. Comaroff, eds., *Law and Disorder in the Postcolony*. Chicago, IL: University of Chicago Press, pp. 299–335.

Methmann, C. and Rothe, D. (2014). Tracing the Spectre that Haunts Europe: The Visual Construction of Climate-induced Migration in the MENA Region. *Critical Studies on Security*, 2(2), pp. 162–179.

Miles, W. F. S. (1989). The Rally as Ritual: Dramaturgical Politics in Nigerian Hausaland. *Comparative Politics*, 21(3), pp. 323–338.

Mitchell, L. T. (2014). The Visual Turn in Political Anthropology and the Mediation of Political Practice in Contemporary India. *South Asia: Journal of South Asian Studies*, 37(3), pp. 515–540.

Möller, F. (2013). *Visual Peace: Images, Spectatorship, and the Politics of Violence*. Basingstoke: Palgrave Macmillan.

O'Reilly, C. (2008). Primetime Patriotism: News Media and the Securitization of Iraq. *Journal of Politics and Law*, 1(3), pp. 66–72.

Parkin, D. (1996). Introduction: The Power of the Bizarre. In: D. Parkin, L. Caplan, and H. Fisher, eds., *The Politics of Cultural Performance*. Oxford: Berghahn Books.

Raineri, L. and Strazzari, F. (2015). State, Secession, and Jihad: The Micropolitical Economy of Conflict in Northern Mali. *African Security*, 8(4), pp. 249–271.

Reed, I. (2006). Social Dramas, Shipwrecks, and Cockfights: Conflict and Complicity in Social Performance. In: J. C. Alexander, B. Giesen, and J. L. Mast, eds., *Social Performance: Symbolic Action, Cultural Pragmatics, and Ritual*. Cambridge: Cambridge University Press.

Salter, M. B. (2008). Securitization and Desecuritization: A Dramaturgical Analysis of the Canadian Air Transport Security Authority. *Journal of International Relations and Development*, 11(4), pp. 321–349.

Sandor, A. (2016). Border Security and Drug-Trafficking in Senegal: Global Security Assemblages and AIRCOP. *Journal of Intervention and Statebuilding*, 10(4), pp. 490–512.

Schatzberg, M. G. (2001). *Political Legitimacy in Middle Africa: Father, Family, Food*. Bloomington, IN: Indiana University Press.

Shaw, M. (2015). Drug Trafficking in Guinea-Bissau, 1998–2014: The Evolution of an Elite Protection Network. *The Journal of Modern African Studies*, 53(3), pp. 339–364.

Smith, A. D. (2014). The Rites of Nations: Elites, Masses, and the Re-Enactment of the 'National Past'. In: R. Tsang and E. T. Wood, eds., *The Cultural Politics of Nationalism and Nation-Building: Ritual and Performance in the Forging of Nations.* London: Routledge, pp. 21–37.

Stritzel, H. (2007). Towards a Theory of Securitization: Copenhagen and Beyond. *European Journal of International Relations*, 13(3), pp. 357–383.

Stritzel H. (2011). Security, the Translation. *Security Dialogue*, 42(4–5), pp. 343–355.

Turner, V. (1967). *The Forest of Symbols: Aspects of Ndembu Ritual.* Ithaca, NY: Cornell University Press.

Turner, V. (1969). *The Ritual Process: Structure and Anti-Structure.* Ithaca, NY: Cornell University Press.

US Embassy Conakry. (2008). Seized Drugs Finally Incinerated … Or Were They? *Wikileaks Cable: 08CONAKRY184.* 6 March. https://wikileaks.org/plusd/cables/08CONAKRY184_a.html [Accessed 5 April 2017].

Wæver, O. (1995). Securitization and Desecuritization. In: R. D. Lupschutz, ed., *On Security.* New York: Columbia University Press.

Wæver, O. (2011). Politics, Security, Theory. *Security Dialogue*, 42(4–5), pp. 465–480.

WACD (West African Commission on Drugs). (2014). *Not Just in Transit: Drugs, the State and Society in West Africa.* June. Geneva: WACD.

Williams, M. C. 2003. Words, Images, Enemies: Securitization and International Politics. *International Studies Quarterly*, 47(4), pp. 511–531.

Williams, M. C. (2007). *Culture and Security: Symbolic Power and the Politics of International Security.* London: Routledge.

7 Collaging Iranian missiles

Digital security spectacles and visual online parodies

Saara Särmä

Introduction

In early July 2008 Iran tested nine missiles, and an image depicting the test was released to the world. The image showed four missiles taking off and was published widely in global media. Very soon after, it became clear that one of the missiles in the image was digitally manipulated. In reality, the missile had failed to take off, but the image covered up the failure.[1]

As is often the case in internet culture that follows public failures, a surge of parody images of the missile test emerged immediately after the cover-up attempt was discovered. Various blogs and discussion forums published collections of parody images, which aimed at ridiculing the digitally manipulated missile image and/or the failed missile launch. The makers of these parody images can be seen as participants in world politics, even when they hardly register as such when world politics is taken as something that happens at the level of high politics.

In this chapter I introduce a playful visual method, collaging, to the study of everyday security spectatorship and the 'common sense' regarding global nuclear politics that is (re)produced by the parody images. The parody images make sense (and nonsense) of the ways in which notions related to gender and sexuality underpin global (nuclear) hierarchies. The chapter proceeds by first arguing that studying internet parody images is a worthwhile endeavour, which complements visual security studies by bringing in a low theory dimension of security spectatorship and participation. The chapter then introduces the methodology of visual collaging before delving into the masculinity game of nuclear proliferation and its visualizations into collages dealing with missile envy and feminizations. The last part of the chapter comes back to methodological issues and in it I ruminate on how IR research is personal and how the personal turns into IR research.

Studying missile parodies

Memes and other internet parody images make a fascinating case for a study of visual security. They are easily seen as something light-hearted and only entertaining, and thus dismissed as spectacles not belonging to the serious world of world politics and security research. The hierarchies of knowing in IR (and elsewhere in academia too) set up and maintain the 'high' in high politics, data, and theory, and thereby closely relate to an understanding of what is serious and what and who should be taken seriously. In a field concerned with life and death issues, focus on the trivial may feel even dangerous – a distraction from 'the real issues'. However, when seriousness is defined in narrow terms, many insights may remain unseen and questions unasked (see Enloe 2013: 7; Rowley 2015: 363). It may be this desire to be taken seriously that has prevented IR scholars from fully embracing the study of funny digital images. If the accolade of 'serious enough' can be withheld even from those daring to study gender (Enloe 2013: 5), surely those studying something that is seen as enjoyable or a light relief in the everyday are at great risk of being dismissed as certainly *not* serious enough.

However, I argue that internet parody images are important and should be paid attention to, first because of the speed at which they circulate (see also Brennan 2015). Back in 2008, social media feeds such as Facebook newsfeed looked different. In the early years of Facebook, interaction happened through individual profiles. Once the newsfeed, comment function on individual posts, and the publishing tool that enabled link sharing were introduced along with users' networks expanding, interaction relocated mainly to the newsfeed. Link previews (including images) and photos and videos have gained more visibility on the newsfeed. In 2009 pages where introduced, when also media could start sharing content on Facebook through their pages. Mobile apps have since taken social media from our computers to our phones, and thus everywhere we go.

Social media's significance as sources for information and news has increased a great deal due to these changes. Today, for those of us who spend a lot of time daily scrolling social media feeds on our computers or phones, social media is in many cases the main channel of news. At the same time, as the amount of visual content and links has overtaken social media feeds, meme-like parody images have gained importance as means for political commentary and criticism (see e.g. Bayerl and Stoynov 2016: 1007; Highfield and Lever 2016: 48). Often these days we encounter a parody image before we encounter the event that gave rise to the parody. This may have consequences for how we understand international security and what we know of the international.

Furthermore, in all their banality, internet parody images and memes that we encounter online everyday are similar to other pop culture products which, as Judith Halberstam (2011: 60) argues, directly tap into mass culturally shared assumptions. For Halberstam (2011: 60) SpongeBob SquarePants, for example, and other 'seemingly banal pop culture text[s]' are 'far more likely to reveal the key terms and conditions of the dominant than an earnest and "knowing" text'. The internet parodies and memes are digital artefacts that can be sites of analysis, but also sources of theorizing, in a 'low theory' sense.

IR as an academic discipline generally has a strong preference for 'high theory', 'high politics', and 'high data' and scholars engaging with popular culture have argued for the need to bring in 'low data' to get a fuller picture of 'high politics' (see also Weldes 2006). Introducing parody images and meme-making as everyday participation and spectatorship of world politics generates low data and low theorizing and consequently adds a new dimension to how IR perceives high politics issues such as nuclear politics and security.

'The key terms and conditions of the dominant' (Halberstam 2011: 60) that interest me in the case of nuclear wannabe Iran and parody images inspired by the digitally manipulated missile incident have to do with gendered and sexualized imagery. When an actor, such as a state, does something in the arena of global politics, which is already saturated with gendered meaning, the actions can be interpreted as, for example, manly or wimpy (see Cohn 1993; Wadley 2009). I call Iran a 'nuclear wannabe' to indicate its in-between status in the global nuclear order. The global nuclear order is a hierarchy institutionalized in the Nuclear Non-proliferation Treaty, which divides the world into nuclear haves and have-nots. Nuclear wannabes are those states that want to move from have-not to have by acquiring nuclear arsenals, i.e. Iran and North Korea.

Even when Iran has not developed full nuclear capabilities in a technical or technological sense, its nuclear weapons exist and are working in our political and popular imagination. These imaginary nuclear weapons already work to construct how we understand the realities of nuclear proliferation and nuclear order, how we understand global security, and how we understand our and Iran's place in the world (see also Masters 2003: 5). The nukes are already operating on this level, even if not realized materially, through the metaphors and images evoked when they are talked about and visualized in parody form: 'Metaphors and imagery are not merely inert devices which aid description and explanation; rather they are doing discursive work through their significations and circulations' (Masters 2003: 5).

Missiles do not, of course, equal nuclear weapons. But because nuclear programs are hardly visual in the public imagination, images of missiles are often used as substitutes for nukes when proliferation is visualized in popular discourse. When the nukes already operate on the imaginary level, they are significant in terms of arousing and intensifying political sentiments about global security. They may intensify or lessen fears or effect threat creation vis-à-vis the nuclear wannabes. The ways in which the particular parodies under examination in this chapter make sense (or non-sense) of the Iranian failed missile test simultaneously contribute to the broader understandings of global nuclear politics and the hierarchies it entails and the wannabe's position in the hierarchy.

Collaging as a playful methodology

Collage-thinking as introduced to IR by Christine Sylvester (2007, 2009) is a theoretical and thematic mode of thinking. *Theoretical collaging* allows for a discussion to emerge between different schools of thought despite and through disciplinary barriers and thus the camp structure, which she describes to be a defining feature of the current IR discipline, can be overcome in a fruitful manner. Theoretical collaging aims to avoid unnecessary competition between differing approaches, even when it highlights contrasts between them. The key point of doing collage work, theoretically and methodologically, lies in the possibility of keeping one's imagination alive: 'Borders between the elements can seem intact and possibly even impermeable, yet the unexpected juxtapositions alter meanings and enable new relationships to be imagined or invented' (Sylvester 2009: 170). This sort of theoretical collaging is ultimately about learning and thinking rather than mere accumulation of knowledge (Bleiker 2006: 94; Shapiro 2012: xv). It is about mediating understanding in new and interesting ways for both the author and the audience (Butler-Kisber 2008: 265). Reinterpretative works help us to search new perspectives and teach us to listen carefully, rather than only offer new facts (Bleiker 2006: 94).

Thematic collaging is a methodological experiment, which brings together seemingly separate topics and maps their 'shadowy mutualities'. Both of these strands of collage-thinking are based on Max Ernst's definition that the purpose of a collage 'is to create a meeting of two distant realities on a plane foreign to them both' (Sylvester 2009: 21, 177).

Putting seemingly separate and incommensurable things together in this way can reveal new connections and things can start making sense in new ways. In a way my choice of topics for my doctoral dissertation (Särmä 2014) – nuclear wannabes, gender, sexuality, and laughter – initially may have not made any sense, as it did not for many people who asked me what my dissertation project was about. Once you see an image of 1980s David Hasselhoff with a missile shooting out of his pants, it may become strikingly obvious how these issues are related. When this particular image is made part of a visual collage, space is opened up for new connections to emerge.

Visual collaging is a playful and creative methodology, which can be fruitful for investigating security spectacles and spectatorship. The methodology has several aims. First, it allows me to *experiment* with art-making as part of a research process to get beyond language-based IR (which is the norm even when studying visuality). It is an art-based intervention, which disrupts the text-based modes of doing and writing up research. These text-based modes are dominant even in research, which focuses on visuality and images; for example, a book titled *Nuclear Fear: A History of Images* (Weart 1988) has about 400 pages of text but no images. Often images are left out because printing is costly or the copyright is either expensive or impossible to trace. The latter reason often applies to internet images. Conventional academic writing can be said to represent and reproduce masculine ideals and feminist scholars have for long experimented with finding feminine ways of writing (e.g. Cixous 1976) to counter the representational demands of masculinized knowledge and reason.

Collage methodology does not aim to hold up a dichotomous either/or thinking, setting up 'feminine' ways of doing research as opposite to 'masculine' ways of doing research. Rather, like other art-based research practices, it calls 'our attention to the polarizing notions that distinguish art and science from each other in ways that have prevented the kinds of cross-breeding that might advance conversations about the human condition and our study of it' (Leavy 2015: 301).

Second, it seeks to promote *accessibility* as it attempts to make academic discussion easier to approach for anyone through light-hearted visualizations, seeking not so much to explain but to involve (see Halberstam 2011: 15 on 'low theory'). Because of its playful nature, collaging is suitable for studying digital artefacts. Digital media systems are built on the idea of playfulness and on the principle of involving people. Similar to the early collagists, my use of everyday digital stuff as research material also aims for accessibility, both in that the stuff used in this work is accessible to anyone with an internet connection, and that what I produce from the stuff aims to be accessible to readers and viewers beyond academia. In this sense, the research attempts to speak back to the popular everyday representations of world politics when I present pieces of art as part of the research. Furthermore, as a data generative process, this kind of research and I-the-researcher/artist become participants in the 'low' international politics, similarly to those who have made the parody images I have reused in my collages.

Through the visual collages, I aim to make accessible feminist critiques of nuclear proliferation by making visible, and funny, the way in which gender and sexuality underpins the thinking about nuclear proliferation. Abstract theorizing about issues of high politics and feminism thus becomes concrete in new ways. Visual art forms are powerful in that they evoke sensory and emotional responses. These embodied responses, such as laughter, can incite meaning-making in the viewer in very concrete ways. Collage emphasizes and gives room to relations arising from juxtapositions. Instead of single coherent notions, differences and shadowy and playful mutualities draw our attention to multiple directions at once (see Butler-Kisber 2008: 268).

Third, it *(re)politicizes the images* and invites the reader/viewer to pay attention, critically, to these kinds of images in the everyday, for example what kind of international they constitute, and what kind of laughter they incite. In the contemporary moment, we are constantly surrounded by the visual or by visual culture, and perhaps it is not an overstatement to say that we are constantly bombarded by the visual. We do, indeed, have more and more skills to critically engage with the visuals we encounter in the everyday, yet we do not always necessarily notice what it is that we see (Weber 2008: 42). Seeing and looking, or seeing and paying attention are different modalities, similarly as hearing and really listening are; it is the paying attention part that makes images particularly important to scholarship and research. When we do not merely see, but rather look and take note of what we see, we already enter a mode of analysis. Light-hearted play and low theorizing in the form of parody images is also already a mode of analysis, but it rarely gets noticed as such. Thus, the point of paying attention is also to persuade others, in academia and beyond, to pay attention as well (Weber 2008: 42). Entering a mode of analysis by paying attention, we can also take a note of what we do not see.

Finally, it constitutes an *IR intervention* that emphasizes the possibilities of playfulness and creativity. In this sense collaging is a method that aims to rupture; it is a method-as-act, instead of method-as-device, as Claudia Aradau and Jef Huysmans (2014: 610) posit Enloe's feminist curiosity. Collage methodology functions as a way to counter and disrupt the representational demands of conventional academic writing, in other words, it aims to challenge what we think counts as Research, with a capital R. The actual visual collages are not mere illustrations, nor research material in the usual sense, but both of these and something more. The art pieces are pop culture products or artefacts at the same time as they function methodologically as vehicles for further thought, both for me as the researcher and for the reader/viewer. With the collages, which are full of everyday internet stuff familiar to those of us who spend much time online, I want to invite even non-academic reader/viewers into the discussion.

Collaging is a specific mode of paying attention; through juxtapositions it can simultaneously emphasize similarities and differences, and the playful and shadowy mutualities between seemingly separate topics. Concrete pieces of collage also demand the reader/viewer pay attention in order to see what is going on in the piece. They require active participation from the spectator.

The masculinity game of proliferation

What unfolded in mainstream media when the Iranian missile tests were first reported in the summer of 2008 reads like a typical episode in what I call the 'masculinity game of proliferation', a term that draws on Agathangelou and Ling's (2004) notion of the 'masculinity game in world politics'. The masculinity game involves hypermasculine jousts in politics, erases alternatives, and manifests in transnationalization of militarization (Agathangelou and Ling 2004: 40). In this particular episode of the masculinity game of proliferation, Iran was seen as attempting to defiantly show its might and to boldly flex its military muscle. Muscle flexing and defiance are actions coded as masculine, as feminist critics of gendered security discourses have for long highlighted (e.g. Duncanson and Eschle 2008). Moreover, the linkages between sexualized phallic imagery and legitimation of nuclear proliferation have been demonstrated on many occasions (e.g. Cohn 1987; Cohn and Ruddick 2004). The original image of four missiles taking off, published by Iranian officials, was in mainstream media seen as a provocation. Although visuality was not addressed explicitly, its role was central in this attempt to send a message to the rest of the world. In terms of the masculinity game, this message was an attempt to establish manliness and manly potency in order to be taken seriously in the global arena.

I read the parody images as reactions to this attempt to 'make it' in the masculinity game. In line with the 'low theory' conceptualization, the parody images can help reveal aspects of the 'common sense' that surrounds gendered nuclear politics. The creators of the parody images are everyday participants of 'low' world politics and produce digital artefacts into the global arena. Paying attention to these everyday participants of world politics and the digital artefacts they produce, can result in a different picture of 'high politics' of nuclear proliferation than more conventional security studies analysis would.

As Carol Cohn (1987: 693) points out, the intent of the individuals who use explicitly sexual imagery in their speech cannot be read from the imagery itself, no matter how tempting it might be. Similarly, in this case, we cannot draw any conclusions about the individuals who participate in world politics by producing the images. In other words, by looking at the parody images, we cannot judge the individuals behind them, or know of their character or motivations. Rather, their participation as spectators of world politics and producers of parody images can be read as a source of popular knowledge about nuclear and security politics. The production of these parody images reflects and reproduces this popular knowledge. Thus, the images analysed through collage methodology reveal gendered and sexualized ideas relating to nuclear politics that are culturally prevalent.

The explicitly sexual imagery does not originate from the individuals producing these parody images, but arises from a broader cultural context in which certain ideas, concepts, and practices are coded masculine and others feminine in the frame of heteronormativity (Cohn 1987: 693–694; Peterson 2009). Moreover, to turn this around, this is precisely why these images can tell us something about the broader cultural contexts and the 'key terms and conditions of the dominant' (Halberstam 2011: 60), which are about the ways in which the global nuclear order is gendered and sexualized, and how the hierarchical global nuclear order is maintained.

What is common to all the parody images in this case is that none of them evokes the consequences of using missiles and/or nuclear weapons. In this sense they transcode technostrategic language into visual form. This preference for abstraction, euphemistic language, and explicit focus on technology when talking about nuclear weaponry, hides the human costs of their development and possible use (Cohn 1987). For feminist anti-militarism, this is problematic because the association of abstract thought and sophisticated technology with masculinity privileges talking about these issues rather than about feminized issues, such as concern over potential physical and emotional damage to people. In other words, all of the parody images as a whole do not do much to dismantle the masculinity game of proliferation. They are visual iterations of the technostrategic discourse and reiterate the no-alternatives view in hypermasculine and deeply militarized global politics. As reactions and countermoves to Iran's masculine identity avowals, the parody images as a whole maintain the masculinity game of proliferation rather than provide alternatives to it. Taking a closer look at groupings of the parody images by using collage methodology may, however, open up space for something else.

Missile envy

It is not always clear to either casual or professional followers of global politics how gender and sexuality are relevant in relation to nuclear weapons and proliferation. This has become apparent to me over the years when I have had to explain what exactly it is that I am researching. I have been met with much bafflement and questions about how on earth nukes have anything to do with gender. However, in the case at hand, there are images that manifest the connections between gender, sexuality, and nukes very clearly. The first example of overtly sexualized imagery was found on a discussion forum. It depicted the missile (that was digitally added into the first image Iran released to the world) shooting out of 1980s David Hasselhoff's (these days known as 'the Hoff') crotch with the caption: 'Words cannot begin to describe how awesome this pic is'. Why we would find this awesome, or hilarious, has to do with the obviousness of these connections that draw upon a cultural reservoir of meanings attached to both the Hoff and nuclear weapons and proliferation.

Parody functions in reference to already existing imagery. In other words, the link between male sexuality and missiles as phallic symbols is quite self-evident when the missile is added on to an image of 80s Hoff, who as Knight Rider was a very macho character and an epitome of straight white masculinity (Särmä 2016: 473). In this millennium, the Hoff has become more of a camp character, which brings other layers to the hilariousness of the described images. Read as a macho character and epitome of straight white (hegemonic) masculinity, the Hoff is on top of the gender hierarchy. Such a character can easily become an object of envy, and thus this image brings me to the concept of missile envy.

Although missile envy as a sole explanation for nuclear proliferation is insufficient and overly reductionist, it pops up regularly in both more and less serious popular discourse about horizontal and vertical proliferation, including Iran's wannabe nuclear status (Caldicott 1986; Cohn 1987). Helen Caldicott (1986) coined the term 'missile envy' during the Cold War, which offered a Freudian perspective on the arms race, according to which acquirement of nuclear weapons, and parading of missiles were attempts to establish masculine prowess in the global arena. According to Caldicott, the psychocultural rationale underlying the arms race between the two superpowers, and especially the US position, was missile envy, that is to say, an idea that bigger is better when it comes to both the size of the bombs themselves and the size of the arsenal.

The figure that the 1980s Hoff evokes is the Knight Rider (Michael Knight), which interestingly enough originates from the same Cold War era as the concept of missile envy, as the original TV series ran 1982–1986. At the time the US was led by President Reagan, who used to play a cowboy in Hollywood movies, and the fictional individual political body of the Knight Rider symbolized a modern and more high-tech version of the lonely rider or of cowboy imagery. Central to these masculinities is both individualism and mastery over nature in the case of the cowboy, and technology in the case of the more high-tech version. Whether the lonely rider rides a horse or a highly intelligent car, such as Michael Knight's, this imagery is central to popular culture masculinities that originate in the US. Simultaneously, the particular image I have used in the collage *Orange Iran* (Picture 1) portrays a hypersexualized masculinity.

> Picture 1: detail from 'Orange Iran', an original collage by Saara Särmä 2014 (see www.huippumisukka.fi/ch7). While the collages are constructed from found images that have been collected from the internet, they are original artworks and have been displayed in art exhibitions multiple times,

thus under fair use and artistic and academic freedom the copyright should fall solely unto the artist. However, according to the publisher's legal department's interpretation of copyright the collages cannot be printed here, because the author/artist does not have permission from the original creators of each individual image that appears as part of the collages.

By using exaggeration as a method of composing an image, this collage makes the obvious connections between machismo and (nuclear) weaponry hypervisible. Looking at this image, it is impossible not to make those connections, at least if the viewer is at all immersed in Western popular culture, which most of us are. This image easily reads as boasting, that 'ours are bigger than yours' in the context where Iran failed to 'get it up' (as discussed in more detail later), thus 'our' masculine being in the world is secured. As Miettinen argues in regard to superhero comics and the geopolitical fictions of the US, the superhero masculinities constitute a particular vision of idealized national identity (see Miettinen 2013: 18). Therefore, the 'us' can in this case, on the level of everyday popular imagery, be understood as both the US national political body and also the hegemonic political body of the West, which is led and protected by the US. This is because the figure of the Hoff that evokes the Knight Rider in the image resonates with political sentiments beyond the US.

> Picture 2: 'Missile Envy', an original collage by Saara Särmä 2013 (see www.huippumisukka.fi/ch7).

The collage *Missile Envy* has been constructed utilizing images from a Google search with key word 'missile envy' (Picture 2). It visualizes the concept and shows that both nuclear wannabes, Iran and North Korea, are linked to the concept. It also points us towards another layer of gendered cultural logic beyond the most obvious layer of sexualized phallic masculinity illustrated by the Hoff–Knight Rider image. Collaging is both an aesthetic and a conceptual method. Furthermore, as I use it, it is also a playful method. When playing around with found images, such as the ones resulting from 'missile envy' Google search, and putting the images on the same surface (canvas in this case), connections start to appear. Proximity of particular images to each other, juxtapositions, and repetitions can provoke conceptual thinking.

This particular collage, combined with my theoretical background and knowledge, reveals in visual form that there is more beneath the surface of the masculinity game of proliferation and explicit jolts of hypermasculinity. The deeper layer that emerges when one scratches the surface of obviousness is the performance-based masculinity and the ways in which it constitutes militarism and global politics. In other words, masculinity has to be enacted and constantly proven to others, which is not only something that applies to the collective political bodies, but to individual ones as well. On the individual level, ordinary spectators of world politics participate in the reproduction of performance-based masculinities by making and circulating the parody images, which are here taken as low theory imaginations of nuclear wannabes and their place in global hierarchies. Furthermore, the militarized performances of masculinity can become addictive and thus hard to dismantle.

Hello Kitty missiles

Other kinds of parody images that utilized familiar popular culture imagery circulated in this instance too. Some of them are more and some less iconic and immediately recognizable, which of course depends largely on the viewer's knowledge of US pop culture. The more easily recognizable imagery originates in science fiction and action movies, and includes images for example from 'Star Wars' and the 'Matrix'. Godzilla, dragons, and other monsters are also featured in many of these images, along with imagery from video games. I view and analyse these images from the point of view of fairly general pop culture knowledge. Someone with more expert knowledge on the specific pop culture artefacts referenced in these images could perhaps do a more nuanced reading of the images. As my interest lies in getting at the general gendered and sexualized understandings of world politics in the everyday, and not the pop culture expert view, this overall analysis remains superficial rather than going deep into the pop culture references.

In terms of analysing masculinities and femininities in this particular instance there are internet specific pop culture images that I group with the images referencing movies and video games. These images belong to internet specific genres such as 'LOLCat', demotivational posters, and 'Epic Fail'. While these genres originate on the internet, they of course also 'leak' from it to other spheres, as various still images and gifs are increasingly used in chats and texting, some are printed out, and also commercialized in various products. These internet parody genres encompass any and every topic imaginable; therefore, it is no surprise that they appear in this case. Nonsensical placement of objects in place of missiles (see Picture 3) or using the missile test photo(s) as the basis for these genres can be playful fun-making; yet again, they also play a part in making sense of nuclear proliferation as a whole and, by extension, of global hierarchies.

What is common to these parody images that draw upon pop culture, is the way in which they can be seen to position some political bodies in relation to others. That is to say that, although there is no certainty of who exactly the creators of these parodies are, it is clear that they are considered as somewhat technologically savvy. Technological skills and expertise are qualities strongly associated with masculinity. Similarly, sci-fi as a genre and video games have been typically perceived as manly. While gaming and geek culture are no longer solely manly terrains as women's participation has increased a great deal, these cultures still continue to be heavily influenced by masculinist discourses (Todd 2015: 64). Women's increased participation in gaming and geek culture is sometimes met with hostility ranging from dismissals to harassment and violence, as evidenced by accusations of girls being fake geeks and what became known as #gamergate (see e.g. Chess and Shaw 2015: 209–210). Furthermore, geek culture and these internet genres, along with technological skills, are associated with a specific kind of masculinity. This geeky masculinity might be often presented as non-hegemonic masculinity when contrasted with 'manly men'. However, on most axes of intersectionality the individual political body of the geek comes out as privileged. The stereotypical geek, after all, is a white educated heterosexual male in a Western country, who has enough time on his hands and enough technological know-how to create these parody images.

In contrast to the political body of the individual geek or group of geeks, Iran emerges in these parodies as technologically backward. Not only does it fail to launch all the missiles, but it also fails at computers and digital image manipulation. So much so 'that even Ray Charles can see that fuck-up' (FARK 2008). By making fun of Iran's failures, the individual selves (geeks) and the wider political bodies (national or the West more generally) they belong to are collectively posited as technologically capable. When the technology, for example, in this case digital image manipulation, is presented as a very simple tool, Iran's failure to use it results in implicit feminization. In the wider cultural realm, tropes that deny women and girls technical skills are plentiful and geek culture typically excludes women. While women and girls do not equal femininity, technical inability is typically associated with femininities through these tropes and practices.

An even more straightforward and explicit linkage to femininity appears in groups of images that feminize through infantilization and domestication. Similarly, as in the referent object of security in the technostrategic language Cohn (1987: 711–712) studied being the weapons, and weapons systems themselves, not human beings as such, the main point of focus in this group of parody images are the missiles themselves. The missiles have nonsensically and playfully been replaced with various objects including babies, bananas, oilcans, pacifiers, cows, Teenage Mutant Ninja Turtles, cats, twitter birds, Hello Kitty Pez-dispensers (see e.g. Alsays 2008), and even George W. Bush. Not all of the imagery seems to make a whole lot of sense; it rather looks like replacing the missiles with random objects.

Without drawing out all the possible intervisual linkages, it is safe to say that at least the babies, pacifiers, and toys infantilize, while the animals and bananas have a domesticating effect through replacing the missile with something that could be patted (cf. Cohn 1987), or petted, or consumed. Both infantilization and domestication diminish the threat of these specific missiles and by extension other missiles as well.

Associating missiles and nuclear proliferation with something furry, cute, and domesticated, for example, when cats of the LOLCat genre are used in some images, further domesticates the missiles. Cats are also commonly linked to femininity while dogs, particularly big dogs, are perceived as masculine (see e.g. Mitchell and Ellis 2013), so domestication and feminization work together here.

Picture 3: 'Hello Militarized Kitty', an original collage by Saara Särmä 2013 (see www.huippumisukka.fi/ch7).

The collage *Hello Militarized Kitty* (Picture 3) exaggerates the pink glittery femininity associated with the Hello Kitty figures and all the paraphernalia in which the figure appears. The collage started with the image in the middle, which was part of the collection of parody images that appeared after Iran's unsuccessful missile test. The rest of the images in the collage were found through a Google search with keywords "hello kitty missile". It was quite surprising to see how many different images this search produced. Some are toys, but some are not.

The cuteness of the pink Hello Kitty Pez-dispensers diminishes the threat by explicitly feminizing and infantilizing simultaneously. Pez-dispensers are refillable candy dispensers, which are mainly seen as children's toys, but are also collectors' items. Hello Kitty as a character is gendered and strongly associated with femininity. But she is not sexualized, partly because she, as many other cartoonish characters, lacks genitalia (cf. Hjorth 2003). Asexual and childlike femininity is commonly perceived as harmless and unthreatening in contrast to various sexualized femininities commonly found in popular culture. In other words Hello Kitty is no femme fatale.

To reiterate, by way of feminization, infantilization, and domestication these kind of images function in diminishing both the threat of nuclear Iran and missiles as weapons in general, because missiles appear through these parodies as something harmless, toy-like, 'randomly' funny, and something easily controlled because they can be petted, patted, or consumed.

The personal is International Relations research

Feminists have for long proclaimed that the personal is political, and Cynthia Enloe reformulated the phrase into 'the personal is international' (Enloe 1989: 196). Both of these phrases also work the other way around: political is personal and international is personal. Drawing from my experience during my doctoral dissertation project, and how my personal social media use turned into 'data', and interest-driven collection into 'method', I would like to offer another reformulation of the feminist classic: the personal is International Relations research and vice versa. Of course, there is nothing new in the idea that we research topics that fascinate or frighten us (Lehtonen 1999: 138 paraphrasing Roland Barthes), and in that sense research is always personal. However, with social media, the personal can intertwine with the research process in new ways. If one chooses so, her researcher identity may be part of everyday social media use; not just as a means of advertising one's work or engaging in public discussions as an expert, but as part of a data collection method. Or, as Patricia Leavy aptly points out, rather than data collection, as when using other arts-based methods, it would be a better description to call it 'data generation', or a content generation method. This implies the researcher is herself an active agent in generating data, not merely collecting it (Leavy 2015: 295). Thus the collages themselves become part of this 'data' generated during the research process, and a clear demarcation between research material and end results produced in the research process becomes undone.

It is impossible to collect a systematic and coherent 'data-set' of internet parody images and memes, because these things always shift and move. Internet parodies – images, videos, and texts – circulate at an incredible speed and yet do so sporadically; they might circulate initially at the moment of their creation and recirculate at any time. The context or recirculation might be similar or different; when it is different, of course, a parody image then may gain totally different meaning. Some parody images, for example, disappear altogether from the digital sphere after a while, for one reason or another (or finding them takes effort and skills that not all everyday users of the internet have). This requires a methodological approach that is both flexible and suitable for the artefacts. Relatedly, as Roland Bleiker argues (2015: 877),

> [t]he world of visual politics is, indeed, so complex that there is only one logical conclusion: to recognise that there is no one method, no matter how thorough or systematic, that can provide us with authentic insights into what images are or how they function.

He goes on to argue for a pluralistic methodological framework while recognizing the many practical problems a scholar may face when attempting to undertake such research. In what follows, I describe some of the practical solutions I have come up with for collecting internet parody images and memes in my research.

For collecting the digital stuff, I have used a method I call *reverse snowballing*. This means in practice that I have done Google image searches with various relevant key words and that I have collected images by following links from one page to another; quite 'normal' web-surfing, in other words. The 'reverse' in 'reverse snowballing' refers to the way that the metaphorical snowball has rolled *towards* me and this is where the personal becomes highly relevant.

Instead of the metaphorical snowball rolling away from me and gathering more informants/interviewees along the way, the snowballs roll towards me and add to the collection of stuff. When this happens indirectly my social media contacts have shared links and they show up on my newsfeeds (and they have therefore indirectly added to my collection of stuff). In this way, data collection can happen unexpectedly and is not limited only to work hours, contrary to other kinds of data collection, for example, archival work.

When the metaphorical snowballs roll towards me or fly at me directly, it means that my friends have directly shared links to my timeline/wall or in a private message. Especially publicly shared content (to e.g. a Facebook timeline) indicates a few things: my research topic has been well known to my social media contacts. Furthermore, in a way, it has become a part of my social media persona or identity to the extent that people feel comfortable sharing links or images to me publically. This may have something to do with the light-hearted and playful nature of the topic and data itself, and a lot to do with my social media usage habits where work and play are co-mingled.

Through the reverse snowballing method, material keeps on piling up, especially when political topics live on and shift and change.

The personal is IR research and IR research is personal in another, more disturbing way too. When social media and web searches are used in data gathering, there are obvious limitations, which have broader impacts beyond research. Google's customization and personalization of search results influences what we see, learn, and know about world events (see also Kaempf 2016). This personalization of internet content in our everyday life creates personal bubbles where we ultimately will have no control over what remains unseen and outside of the search results, for example. We each might be getting at least a slightly different perspective, depending on the media we use and follow and the intensity of our use of media. The size and type of networks we are part of also affects the perspective(s) we might be encountering. Google does not reveal the algorithms it uses, but the most popular items come up top in the searches and in the autofill search function.

Furthermore, when I am logged on to Google and do a search, I get different results than when using an anonymous browser. Results may also vary according to my physical location: in Tampere, Finland I get different results than in Minneapolis, USA. The customization and personalization may reinforce the existing power structures, if the search results are largely based on popularity. They may also reinforce polarization between different groups of people who have differing ideological stances, if it is hard to find information and viewpoints outside of your own bubble. This has implications for the research material that we acquire online, but more broadly it increases the fragmentation of knowledge in our everyday encounters with the world and international politics.

Conclusion

This chapter's starting point was one specific event taken as an international security spectacle, namely Iran's (failed) missile test. The parody images that ensued were taken as sources of low theorizing and indicative of some of the common sense surrounding global nuclear politics as it is underpinned by gender and sexuality. The producers of the parody images were seen as spectators of world politics, whose participation in world politics on the everyday level produces digital artefacts not usually paid attention to in security studies, critical or otherwise inclined.

Art-based methods such as collage methodology differ from the more conventional academic writing and mode of presenting research in that they attempt to open space for multiple possible interpretations rather than presenting one line of argumentation, which closes off other possibilities. This chapter has presented several insights into the masculinity game of nuclear proliferation, which are made visible through visualization, when collage methodology is used as a mode of artistic inquiry in visual security studies. The parody images are a genre that is often most prolific when something has failed. A missile failing to take off might constitute a deficient security spectacle and an unsuccessful move in the masculinity game of nuclear proliferation.

When the parody images are read as reactions to nuclear wannabe Iran's attempt to 'make it' in the masculinity game, the previously invisible role of internet users as everyday participants in 'low' global politics can be highlighted. Yet again, as Cynthia Enloe has argued on numerous occasions, piece by piece, we get a fuller picture of global politics and of global security, when all the participants, not just the high politics ones, are seen as part of it.

Note

1 See the images e.g. on the *New York Times* blog "The Lede" http://thelede.blogs.nytimes.com/2008/07/10/in-an-iranian-image-a-missile-too-many/

References

Agathangelou, A. M. and Ling, L. H. M. (2004). Power, Borders, Security, Wealth: Lessons of Violence and Desire from September 11. *International Studies Quarterly*, 48(3), pp. 517–538.
Alsays. 2008. "Iran: requires photoshop lessons" Website. http://portablecontent.wordpress.com/2008/07/11/iran-requires-photoshop-lessons/ [Accessed 12 April 2010]
Aradau, C. and Huysmans, J. (2014). Critical Methods in International Relations: the Politics of Techniques, Devices and Acts. *European Journal of International Relations*, 20(3), pp. 596–619.
Bayerl, P. S. and Stoynov, L. (2016). Revenge by Photoshop: Memefying Police Acts in the Public Dialogue about Injustice. *New Media & Society*, 18(6), pp. 1006–1026.
Bleiker, R. (2006). Art after 9/11. Alternatives: Global, Local, Political, 31(1), pp. 77–99.
Bleiker, R. (2015). Pluralist Methods for Visual Global Politics. *Millennium: Journal of International Studies*, 43(3), pp. 872–890.
Brennan, K. P. J. (2015). MemeLife. In: M. B. Salter, ed. *Making Things International I: Circulation*. Minneapolis, MI: University of Minnesota Press, pp. 243–254.
Butler-Kisber, L. (2008). Collage as Inquiry. In: J. G. Knowles and A. L. Cole, eds., *Handbook of the Arts in Qualitative Research: Perspectives, Methodologies, Examples, and Issues*. Thousand Oaks, CA: Sage Publications, pp. 265–276.
Caldicott, H. (1986). *Missile Envy: The Arms Race and Nuclear War*. New York: Bantam Books.
Chess, S. and Shaw, A. (2015). A Conspiracy of Fishes, or, How We Learned to Stop Worrying About #GamerGate and Embrace Hegemonic Masculinity. *Journal of Broadcasting & Electronic Media*, 59(1), pp. 208–220.
Cixous, H. (1976). The Laugh of the Medusa. *Signs*, 1(4), pp. 875–893.
Cohn, C. (1987). Sex and Death in the Rational World of Defense Intellectuals. *Signs: Journal of Women in Culture and Society*, 12(4), pp. 687–718.
Cohn, C. (1993). Wars, Wimps, and Women: Talking Gender and Thinking War. In: M. Cooke and A. Woollacott, eds., *Gendering War Talk*. Princeton, NJ: Princeton University Press, pp. 227–246.
Cohn, C. and Ruddick, S. (2004). A Feminist Ethical Perspective on Weapons of Mass Destruction. In: S. Lee and S. Hashmi, eds., *Ethics and Weapons of Mass Destruction: Religious and Secular Perspectives*. Cambridge: Cambridge University Press, pp. 405–435.
Duncanson, C. and Eschle, C. (2008). Gender and the Nuclear Weapons State: A Feminist Critique of the UK Government's White Paper on Trident. *New Political Science*, 30(4), pp. 545–563.

Enloe, C. H. (1989). *Bananas, Beaches & Bases: Making Feminist Sense of International Politics*. London: Pandora Press.
Enloe, C. H. (2013). *Seriously! Investigating Crashes and Crises as if Women Mattered*. Berkeley, CA: University of California Press.
FARK. (2008). "Iranian missile photo 'shopped to cover botched test fire". Website. www.fark.com/cgi/comments.pl?IDLink=3726113andviewmode=1andcpp=1 [Accessed 12 April 2010]
Halberstam, J. (2011). *The Queer Art of Failure*. Durham, NC and London: Duke University Press.
Highfield, T. and Leaver, T. (2016). Instagrammatics and Digital Methods: Studying Visual Social Media, from Selfies and GIFs to Memes and Emoji. *Communications Research and Practice*, 2(1), pp. 47–62.
Hjorth, L. (2003). Pop and Ma: The Landscape of Japanese Commodity Characters and Subjectivity. In: C. Berry, F. Martin, and A. Yue, eds., *Mobile Cultures: New Media in Queer Asia*. Durham, NC: Duke University Press pp. 158–179.
Kaempf, S. (2016). The Potentiality and Limits of Understanding World Politics in a Transforming Global Media Landscape. In: L. J. Shepherd and C. Hamilton, eds., *Understanding Popular Culture and World Politics in the Digital Age*. New York: Routledge, pp. 14–31.
Lehtonen, M. (1999), Sinun tekstisi eivät ole sinun tekstejäsi. In: M. Kinnunen and O. Löytty, eds., *Iso gee. Gradua ei jätetä!* Tampere: Vastapaino.
Leavy, P. (2015). *Method Meets Art: Arts-Based Research Practice*. 2nd edition. New York: The Guilford Press.
Masters, C. (2003). Tales of the Shield: A Feminist Reading of Ballistic Missile Defence. *YCISS Working Papers*, (23).
Miettinen, M. (2013). *Truth, Justice, and the American Way? The Popular Geopolitics of American Identity in Contemporary Superhero Comics*. Tampere: Tampere University Press.
Mitchell, R. W. and Ellis, A. L. (2013). Cat Person, Dog Person, Gay, or Heterosexual: The Effect of Labels on a Man's Perceived Masculinity, Femininity, and Likability. *Society & Animals*, 20(1), pp. 1–16.
Peterson, V. S. (2009). Interactive and Intersectional Analytics of Globalization. *Frontiers – A Journal of Women's Studies*, 30(1), pp. 34–65.
Rowley, C. (2015). Popular Culture and the Politics of the Visual. In: L. J. Shepherd, ed., *Gender Matters in Global Politics: A Feminist Introduction to International Relations*. Abingdon: Routledge, pp. 361–374.
Shapiro, M. J. (2012). *Studies in Trans-Disciplinary Method: After the Aesthetic Turn*. Interventions series. Abingdon: Routledge.
Sylvester, C. (2007). Whither the International at the End of IR. *Millennium: Journal of International Studies*, 35(3): 551–573.
Sylvester, C. (2009). *Art/Museums: International Relations Where We Least Expect It*. Boulder, CO: Paradigm Publishers.
Särmä, S. (2014). *Junk Feminism and Nuclear Wannabes – Collaging Parodies of Iran and North Korea*. Tampere: Tampere University Press. Also available electronically at: http://urn.fi/URN:ISBN:978-951-44-9535-9 [Accessed 5 April 2017]
Särmä, S. (2016). Congrats, You Have an All Male Panel! A Personal Narrative. *International Feminist Journal of Politics*, 18(3), pp. 470–476.
Todd, C. (2015). Commentary: GamerGate and Resistance to the Diversification of Gaming Culture. *Women's Studies Journal*, 29(1), pp. 64–67.

Wadley, J. D. (2009). Gendering the State: Performativity and Protection in International Security. In: L. Sjoberg, ed., *Gender and International Security: Feminist Perspectives*. London & New York: Routledge, pp. 38–58.

Weart, S. R. (1988). *Nuclear Fear: A History of Images*. Cambridge: Harvard University Press.

Weber, S. (2008). Visual Images in Research. In: J. G. Knowles and A. L. Cole, eds., *Handbook of the Arts in Qualitative Research: Perspectives, Methodologies, Examples, and Issues*. Thousand Oaks, CA: Sage Publications, pp. 41–53.

Weldes, J. (2006). High Politics and Low Data: Globalization Discourses and Popular Culture. In: D. Yanow, ed., *Interpretation and Method: Empirical Reseacrh Methods and Interpretative Turn*. Armonk, NY: Sharpe, Inc., pp. 176–186.

Part III
Making security visible

8 Leonardo's security
The participant witness in a time of invisibility

Frank Möller

Introduction: the invisible and the unphotographable

In *Treatise on Painting*, Leonardo da Vinci argues that obscure things can stimulate the mind to new inventions. Similar to da Vinci, W. J. T. Mitchell (2011) suggests that the mind can actually be stimulated, not by that which can be seen but instead by what can*not* be seen. 'Obscure' means to hide from view, to conceal from knowledge, or to render vague or unintelligible. Obscure is an apt term to designate specific developments in contemporary security policy characterized by permanent invisibility (Mirzoeff 2005: 149) aiming to 'disappear' people and material objects. However, as da Vinci argues, obscurity may also have a stimulating effect on viewers. Obscurity, thus, may help to 'reappear' the disappeared in viewers' imaginations. In this chapter, I want to think about the viewer's subject positions when exposed to obscure images, especially photographs, in the context of security policy. The viewer I have in mind is what I call elsewhere a participant witness (Möller 2013) – someone who self-critically engages with the conditions depicted in a given image, including his or her own subject positions in connection with these conditions. As the participant witness, as an ideal type, is unattainable, the issue is one of moving along the trajectory from the subject position of a (passive, observing, neutral) spectator in the direction of the subject position of a 'responsible, ethical, participant' witness (Taylor 2003: 243). In what ways do obscure images help spectators both to move along this trajectory and, ultimately, to transfigure into participant witnesses?

The combination of obscurity, invisibility, and stimulation also aptly describes visual strategies in recent photographic approaches to the politics of security, especially technological and infrastructural developments mostly hidden from view or '"unphotographable" for reasons of security, secrecy or law' (Bridle 2015). These approaches, paradoxically, make these developments visible without liberating them from obscurity; they expose them without making them intelligible. They do not give viewers assurance but they stimulate them all the same to look behind the photograph, searching for that which cannot be seen in the picture. This chapter investigates Edgar Martins' photographs of airfields, selected works by Simon Norfolk visualizing technologies and the aftermath of war, and Trevor Paglen's photographs of military installations in the American West. I discuss this photography in terms of photographic representations decoupled from seemingly straightforward knowledge-production: construction and simultaneous deconstruction of photographic knowledge.[1] Traditional photojournalistic approaches to war and security in search of 'great' shots close to 'action' are still capable of producing important and stimulating images (Tucker and Michels with Zelt 2012). However, many trends in recent security policy cannot be captured photographically by such an approach because 'action' in any conventional sense is absent, thus making 'great' shots, traditionally defined, impossible. Obscure photography builds on and expands the photojournalistic tradition by violating its basic, Capa-inspired credos. It explores, challenges, and exposes the space of representation, thus testing and expanding the limits of both representation and visibility.

Obscure photography, or: it is not easy being a spectator

For Simon Norfolk, 'traditional war reporting risks irrelevance if it only concentrates on what can be seen, what can be photographed and filmed when the "real" war is taking place elsewhere.'[2] Such warnings lead us to consider which kinds of images motivate viewers to investigate current forms of warfare and security policy. Photojournalism and social documentary, concerned photography, have always been interested in *revealing* things – for example, the gruesome horrors of war, social inequalities, poor living conditions, discrimination, and exploitation (Stomberg 2007) – so as to make others, non-photographers, intervene in the scenes depicted with non-photographic means. If, however, as da Vinci (quoted in van Alphen 2005: 1) argued with regard to painting, 'the mind is stimulated to new inventions by obscure things', then the simple dichotomy visibility vs. invisibility underlying many writings on photography appears as insufficient as the connection in liberal political thought between visibility and politics.

Visibility would even seem to be counter-productive because it reveals things rather than obscures them, thus operating in opposition to a search for new things. Making things visible and photographically representing them truthfully, unaltered and realistically, that is, as they are (or as they seem to be; this is the old but still powerful myth underlying photojournalism and concerned photography) is often seen as the first step in the process of changing things by raising political awareness and motivating thought. According to this line of thought, that which cannot be seen and which is not made visible does not exist in public imagination. To make something known, thus requires visibility. In this understanding, invisibility is the main culprit. However, the resulting idea that any kind of visibility is better than invisibility is not compelling, for at least three reasons. First, invisibility might be equated with obscurity, thus stimulating the search for new things. There is a growing body of literature on the merits of invisibility (Saltzman 2006; Mitchell 2011; Shell 2012; Andersen and Möller 2013; Campany 2013). Second, there is a vast body of literature criticizing specific forms of visual representation, in particular photographic representations of human suffering and people in pain, on ethical grounds (see Reinhardt *et al.* 2007; Grønstad and Gustafsson 2012). Third, photojournalism is said to be exhausted, failing to address viewers as it used to do, precisely because of its success, which is alleged to have resulted in desensitized and dulled viewers (Sontag 1979). As a consequence of the above, many photographers are searching for alternative ways of representing the politics of security. Some of them are inspired by the power of invisibility and obscurity currently investigated in the humanities and social sciences.

Mitchell, for example, argues that what cannot be seen is more powerful than what can be seen. Making things visible would undermine their power: the 'invisible and the unseen has, paradoxically, a greater power to activate the power of imagination than a visible image' (2011: 84). Suppressing undesired or particularly gruesome photographs – for example, Richard Drew's 'Falling man', taken in New York City on 11 September 2001 – would be counterproductive, activating imagination and thus increasing (imagined) visibility. The photographer (quoted in Friend 2006: 136) misses this point when commenting on this photograph to the effect that it is 'the most famous picture nobody's ever seen' – indeed, many people have seen or imagined it once they learned of its existence or were informed that people did in fact jump out of the windows of the twin towers.

Mitchell develops his argument with reference to the horror film. The horror film is a genre playing exceedingly with and relying on viewers' expectations and anxieties, which the genre itself has created in the first place and without which it could not fully operate. It operates successfully, although its operating mechanisms are no mystery to most viewers. The success of the horror movie depends on both viewers' willingness to accept the genre's operating mechanisms and their socialization into specific ways of seeing. This socialization makes them see (or feel or anticipate or imagine) even that which cannot be seen on screen: they know, or are socialized into knowing, what to expect; they are socialized into seeing what cannot be seen: it can be seen because it is absent from representation. However, more is at stake than just seeing. Once we know how to watch a horror film,

> our eyes are functioning to perceive the matter on the screen, and our brain is decoding what we see; but at the same time our emotions are brought into play, our heart is racing, our stomach is twisting, our whole self is involved in what is no more than the play of light and sound.
>
> (Schirato and Webb 2007: 55)

None of the above can be explained exclusively as a result of what we see in a given situation. Lisa Saltzman argues that, as 'a genre […] the horror film unabashedly exploits the traumatic potential of the visual field, deploying techniques that blur, if not level, the distinction between real and paranormal, animate and inanimate, live and dead.' According to Saltzman, the horror film gives back to the domain of the visual a body whose radical non-being defies the very notion of representation, even as it appears in cinematic form. Indebted to the mechanism of haunting, the metaphor of haunting, the horror film represents and re-members the unrepresentable body, the body at once ghastly and ghostly. For it is the horror film that gives the absent and unrepresentable body back to the domain of the visible, to the realm of representation.

(2006: 77)

The horror movie returns to the realm of representation what cannot be represented and it does so by both employing the mechanisms of haunting and returning the body to the domain of the visual while simultaneously sticking to the ('ghastly and ghostly') body's obscurity.

While the horror movie exemplifies Mitchell's argument, Mitchell does not limit his argument to horror movies. By so doing, he opens up important questions regarding visibility and invisibility also in connection with the visualization of security policy. Applied to visual aspects of security, the comparison with the horror movie is not meant to imply that security policy necessarily likens the horror movie. However, it would not be entirely inappropriate to reflect upon the horror of security: the use of drones comes to mind (see Shapiro, this volume), pure horror for those targeted, as drones are audible all the time and can strike at any moment (Chamayou 2015: 44).[3] Furthermore, many photojournalistic images are 'close-up[s] of a real horror' (Sontag 2003: 42) inflicted on people in the name of security. Yet, the question here is: is it possible to reveal something about the politics of security by visualizing security in a manner that is informed by the workings of the horror movie, that is, by the conflation of visibility and invisibility and by adherence to (some degree of) obscurity? Thus, do obscure photographs, when visualizing the politics of security, show viewers something that other forms of visual representation do not – cannot? – show them? And if so, do obscure photographs help viewers morph into participant witnesses? To begin this investigation, it is useful to recall what 'obscure' means precisely:

Obscure: 1. Devoid of light; dim; hence, gloomy, dismal. 2. Of, pertaining to, or frequenting the darkness; hence, eluding sight 1605. 3. Of colour, etc.: Dark, somber; in later use, dingy, dull 1490. 4. Indistinct, undefined; hardly perceptible to the eye; faint, 'light' 1593. b. Indistinctly perceived, felt, or heard 1597. 5. Of a place: Hidden, retired; remote from observation 1484. 6. Inconspicuous, undistinguished, unnoticed 1555. b. Of persons, their station, etc.: Unknown to fame, humble, lowly 1548. 7. *fig.* Not manifest to the mind or understanding; hidden, doubtful, vague, uncertain 1432. b. Of words, statements, etc.: Not perspicuous; hard to understand. Also, of a speaker or writer. 1495.[4]

Obscure photography, paradoxically, makes things visible without liberating them from obscurity; it exposes them without making them intelligible. Things remain hidden, doubtful, vague, uncertain, and hard to understand. Approaching such photography in terms of *understanding* and *explaining* is based on misunderstanding: such photographs do not intend to explain anything; they are not meant to be understood in any conventional way. At the same time, they are neither mere abstraction nor art; they are not meant to be approached in terms of beauty or be admired for the technological sophistication of the photographer. Such photography is a stand-in for something more real, the existence of which, while not being made explicit, is alluded to in the photographs. While not giving viewers assurance, such photographs, by means of obscurity, nevertheless stimulate them to look behind the photographs in search of what cannot be seen in the picture, the existence of which the viewer is nonetheless aware of because without it, the photograph would not exist.[5]

Obscure images operate in ways other than those employed by photojournalism. Photojournalism succeeds on condition that texts and pictures, based either on the 'intellectual stereoscopic effect' (Gilgen 2003: 56) or on similar effects, seem to be mutually supportive, telling the same story. Such effects are especially important with regard to photographic representations of people in pain, which are said to be largely useless and highly exploitative without explaining captions, triggering only 'bewilderment and hopelessness' if not 'disgust and contempt' on the part of viewers (Linfield 2010: 217).[6] Commenting on a Muzaffar Salman photograph, Linfield, referring to Susan Sontag's work, notes that

> without a political context [presumably to be provided by text] it is impossible to understand a photograph. This is true even – or especially – of political photographs themselves. Salman's picture can't answer the key questions – who are the rebels? what is their agenda? what kind of country are they fighting to create? – that surround the Free Syrian Army, and that have befuddled so many in the West (including me).
>
> (Linfield 2013: 14)

There is no doubt that Salman's picture cannot answer these questions; no picture can answer such questions. However, if the political context is already provided by text, if viewers are taught or told what pictures mean – what is the value of the photograph other than confirming the text and strengthening its message?[7] Information may suppress curiosity: when I am already told what I see, why should I bother to start my own visual investigation? Indeed, preventing viewers from starting their own investigation may be seen as one of the reasons for the scepticism of images articulated in parts of the photographic discourse. The photograph 'draws the viewer into an interpretive relationship that bypasses professional mediation' (MacDougall 1998: 68) but it is precisely professional mediation photography critics insist on. In Linfield's approach, (con)text – to be provided by photography critics or other commentators speaking with sufficient authority – provides the frame within which viewers are supposed to look at an image. The image is subordinated to the text, illustrating the text,[8] rather than operating independently on the viewer – within certain limits as there is no such thing as pure viewing and all media are mixed media (Mitchell 1994) – and the viewer's interpretation is subordinated to the interpretation provided by the professional commentator.

There is, however, something in a photograph – in many photographs – that speaks to viewers and affects them even *without* knowledge of the political context and *without* professional mediation and that stimulates them to do something they would not otherwise do. This 'something' is marginalized in such approaches as Linfield's where text domesticates the surplus of meaning and the 'unintended sites of connotation' images carry with them (MacDougall 1998: 68). Indeed, Linfield articulates what the photograph does *not* tell us without additional information but she does not ask what the photograph *does* tell us or how it operates on us.[9] While reflecting on what this photograph does *not* do without text, she has little to say about the question of what it *does do*. This question is ultimately the more important one if we want to approach an image as an image, not as an illustration of text, and the question is relevant with regard to both photojournalistic work in general and obscure photography in particular (because even if we know the political context, it is often difficult to connect this context to the obscure photograph; see below). There is something elusive and evasive in images that no text can grasp (Reinhardt 2007: 25). An image's elusive elements are possibly more important for understanding both its relationship to the equally elusive world of security and its power on the viewer than those elements that can (seemingly easily) be grasped by means of language. Obscure photography capitalizes on elusiveness and requires curious and patient viewers.

To be sure, obscure photography requires viewers interested in the exploration of different ways of seeing. In an *Aperture* issue dedicated to curiosity, David Campany notes that the 'politics of [photographic] abstraction' – 'Habits of seeing are estranged strategically in the hope of opening up a space to think differently (about warfare, about landscape, about photography, about vision)' – is 'a risky strategy, always provisional and contingent upon the cultural norms that are being challenged' (2013: 51). Catering photographically to 'habits of seeing' (Campany) when representing conflict and war, however, is equally risky as it tends to result in 'generally interchangeable images of violence's apex' (Ritchin 1999: 27), which, owing to predictability and visual habituation, might fail both to attract viewers and to make them think about the conditions depicted in a given image including their own responsibility for the conditions depicted. A sense of responsibility follows from a process of reflection about the conditions depicted in an image, triggered by the act of seeing. The act of seeing, thus, is the condition for the possibility of reflection but without transformation into a process of reflection, the act of seeing will largely be inconsequential (Möller 2013: 36–55). To be sure, expert viewers may be able to understand or explain obscure photographs on the basis of knowledge acquired prior to and independent of the act of seeing but for non-expert viewers, understanding obscure photographs is not the main issue: even without understanding them, obscure photographs may affect viewers in a way more concrete photographs may not. My point here is not that obscure photography should replace conventional forms of photographic representation (which are still needed). Rather, obscure photography should supplement such conventional forms and become an ingredient of photojournalistic work rather than being delegated to the realm of art photography (Philips 2010: 143), seemingly remote from politics. In other words, I would like photojournalism to escape from the straightjacket of the tradition and to capitalize on the endless possibilities photography offers so as to open up space for engagement on the part of viewers. There is no reason to assume a priori that viewers interested in engagement and reflection do not exist anymore although digital culture does not favour 'viewers who scrutinize [photographs] with concentrated interest' (Lister 2013: 7).

Indeed, why should we reduce viewers to people who watch and *only* watch? Why should we assume that people are neither interested in the ways images operate on them nor in their own habits of viewing? And why should we assume that people do not care about what they see? 'Spend time pondering photographs of things other than people (…) and your habits of seeing will slowly become visible' (Elkins 2011: 152). In Campany's words, 'those moments when our basic recognition is challenged' – those moments when we do not even know what a photograph 'is *of*' – 'may tell us a lot about the ways in which habits of seeing shape the pleasure and knowledge offered by photographs' (2013: 48). We are nowadays exposed to – just as we contribute to – sophisticated forms of image production but our ways of seeing do not seem to keep pace with these developments. Being or becoming a spectator (Emerling 2012: 165) means occupying an unfavourable place or condition, and revealing one's habits of seeing may be uncomfortable. Sean O'Hagan, for example, commenting on Donovan Wylie's photographs of military surveillance installations, notes that the absence of people adds to the 'haunting power' of these photographs but, reflecting on photographs of the conflict in Northern Ireland, he also observes 'a perverse feeling of nostalgia for those troubled times' (2013). It is not easy being a spectator.

Obscurity in the work of Edgar Martins, Simon Norfolk, and Trevor Paglen

The combination of obscurity and stimulation aptly describes visual strategies in recent photographic representations of security policy, especially technological and infrastructural developments, in the work of Edgar Martins, Simon Norfolk, and Trevor Paglen. A good starting point for discussion is Peter Gilgen's characterization of film (2003: 58–59): 'Film supplements the anatomy of the body. […] Through film it becomes possible to isolate and dissect a specific behavioural pattern' thus rendering visible '[n]ormally neglected details.' Photography, too, makes visible what is invisible to the human eye. Microscopic photography of tiny water creatures, for example, 'reflects photography's capacity to present things that could otherwise barely be described' (Elkins 2011: 149) and the extremely fast shutter speed of a Rapatronic camera revealed things that no human eye would otherwise have seen (Elkins 2011: 168). Film and photography do not only supplement 'the anatomy of the body' (Gilgen) but also the anatomy of the society by isolating and dissecting societal behavioural patterns, thus making visible, and socializing viewers into regarding, details. The conditions for the possibility of modern warfare, however, are hardly details. Weapons testing grounds, communications facilities, satellite technologies, eavesdropping facilities, detention centres, and airfields are hidden from view and remote from observation, thus obscure. They are, however, indispensable for the operation of the current security-state which, in contrast to earlier forms of population control relying on visibility, relies heavily on invisibility (Mirzoeff 2005: 124, 149).

Obscure photography of security stands outside the visual-discursive frame within which images of war and security are normally produced and received according to standard, simplistic, ready-made patterns (see Chouliaraki in this volume) – both textual and visual – preventing rather than encouraging thinking and channelling viewing into specific patterns from which critical investigation can hardly emerge. Viewers' right to autonomous interpretation is denied and photography's capability 'to engage itself otherwise, less obviously, in subtle ambiguity, in soaring metaphor, in questioning the nature of reality rather than delineating conventional responses' is ignored (Ritchin 1999: 126). With regard to obscure photography, what is required is interpretative ingenuity or at least curiosity: the wish to see more than can be seen at first sight, the wish to interrogate the conditions depicted in a photograph, the wish to engage with the limits of both representation and visibility (Andersen and Möller 2013). Such interpretative ingenuity is required, for example, in connection with Edgar Martins' work. His untitled photographs of runways at night from the series *Approaches*, 2006, resemble abstract, geometrical patterns (Martins 2008: 95–103). These photographs are dominated by black – black tarmac (constructed space/built environment) and black night (nature/surround) merging, blurred, disorienting viewers. There is little light and the little light there is does not reveal much: some signs on the ground, some position lights, the moon half hidden behind clouds, a wind gauge, a vehicle (looking like a miniature, a toy vehicle – the scale is difficult to discern[10]), technical devices. These devices are indispensable for the operation of airports but they are neither normally observed with much interest nor visualized as ingredients of security policy. In Martins' photographs, they are photographed and observed with interest (and technological sophistication). Lack of additional information makes the viewing experience difficult and, therefore, irresistible. These photographs address viewers, not readers. Viewers have to look carefully because there is no accompanying text seemingly offering refuge: no date, no location, nothing that would help them feel at home in these photographs. Thus, the viewer has to do the work of interpretation but cannot: 'this is a landscape of signs that can be read by the knowledgeable – pilots and air traffic controllers, for instance – but that remain perplexing to the uninitiated' (Beardsley 2008: 23). The viewing experience, therefore, is as pure as possible (although pure viewing is impossible). Viewers are sucked into these pictures while at the same time being kept at some distance; they are given space for their own inventions:

MARTINS: I am interested in a space between reality and imagination.

CAMPANY: ... And the more apparently simple the reality, the more space for the imagination.

MARTINS: Exactly, and it is valid as both.

(Martins and Campany 2008: 115)

This photography is relevant in the context of visual aspects of security because Martins' work is a photographic study of a particular locality (hence the title, *Topologies*) that can be assumed to fulfil a certain function in the global politics of security. This function could be analysed, provided that we knew the locality. However, Martins does not reveal the location; the statement he wants to make is decoupled from any given place. It is, therefore, more important to study Martins' photography in light of what it shows us about 'the ambiguous history of human impact on nature' (Beardsley 2008: 26) and what it reveals about the impact of human behaviour on humans. Like Norfolk's and Paglen's work to be discussed below, it is a symbol for current developments in modern warfare independent of the specific location where a given photograph was taken: the replacement of bodies by technology, the extent to which current societies are dominated by and exposed to the politics of security including ubiquitous warfare, and the increasing invisibility of this warfare. Indeed, what used to be referred to as 'the War on Terror' is a 'war that is everywhere and yet largely invisible' (Paglen 2012: 78). As Paglen notes (2011: 68), this invisibility is something 'photographers should critically reflect upon' especially because 'photography has become a relational medium – a meta-network of machines, politics, culture, and ways of collective seeing' that is likely to dominate the ways we are going to perceive our everyday lives in the twenty-first century.

Likewise, it is difficult to connect such a photograph as Simon Norfolk's 'The BBC World Service Atlantic Relay Station at English Bay' on Ascension Island with current warfare. This photograph may epitomize current warfare's 'really interesting developments: submarine warfare, space weapons, electronic warfare and electronic eavesdropping [all of which] are essentially invisible'.[11] However, without further investigation, stimulated by the image's obscurity, viewers, used to visual representations of war as 'showbiz' (Norfolk) or video game, will see only 'a web of tiny wires, an almost invisible net' (Phillips 2010: 143) in front of grey clouds. Reflection starts when seeing stops, when the 'initial spark' (Sontag 2003: 103) that photographs are said to be capable of triggering is translated into a process of reflection, but seeing will be resumed in this process, revealing formerly obscure things (which may very well be imagined) without increasing their perceptibility to the eye. It is difficult, too, to connect Norfolk's photograph 'Bratunac soccer stadium' with the brutality of the war in Bosnia even if viewers pay close attention to the photograph's complete title: 'Bratunac soccer stadium. MSF [Médicins Sans Frontières] reported having seen 700 prisoners at this site. A UNHCR [United Nations High Commissioner for Refugees] team, in a nearby hotel, reported hearing gunshots all night from the direction of the stadium.' The seeming peacefulness of the photograph does not reveal the above. The image is reminiscent of the 'loudness of silence', described by UNAMIR (United Nations Assistance Mission in Rwanda) commander Roméo Dallaire as unbearable in connection with his memories of the 1994 genocide in Rwanda.[12] It is the tension between what viewers see and what they expect to see that makes Norfolk's work powerful and compelling. Indeed, to 'be compelling, there must be tension in the work; if everything has been decided beforehand, there will be no tension and no compulsion to the work' (Strauss 2003: 10). Norfolk's photography invites what Strauss calls 'a more complex response' than accepting or rejecting a message.

It is ultimately up to viewers to accept this invitation – and the question of why they would want to accept this invitation is a difficult one since such acceptance is likely to render their subject positions more difficult – and to start a process of reflection. But photographers have many means at their disposal with which to trick viewers into engagement. For example, photographers may seduce viewers into a photograph's space. Or they may refuse them entry into that space. Among the photographic strategies of seduction and refusal, the space of architecture deserves special attention not only because the grid-like structure in Norfolk's Ascension Island photograph referred to above points at architecture but also because it is closely related to the idea of obscurity. When discussing the representation of space and the space of representation within a larger exploration of the ways art thinks, Ernst van Alphen (2005: 71–95) differentiates the space of landscape from the space of architecture. Both spaces operate on viewers by engaging vision but they do so differently. With regard to works of visual art utilizing the space of architecture, the work 'keeps setting up obstacles that make the viewer more and more eager to look behind them'. Works of art utilizing the space of landscape, on the other hand, emphasize attraction and seduction by means of which they invite the viewer 'to merge into space' (van Alphen 2005: 72).[13] Norfolk's work in Afghanistan in the footsteps of John Burke exemplifies the space of landscape, explicitly utilizing beauty so as to seduce viewers into engagement, not with the photographer's aesthetics but with his politics (Norfolk 2011). His work on Ascension Island epitomizes use of the space of architecture. Neither the space of landscape nor that of architecture is 'an end in itself as a representation of space, but it is the means by which the space of representation is explored, challenged, and exposed' (van Alphen 2005: 73). The distinction between the space of landscape and the space of architecture is, as van Alphen notes,

> not a distinction between good and bad, between stimulating vision and frustrating it. They are both effective ways of engaging vision but according

to different principles. [...] Architectural space engages vision by raising obstacles. And obstacles encourage the desire to conquer them, to do something when it is forbidden, to try something when it is impossible, to intrude on a space that is not yours and has to be respected as secret or somebody else's. In contrast, the space of landscape engages vision by seducing you or inviting you. Both can be effective, but the effects differ.

(2005: 91–92)[14]

Just like the work discussed above, Trevor Paglen's geo-photographic works, and especially the *Limit Telephotography* series focusing on classified military installations located mostly in the southwestern part of the United States of America (2010: 19–53), although aesthetically appealing, operate largely within the space of architecture. They engage vision by raising obstacles; they are obscure and they are hard to understand. They explain nothing but their purpose is neither to explain anything nor to be understood: Paglen 'welcomes distortion in his images' – and dislikes clearness – as 'his aim is not to expose and edify so much as to confound and unsettle' (Weiner 2012: 56). The blurriness characterizing his photographs 'serves both an aesthetic and an "allegorical" function. It makes his images more arresting while providing a metaphor for the difficulty of uncovering the truth in an era when so much government activity is covert' (Weiner 2012: 56–57). The military installations Paglen photographs are off limits to the public; they are almost unphotographable: they can be accessed only with security clearances or photographed from afar.[15] Most space within these military ranges is devoted to combat training 'but the ranges also serve as home to obscure facilities associated with "black" or classified military projects' (Paglen 2010: 19). All these installations are characterized by large spatial distance from urban conglomeration in rather remote areas of the country. They are remote from observation, inaccessible, and invisible: 'there is often no place on public land where a member of the public might see them with an unaided eye' (Paglen 2010: 19). The photographer's efforts to bridge this distance are immense. Line-of-sight views were few and far between and astronomical and astrophotographical devices were required (just as Martins' work at night required extreme long exposure times of up to three hours).

Paglen's photography is based on thorough research and a geographical approach to the world: whatever happens, it has to happen somewhere; or, in Paglen's words: 'if you're going to build a secret airplane, you can't do it in an invisible factory' (quoted in Weiner 2012: 60). His work shows that it is not impossible to transform the invisible into the visible but it requires a lot of work and a lot of research before the first photograph can be taken. It necessitates 'countless hours spent in libraries, sifting through documents, conducting interviews, repeated site visits, careful planning and project management, and personal relationships developed over years of dedication to the material.' It also requires learning both a new language – a technological one that is not meant to be understood by outsiders – in order to make sense of all the documents and project descriptions and a new visual language: it necessitates photographic ingenuity because traditional knowledge on, for example, landscape photography is basically useless when taking photographs at extreme distances. For example, there is no such thing as depth of field at extreme distances; locations from which to take photographs were limited; 'possible composition, colour, and exposure choices' were dictated by 'atmospheric conditions and temperature differentials between air and land' (Paglen 2010: 144–145).

Does Paglen's photography, by transforming the invisible into the visible, also render intelligible the once invisible and now visible? Hardly, and that's the point. Although the photographs transform invisibility into visibility, viewers are none the wiser after the viewing experience. Paglen's photographic work does not transform incomprehensibility into comprehensibility: we cannot recognize what we see and we cannot identify it as ingredients of security policy. Indeed, if the work is blurry, 'that is because it has to be. It would not be the same were clarity to be achieved' (Keenan 2008: 38) because clarity would give viewers only the illusion of comprehensibility. Consequently, Paglen rejects technologies with which to produce clearer images (Weiner 2012: 57). The images' obscurity invites viewers to engage with them and the artist's use of the space of architecture tricks them into engagement. The photographs refuse simple answers to the question of how current security policies operate and whether these policies are desirable or not; they render easy responses impossible and, however the viewer responds, it is his or her response, not the photographer's or a commentator's. Thus, the responsibility of the viewer increases in the process of co-constructing meaning. Paglen's photographs 'constitute a provocation, a question for us … or, actually, a question about us' (Keenan 2008: 39). The visual arts, as has been noted in a different context, 'complexify the perceptual experience of the spectator' (Ross 2008: 7). This is exactly what the photography discussed above does. Such photography is demanding, it is inexplicable, and it complicates viewers' visual experience:

> I embrace the epistemological and visual contradictions in my work and am most compelled by images that both make claims to represent, and at the same time dialectically undermine, the very claims they seem to put forth. I think about the images in this book as making claims on both sides of the murky boundaries separating fact and fiction, empiricism and imagination, and literature and science, while insisting on underlying sociological, cultural, and political facts.
>
> (Paglen 2010: 151)

Conclusion: from spectator to participant witness

The spectator I have had in mind in this chapter is not just any spectator; it is definitely not a person who looks and only looks, 'who simply notices but does not act' (Simpson 2006: 3). I would want to think of spectators in terms of participant witnesses who self-critically engage with the conditions depicted in a given image including their own subject positions in connection with the conditions depicted. The participant witness is an ideal type. It is unattainable because nobody can respond to all the images they are regularly exposed to and not every image speaks to viewers in such a way as to trigger curiosity and stimulate visual investigation. The question then is what obscure photography does to transform spectators into participant witnesses. Following Leonardo's advice that the mind is stimulated by obscure things I have discussed selected works of Edgar Martins, Simon Norfolk, and Trevor Paglen in terms of obscurity. I argued that obscure images may stimulate viewers, not only because they are unusual but precisely because they are obscure: their obscurity stimulates people to do something in response to their viewing experience and imparts additional energy to the process of doing something. Paradoxically, obscure photography – operating in the spaces of either architecture or landscape – makes things visible without liberating them from obscurity; it exposes them without making them intelligible. Things remain hidden, doubtful, vague, uncertain, and hard to understand. Viewers are required to engage with the limits of both representation and visibility. Engagement with these limits requires curious and patient viewers who are willing to accept some degree of responsibility for the conditions depicted in a given image. They also have to accept that their own subject positions as spectator/participant witness get complicated. To repeat, it is not easy being a spectator; being a participant witness is still more difficult.

The images discussed above also serve as a reminder of the extent to which our societies are penetrated by the logic, the idea, and the practice of security, including those ingredients that are hardly visible, intangible, and abstract, difficult to grasp, and hard to understand even when they are made visible. In obscure photography there is no immediate connection between making things visible and making them known. This photography shows that visual aspects of security cannot be reduced to what Norfolk calls the 'showbiz of war' but include routine, entirely uninteresting, even boring, seemingly trivial elements that are hard to visualize. Its ordinariness and ubiquity make security policy invisible and, therefore, powerful. The kind of photography introduced here is quantitatively irrelevant when compared with the number of conventional war photographs professional photojournalists and non-professional citizen photographers produce in Afghanistan, Iraq, Syria, and elsewhere, rather disparagingly referred to by Norfolk as 'the work that is pouring out like some kind of sewer pipe with a crack in the side.'[16] It surely is statistically irrelevant when compared with the overall number of photographs nowadays produced. In contrast to most conventional photographs, however, this photography both socializes us into seeing the invisible and helps us to think differently about security, including, but not limited to, its visual aspects. Finally, it should be noted that even if the photography discussed above manages to transform spectators into participant witnesses, there is no guarantee that such witnesses want to change the conditions depicted in a given image: critical reflection may result in the wish either to change or to preserve these conditions. And should the wish to change these conditions occur, it can be translated into either progressive or regressive politics (Möller 2013: 192). Furthermore, most of the photographs discussed in this chapter are photographs without people. Such photographs may mark 'a reappraisal of a progressive notion of landscape as a medium that pushes the limits of perception, and that expands the faculty of imagining' (Gustafsson 2013: 150). While traditional landscape painting and landscape photography have often been criticized as depicting landscapes as spaces without people, seemingly empty spaces to be occupied and colonized by the nation-state (Shapiro 2004; Solnit 2014), the work discussed in this chapter does not function as a provider of legitimacy for the taking-possession and the use of seemingly empty space by the national security-state: this photography, although being largely without people, is ultimately *about* people (Möller 2015).

Notes

1 For a discussion of Norfolk's and Paglen's photography in terms of different epistemological modalities of the visual sign, see Andersen and Möller, 2013.
2 Simon Norfolk, 'Ascension Island: The Panopticon (ECHELON for beginners),' www.simonnorfolk.com (accessed 16 January 2012).
3 See also http://livingunderdrones.org/living-under-drones. Many drones are used for surveillance and reconnaissance but they may sound and look and feel like those equipped with weapons; thus, if they do not in fact carry weapons they nevertheless inflict horror on people.
4 *The Shorter Oxford English Dictionary on Historical Principles*, Vol. 2, p. 1429.
5 Augmented Reality (AR) will soon undermine this awareness as the 'quality of the AR image will soon match that of other digital photographic images' (Mesch 2013: 205). As to the AR image, viewers cannot know if what is depicted in the image actually does exist.
6 Note that most obscure photographs discussed in this chapter do not depict people in pain; in fact, they do not depict any people.
7 Fred Ritchin (1999: 99) writes that photography is 'a medium which is almost everywhere considered secondary to the text' and laments the limited power of picture editors. But also many photography critics – from Benjamin to Sontag to Linfield – seem to be skeptical or afraid of the autonomous power of the image, its uncontrollability. From a photographer's point of view, the addition of text simply signifies the failure of the photograph as a photograph (Adams 1994: 33).
8 See Ritchin (1999: 26) for 'editorial photography' where pre-existing ideas are illustrated by means of images.
9 She acknowledges, however, that viewers' attention may be directed to the ubiquitous presence of camera-phones in conflict situations where two meanings of 'shooting a person' often coincide.
10 Campany (2013: 47) explains that photography is 'a medium of distances and perspectives' and that, therefore, 'making sense of it is never just a matter of recognizing what is depicted: it also involves knowing *from where* it has been depicted. An unorthodox vantage point may render abstract even the most optically clear photograph.'
11 Simon Norfolk, 'Ascension Island: The Panopticon (ECHELON for beginners)', www.simonnorfolk.com (accessed 16 January 2012).
12 See *Shake Hands with the Devil*, White Pine Pictures/Investigative Productions (2004), directed by Peter Raymont, 1:00'15"–1:00'21".
13 Van Alphen discusses paintings but I wish to apply his discussion to photography.
14 Elsewhere, van Alphen suggests that 'when artists set out to explore the two-dimensionality of the picture surface, they end up in the realm of architecture' and when they 'set out to explore the space between viewer and image, they end up in the realm of landscape' (2005: 84).

15 The photograph 'Large Hangars and Fuel Storage, 2005 (Tonopah Test Range, NV)' is taken from a distance of approximately eighteen miles; the photograph 'Chemical and Biological Proving Ground #2, 2006 (Dugway, UT)' from a distance of approximately forty-two miles; the photographs 'San Nicholas Island #1, #2 and #3, 2007 (US Navy-owned facility, Santa Barbara Channel, CA)' from a distance of approximately sixty-five miles.

16 *Burke + Norfolk: Photographs from the War in Afghanistan by John Burke and Simon Norfolk*. Video, http://timemachinemag.com/2011/12/31/simon-norfolk-burke-and-norfolk (accessed 9 January 2012), 8′17″–8′27″.

References

Adams, R. (1994). *Why People Photograph*. New York: Aperture.

Andersen, R. S. and Möller, F. (2013). Engaging the Limits of Visibility: Photography, Security and Surveillance. *Security Dialogue*, 44(3), pp. 203–221.

Beardsley, J. (2008). Topologies of Place. In: E. Martins, *Topologies*. New York: Aperture, pp. 7–28.

Bridle, J. (2015). What They Don't Want You to See: the Hidden World of UK Deportation. *Guardian*, 27 January 2015, at www.theguardian.com/artanddesign/2015/jan/27/hidden-world-of-uk-deportation-asylum-seamless-transistions [Accessed 5 April 2017].

Campany, D. (2013). What on Earth? Photography's Alien Landscapes. *Aperture*, #211 (Summer 2013), pp. 46–51.

Chamayou, G. (2015). *Drone Theory*. London: Penguin, 2015.

Elkins, J. (2011). *What Photography Is*. New York and London: Routledge.

Emerling, J. (2012). *Photography: History and Theory*. London and New York: Routledge.

Friend, D. (2006). *Watching the World Change: The Stories Behind the Images of 9/11*. New York: Picador.

Gilgen, P. (2003). History after Film. In: H. U. Gumbrecht and M. Marrinan, eds., *Mapping Benjamin: The Work of Art in the Digital Age*. Stanford, CA: Stanford University Press, pp. 53–62.

Grønstad, A. and Gustafsson, H. eds. (2012). *Ethics and Images of Pain*. New York: Routledge.

Gustafsson, H. (2013). Foresight, Hindsight and State Secrecy in the American West: The Geopolitical Aesthetics of Trevor Paglen. *Journal of Visual Culture*, 12(1), pp. 148–164.

Keenan, T. (2008). Disappearances: The Photographs of Trevor Paglen. *Aperture*, #191 (Summer 2008), pp. 36–43.

Linfield, S. (2010). *The Cruel Radiance: Photography and Political Violence*. Chicago, IL and London: The University of Chicago Press.

Linfield, Susie (2013). Shooting Conflict. *Aperture*, #213 (Winter 2013), p. 14.

Lister, M. (2013). Introduction. In: M. Lister, ed., *The Photographic Image in Digital Culture*. Second edition. London and New York: Routledge, pp. 1–21.

MacDougall, D. (1998). *Transcultural Cinema*. Ed. Lucien Taylor. Princeton, NJ: Princeton University Press.

Martins, E. (2008). *Topologies*. New York: Aperture.

Martins, E. and Campany, D. (2008). In Conversation. In: E. Martins, *Topologies*. New York: Aperture, pp. 115–122.

Mesch, C. (2013). *Art and Politics: A Small History of Art for Social Change since 1945*. London and New York: I.B. Tauris.
Mirzoeff, N. (2005). *Watching Babylon: The War in Iraq and Global Visual Culture*. New York and London: Routledge.
Mitchell, W. J. T. (1994). *Picture Theory: Essays on Verbal and Visual Representation*. Chicago, IL and London: The University of Chicago Press.
Mitchell, W. J. T. (2011). *Cloning Terror: the War of Images, 9/11 to the Present*. Chicago, IL and London: The University of Chicago Press.
Möller, Frank (2013). *Visual Peace: Images, Spectatorship, and the Politics of Violence*. Houndmills: Palgrave Macmillan.
Möller, Frank (2015). The Power of Obscurity: Trevor Paglen's Geo-Visual Imagination. In: M. Elo and M. Karo, eds., *Photographic Powers –Helsinki Photomedia 2014*. Helsinki: Aalto University, pp. 155–176.
Norfolk, S. (2011). *Burke + Norfolk: Photographs from the War in Afghanistan by John Burke and Simon Norfolk*. London: Dewi Lewis.
O'Hagan, S. (2013). Spies Like Us: Donovan Wylie Captures the Impact of Surveillance. *Guardian*, 24 October 2013, at www.theguardian.com/artanddesign/2013/oct/24/donovan-wylie-vision-as-power-exhibition [Accessed 5 April 2017].
Paglen, T. (2010). *Invisible: Covert Operations and Classified Landscapes*. New York: Aperture.
Paglen, T. (2011). Contribution to *The Anxiety of Images*, *Aperture*, #204 (Fall 2011), pp. 67–68.
Paglen, T. (2012). Images of the Everywhere War. *Aperture*, #209 (Winter 2012), pp. 78–79.
Phillips, S. S. (2010). Surveillance. In: S. S. Phillips, ed., *Exposed: Voyeurism, Surveillance and the Camera*. London: Tate Publishing, pp. 140–144.
Reinhardt, M. (2007). Picturing Violence: Aesthetics and the Anxiety of Critique. In: M. Reinhardt, H. Edwards, and E. Duganne, eds., *Beautiful Suffering: Photography and the Traffic in Pain*. Williamsburg, VA/Chicago, IL: Williams College Museum of Art/The University of Chicago Press, pp. 13–36.
Reinhardt, M., Edwards, H., and Duganne, E., eds. (2007). *Beautiful Suffering: Photography and the Traffic in Pain*. Williamsburg, VA/Chicago, IL: Williams College Museum of Art/The University of Chicago Press.
Ritchin, F. (1999). *In Our Own Image*. New York: Aperture.
Ross, C. (2008). Introduction: The Precarious Visualities of Contemporary Art and Visual Culture. In: O. Asselin, J. Lamoureux, and C. Ross, eds., *Precarious Visualities: New Perspectives on Identification in Contemporary Art and Visual Culture*. Montreal & Kingston: McGill-Queen's University Press, pp. 3–16.
Saltzman, L. (2006). *Making Memory Matter: Strategies of Remembrance in Contemporary Art*. Chicago, IL and London: The University of Chicago Press.
Schirato, T. and Webb, J. (2007). *Understanding the Visual*. Los Angeles, London, New Delhi, Singapore: Sage Publications.
Shapiro, M. J. (2004). *Methods and Nations: Cultural Governance and the Indigenous Subject*. New York and London: Routledge.
Shell, H. R. (2012). *Hide and Seek: Camouflage, Photography, and the Media of Reconnaissance*. New York: Zone Books.
Simpson, D. (2006). *9/11: The Culture of Commemoration*. Chicago, IL and London: The University of Chicago Press.

Solnit, R. (2014). *Savage Dreams: A Journey into the Hidden Wars of the American West. 20th Anniversary Edition, with a new preface*. Berkeley, Los Angeles and London: University of California Press.
Sontag, S. (1979). *On Photography*. London: Penguin.
Sontag, S. (2003). *Regarding the Pain of Others*. New York: Farrar, Straus & Giroux.
Stomberg, J. (2007). A Genealogy of Orthodox Documentary. In: M. Reinhardt, H. Edwards, and E. Duganne, eds., *Beautiful Suffering: Photography and the Traffic in Pain*. Williamsburg, VA/Chicago, IL: Williams College Museum of Art/The University of Chicago Press, pp. 37–56.
Strauss, D. L. (2003). *Between the Eyes: Essays on Photography and Politics*. New York: Aperture.
Taylor, D. (2003). *The Archive and the Repertoire: Performing Cultural Memory in the Americas*. Durham, NC and London: Duke University Press.
Tucker, A.W., Michels, W., and Zelt, N. (2012). *War/Photography: Images of Armed Conflict and Its Aftermath*. Houston, TX/New Haven, CT and London: The Museum of Fine Arts/Yale University Press.
van Alphen, E. (2005). *Art in Mind: How Contemporary Images Shape Thought*. Chicago, IL and London: The University of Chicago Press.
Weiner, J. (2012). Prying Eyes: Trevor Paglen Makes Art out of Government Secrets. *The New Yorker*, October 22, 2012, pp. 54–61.

Film and video

Burke + Norfolk: Photographs from the War in Afghanistan by John Burke and Simon Norfolk. Video, http://timemachinemag.com/2011/12/31/simon-norfolk-burke-and-norfolk
Shake Hands with the Devil. White Pine Pictures/Investigative Productions (2004), directed by Peter Raymont.

Websites

http://livingunderdrones.org/living-under-drones
www.simonnorfolk.com: 'Ascension Island: The Panopticon (ECHELON for beginners)'.

9 Making norms visible

Police uniforms and the social meaning of policing[1]

Xavier T. Guillaume, Juha A. Vuori, and Rune S. Andersen

This chapter takes an approach to visuality that emphasizes how different modalities of security representations and signs are used to make security norms visible in security practices (see Introduction). We examine colour-use as one such modality. In terms of security practice, we discuss how the colours of a police uniform participate in the formation of 'police spaces' (Rancière 2014) in encounters between (uniformed) police officers and citizens. Such encounters are among the most common forms of quotidian (in)security experiences, they take various forms, and they have numerous trajectories over time in different countries. For example, the 'proximity' of the police to the general population, cultures of interaction, and types of quotidian prejudices differ from society to society (on the French case, see for instance, Mouhanna 2011; see also the chapters in this volume that discuss relations between citizens and security professionals in Liberia (Vastapuu) and West Africa (Sandor)). Yet, despite or maybe even because of such plurality, police-citizen encounters are an important site to analyse which kinds of modes of action and being are interpellated by what a police uniform conveys to an audience. In order to analyse such interpellation,[2] or how subjects are constituted through colour use, we pay special attention to the social imaginaries as well as modes of being and action that are linked to specific situations where traditional police uniforms are absent from a situation of policing, e.g. when uniformed police officers are wearing actual battlefield and military tactical uniforms.

The most commonly identified colour-use in police uniforms – dark blue or black – have a rather clear semiotic connection to forms of authority (see Pastoureau 2000: 143; 2008: 114–119, 199): in a Western context, at least, dark blue has replaced black as a colour of authority, though blue itself is a much more fluid colour in semiotic terms (Pastoureau 2000). In this chapter we pay close attention to police uniforms that are adorned in situations of emergency or violence, asking what is the visual agency of replacing common police uniforms, in their specific shape and hues, with battle tactical ones. We do so by focusing on the 2014 demonstrations in Ferguson, Missouri, that sprung up after the killing of Michael Brown by a uniformed police officer. By contrasting an ordinary and an extraordinary social imaginary of the uniformed police officer, we propose that the latter not only makes the orthodox norms of policing visible, but is also revealing in regard to the evolution of the social meaning of policing. Indeed, the wearing of tactical battlefield uniforms by the police produces a specific political space in which the ability to perform one's subjectivity as a political subject is conditioned to an important extent by the contours of the public space interpellated by the interventions of the police. The quotidian police–citizen relation is replaced by an extraordinary imagination where different norms are in play. While the increased militarization of Western police forces and the effects of this on societies have already been noted (see Jefferson 1987, 1993; Kraska 1996; Kraska and Kappeler 1997), less attention has been paid to the differentiated modalities by which the effects of this process of militarization take place.

Therefore, this chapter concentrates on how police uniforms can interpellate specific police spaces. Changes in colour-use in police uniforms, in conjunction with changes in their forms and functionality are a window into the evolutions induced on such spaces by changes in the regime of visibility produced by police forces. They also illustrate the banalization of this militarization that until recently was confined to exceptional situations (e.g. hostage taking or terrorist threats) and did not characterize other more common forms of policing (such as facing demonstrators).

In paying attention to the regime of visibility behind policing, this chapter follows the tradition of studying the police as a force that constitutes societal norms and the social order (see Favre 2009). We draw particularly from Michel Foucault's (2004: 319–370) analysis of the police.[3] As such, the term 'police' has gone through many modifications in its meaning. Until the nineteenth century, the meanings of police included a larger sense of societal development (see Liang 1992: 1–4) that is often detached from our current understanding of the police. Contemporary understandings are largely limited to a specific state institution at the service of the judicial power that wields the legitimate use of force against citizens (Reynolds 1998: 1). Importantly for our argument here, the idea of the police has been, and we argue still is, intimately linked with the governing capacity of the state, and is considered to be the interface between the state and other components of what Foucault terms the 'relational field of forces' (i.e. individuals, groups, companies, and so on) (Foucault 2004: 319). Here, a specific, professional, and centrally organized (not necessarily unitary) 'state civilian force' replaced the existing 'municipal civilian' (e.g. parish constables in England), and 'state military' (e.g. the gendarmerie in France) policing forces in the nineteenth century (see Emsley 1999).

Before the development of what we understand as the police now, the way in which the 'mobile relation' between the 'domestic order of the state and the growth of its forces' was termed in the seventeenth century by a 'strange word': splendour (Foucault 2004: 321). According to Foucault, the idea of splendour in seventeenth- and eighteenth-century treaties about the police designates

> at the same time the visible beauty of order and the glow of a force which manifests itself and radiates. The police is the effect of the art of the splendour of the state as a visible order and a dazzling force.
>
> (Foucault 2004: 321)

Inspired by such a metaphor of visibility, we examine the contemporary institution of the police as a modality of the state's 'splendour' in terms of a regime of visibility. Such a regime is one in which its forces are managed and offered a space. These consist mainly of citizens or residents, but also include those denied formal recognition by the state while still participating in its political economy and social life (see McNevin 2006). Policing is part of the 'iconography of the nation state' and a 'vehicle, through which political communities are imagined' (Loader and Walker 2001: 13). From this viewpoint, the police are a vital visual modality of the state, and concomitantly colour-use is an important modality of the police uniform as a sign-vehicle.

Indeed, in the modern evolution of the meaning of the word and the function of police, the idea of splendour can be transcribed through the aesthetics of politics that Jacques Rancière has analysed. More specifically, Rancière (2014: 37–40) speaks of the way in which the configuration of political space is linked to how politics 'make[s] the world of its subjects and its operations seen'. Police interventions are particularly important for Rancière in this respect, as they are what enables the state to define a specific space as a 'space of circulation', one in which 'there's nothing to see and so nothing to do but move along'. Police interventions thus counter the essence of politics, which is the definition and manifestation of 'dissensus as the presence of two worlds in one'. In other words, police interventions disrupt the ability of the people to make a singular space contain two worlds by disabling the manifestation of dissensus. These two worlds are those of the public space, where political claims are made, and the world of private sufferings and voices. A police force intervention in a space makes it one where everyone has a set position from where to speak and act, cancelling dissensus and the voices of those who have no authority to speak but still exercise that very right. Indeed, for Rancière (2014: 38), dissensus 'is not a confrontation between interests or opinions [, but] the demonstration (*manifestation*) of a gap in the sensible itself'. Therefore, even in a situation where the police act to protect the rights of people to demonstrate, this is still within the sensible and counts as a 'police' rather than 'political' space for Rancière.

The police is central to Rancière's (2014: 42) conception of politics as 'the police is a distribution of the sensible', where there is no void[4] or supplement; the police is a symbolic constitution of how the sensible is divided up in a certain way. Moreover, the police as a profession in its quotidian interactions with the public and by its large autonomy from political authorities have an important role in shaping a social order (Favre 2009). The partition of the sensible allows for both exclusion and participation, and produces a distribution of what is visible and what is not, what can be heard, said, what or who is permissible, authorized or not, and so on. In such divisions, there is no room for voids or supplements: functions, places, and ways of being are matched. Consensus reduces politics to the police (Rancière 2014: 42). In contrast, the essence of politics is to disturb the arrangement of police spaces and to supplement 'it with a part of those without part, identified with the whole of the community' (Rancière, 2014: 36); politics 'is an intervention in the visible and sayable' (ibid.: 37). Politics refigures a space into one where a subject may appear, it reconfigures 'what is to be done, to be seen and to be named in it': it institutes a dispute over the distribution of the sensible (ibid.). Politics forms a shared aesthesis, it makes the unseen visible and turns noise into speech (ibid.: 38). Thus, even in the event that the police arrives to protect rights of protesters to protest, they reduce the space to one where everyone has a set role and position (Rancière 2014) managing who has a part and who does not.

Yet, Rancière remains rather silent on the *visual conditions of possibility* that are conducive to political spaces that enable or disable dissensus, and thus on the *modalities* conditioning the modes of being and action on the part of the police forces and the public. To elaborate this issue, we are investigating the modalities through which operations of security and order are made visible. We argue that the police uniform and its colouration is part of a regime of visibility and is thus a window into the contemporary social meaning of policing. It is important to note however that this possible interpellation of a political space via the public visibility of the police is something that is much more fluid than a simple imposition of an order over subjects, as this would make the latter a simple passive receiver of the splendour of the state. Indeed, Quentin Deluermoz (2008a: 423) notes that in late nineteenth-century Paris, 'the order [the police officers] put in place [was] an order in tension, shared and negotiated' with the people they interacted with in their quotidian routines and interventions, a point that can be extended across historical periods and circumstances.

Thus, to reflect on the norms behind police routines and interventions, this chapter concentrates on a chromatological analysis, and more particularly a visual social semiotics (see Andersen *et al.* 2015), of police uniforms. We use such an approach in order to establish the manners by which colour-use in police contexts is connected to modes of being and action that relate to the definition of political spaces. Building on our previous analysis of colour-use in military uniforms (Guillaume *et al.* 2016), we address the following questions: (1) How does colour-use on police uniforms interpellate police-citizen encounters? and (2) How do changes in such colouring reflect debates in what security means in the context of policing?

As we have demonstrated elsewhere (Andersen *et al.* 2015, 2016; Guillaume *et al.* 2016), the analysis of colour-use in relation to people, or chromatology, has largely been absent from analyses of the international and of security, with the central exception of its use as a stand-in concept for race (see from an international relations perspective, Anievas *et al.* 2014). Colour-use has firmly been relegated on the side of the 'invisible' (Gage 1990: 518), and of 'noise' (Rancière 2009: 24–25). Of course, we do not argue that we can once and for all determine the meaning of a particular colour, as colours are continuously used and reconfigured in political communication and meaning-making in conventional ways. Yet, these conventions and social expectations, and their violation, can be studied, and aid us in understanding how colour-use is power and politics. We will do so by first explaining what a chromatology of policing is. We then situate it in light of the emergence of police uniforms, and the colour-uses linked to them and the specific norms they interpellate. Finally, we will provide an analysis of the 2014 events in Ferguson as a way to illustrate how what has been considered a violation of the orthodox visual modality of policing actually participates in one of the larger transformations in the social meaning of policing.[5] This transformation has been identified by for example Peter Kraska's (1996; Kraska and Kappeler 1997) and Tony Jefferson's (1987; 1993) scholarship on the militarization of the police in the United States and the United Kingdom. This transformation concerns a shift from legitimate to violent ordering that goes beyond the specific patterns of racial prejudice that are apparent in the empirical case we discuss. What our chapter concentrates on is the specific interpellations at work when police uniforms, as a particular semiotic vehicle, are not of the expected colour that fits in the usual, expected legitimate ordering.

A chromatology of policing

Colours are largely omitted as a subject of research in international studies, and more generally in the social sciences (see Andersen *et al.* 2015 for further elaboration of this argument with regard to security studies). IR and security studies do not think about the social and political world around us in terms of how, why, and by whom it has been coloured. The social and political world we study is not even black and white; it is simply a-chromatic. Even when colour has made its way into scholarship on international relations, its social meaning and references have not generally been noted. A partial exception is Elspeth Van Veeren's work on orange jumpsuits. In a compelling article from 2011, she analyses the 'orange series' of photographs from Guantánamo to 'remind us, as IR scholars, to look at the diverse set of practices (beyond simply spoken language) to understand the complexity of international politics' (2011: 1721). While in this work the colour itself is not considered as a signifying practice, but rather 'orange' plays the role of a subject of the signifying photographic practice, her later work attributes more agency to the orange suit, noting how the colouring makes a 'connection between orange and guilt [that] is recognized by the U.S. justice system' (Van Veeren 2016: 126). This gradual move is symptomatic of how colour has been popping up, yet has only recently begun to be considered meaningful when studying the international.

Colours are a social fact as any other; they are a fact of society. Colours, and more specifically colour-use, should thus be an important analytical locus to visually analyse political phenomena, as colours are used as markers of specific qualities or representations of who or what is vested with them. They are also markers of expected modes of being and action connected to those who adorn them. One can think of, for instance, gender (e.g. pink, see Koller 2008), or race (e.g. black in the early modern period, see Deroux 2010) – categories that often intersect practically – in terms of colour-use, whereby the evolution of such meanings can also tell us longitudinal and transversal societal stories about their social and political connotations and use. The aim of this chapter, and more largely of chromatology, is not to produce interpretations about what colours on police uniforms mean per se, but rather to understand how colour-use enables the norms pertaining to institutions, individuals, groups, practices, and so on to be 'intelligible to those who view' (see Bal and Bryson 1991: 184). The police uniform performs such norms both for those who are vested with them and for those who encounter them.

Visuality 'plays a vital role in both the conduct and rationalization' (Gregory 2010: 266) of security practices, including policing. This visuality is linked but not limited to the historical moment when police officers stood out visually, most notably by wearing specifically recognizable uniforms, when the police transformed itself into a 'state civilian force' (Emsley 1999; see below on the historical processes at work in nineteenth-century Europe). The police was transformed into a force that was designed to be in a regular interaction with the inhabitants of cities like London or Paris (Deluermoz 2008b: 81–82). A central development of nineteenth-century police was the introduction of 'beat police'. This meant, according to Deluermoz (2008b: 81), that uniformed police officers implemented 'a new conception of space' that moved 'the centre of gravity that was the police station to the street and from the occupation of a single point to an insertion in urban life'. In this new conception of space, symbolically speaking, the police officer is one of the principal actors of an urban 'social imaginary' (Taylor 2004), which is transcribed in depictions found in newspapers or popular novels (Deluermoz 2008b: 82). In the Parisian case, for instance, it is striking that in the late nineteenth century, this symbolic dimension lead to more comments about the balanced behaviour of police officers rather than their efficiency in fighting crime (Deluermoz 2008b: 82–83). This should not, however, make us think that the image of the police was positive. Quite the contrary (Deluermoz 2008b: 84).

This symbolic dimension can also be found in Annette Pedersen's analysis of the 'iconography of the law in relation to policing' (Pedersen 2001: 29) that she finds in William Strutt's paintings and sketches of nineteenth-century colonial police forces in Australia. Pedersen highlights how these iconographic representations participated in 'the importance of civil policing as a means employed by the state in its search for ideological hegemony – to generate consent for the established order' (Pedersen 2001: 32). This took place in a context where the primary force of policing was 'state military' forces, in the context of Australian colonial enterprise, rather than 'state civil' forces, as in England for instance. The artistic renderings of such police forces are particularly interesting for our argument because they display how the concept of splendour in the nineteenth century still resonated with 'the visible beauty of order and the glow of a force which manifests itself and radiates' (Foucault 2004: 321, see Pedersen 2001: 33, 36, esp. 39–41), that is, the police. This is striking, as, at the same time, the connotation of the idea of the police, and of policing, had evolved immensely from the seventeenth to the nineteenth century (see below). This argument is also echoed in how the 'state military' forces, such as the gendarmes in France, evolved into a uniformed policing force as early as the 1820s. This transformation was linked to the idea of the splendour of the state, and how visuality enacts norms and behaviours (Luc 2008: 396–397).

In effect, the compulsory wearing of the uniform was seen as a visual indicator that police officers and gendarmes were acting in their official capacity. At the same time, it was also seen as a way to distinguish, for instance, the gendarmes from other 'discredited' state agents, and to 'contribute to [the state's] prestige in the eyes of civilians and other military' (Luc 2008: 396). Uniformed military or civil state forces enable conspicuous signalling to the public, and they represent the spatial deployment of the state in 'rural and urban communities' (ibid.). They thus take part in the political deployment of how the French state attempted from the mid-1820s onwards to implement a 'logic of "transparency or at least greater visibility"' that is characteristic of a democratizing state (Pierre Rosanvallon, quoted in Luc 2008: 396). This 'greater visibility' also possesses, in light of this political deployment, a normalizing effect on rural and urban populations. This was accomplished by making the state presence felt on an almost everyday basis through the sheer visual presence of (ideally) disciplined and uniformed police officers in the cities and gendarmes in rural areas. Such a presence enacted the 'exemplary staging [*mise en scène*] of public power' (Luc 2008: 397). In cases where police officers or gendarmes used undercover practices, putting into question the exemplarity sought with this 'greater visibility' and 'transparency', the population reacted quite negatively to them (Lignereux 2008).

The conspicuousness of uniforms makes colour-use an important visual modality, whereby the use of colour in security practice is not innocent. Colour-use is implicated in practices that 'not only detect objects and people but also produce' (Harris 2006: 102) them with certain statuses. This also applies to social situations. Colour-use shapes and participates in social imaginaries about policing, both for those who are policing (see Fassin 2011) and those who are policed (see Nickels 2008; Singer and Singer 2001). In regard to police uniforms, we can enter such imaginaries through three steps of investigation that become more general with every step (see Figure 9.1).

First, colours can be a particular visual modality in human communication (Kress 2011). Second, colour-use can be a part of systems of signification that participate in meaning-making in certain fields (Barthes 1973). Finally, colour-use in systems of signification is part of systems of the sensible (Rancière 2011) that modulate what is considered sensible rather than noise, what can be seen, and so on. Here, we pay attention to policing as a system of the sensible, where the state produces a relationship with citizens and non-citizens alike. A police uniform, or a police vehicle, can be a part of such a system by participating in meaning-making in policing.

Societal understandings about norms, for instance, depend on a certain degree of commonality, which is attained as what Rancière (2011) calls systems of the sensible. Such systems are a part of aesthetic regimes that modulate what is seen and said, and also what is done, and what can be done. In other words, systems of the sensible are productive of normative and meaning(-making) systems. Such regimes work to form a common sense, inclusive of the visual, and of colour in it. Common sense here means 'a community of sensible data': shared visibility,

Making norms visible 157

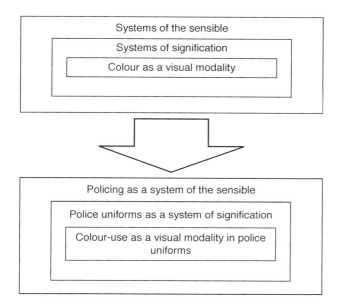

Figure 9.1 From colour-use in police uniforms to policing as a system of the sensible.

modes of perception, and conferred meanings. Concomitantly, it binds individuals or groups together into 'a spatiotemporal system in which words and visible forms are assembled' (Rancière 2011: 99) through different modalities. Here, we see how such 'common senses' construct different realities, and thereby also different *dispositifs* of visibility, which in turn affect and effect how the 'common sense' of certain modes of being and doing behind policing change alongside the 'common sense' of the police uniform. In other words, what the police uniform looks like has an effect on how policing is seen and what it means. While the presence of the uniform as such is to produce a police space in Rancière's (2014) sense, variety in the uniform can also produce variety in the kinds of subjectivities a police space expects.

There are of course multiple analytical positions from which to look at the 'common sense' linked to colour-use in police uniforms. For example, colours can be viewed from the perspective of the police men and women who wear them, from the institutions that commission and deploy them, the citizens and non-citizens that see them, and so on. In this chapter, we are interested in the intersubjective relations between groups that practically constitute the contours of the public space. What is engaged here, following Rancière, are the assumed ideals of what this public space is like, the social imaginaries that are linked to this space as a space of circulation, and how colour-use in police uniforms partakes in the establishment, maintenance and, possibly, transgression of these contours.

Uniforms and the police

Uniforms designate state and non-state, organized and unorganized groups both formally and symbolically (see Craik 2005). More importantly, for the argument here, 'uniforms – and the enforcement of rules about them – are imprinted on our techniques of selfhood through techniques of the body (sociological, psychological, and biological)' (Craik 2003: 128).[6] A police uniform is (or should be) a marker, both for its wearer and for anyone else, of abidance to sets of codes, rules, norms, and laws about society, as well as of modes of action and being that are enacted on behalf of these set of codes, rules, norms, and laws. Indeed, police officers have several 'archetypal' roles: a technician, diplomat, entrepreneur, public-relations expert, legal expert, spy, field operator, and enforcer, which all have intrinsic norms, routines, and value systems (Bowling and Sheptycki 2012: 82). As a marker, however, a police uniform is constituted of different modalities – shape, colour, adornments, insignias, and so on – which, as a whole, make the wearer of the uniform embody, both for her/himself and to the eyes of others, specific modes of being and action, thus interpellating a specific political space. Before exploring this interpellation in connection with colour-use, it is crucial to resituate historically what it socially and politically meant to see police uniforms in the streets and roads of Western Europe.

The first uniformed police units were created around the same time in both London and Paris in 1829. In Paris, there were only a limited number of agents, but London was developing the whole Metropolitan Police of London (Deluermoz 2008b: 77; Luc 2008: 396; see Emsley 1996; Reynolds 1998 on the English case, and Berlière 2011; Deluermoz 2008b on the French case).[7] The new police force, first in England and later elsewhere (though historiography often disputes this single origin narrative), was designed to be primarily dedicated to the prevention of crime not only in light of nineteenth-century urban growth and industrialization, but also to the 'the transformation of the organisation of political power, the extent of violent popular resistance to government, the erosion of the old social bases of community authority, and the creation of new law and order tasks' (Emsley 1999: 30–31). The Metropolitan Police of London was thus developed as a professional force, compared to the parish constables and night watchmen of the time, that was to be very strongly disciplined within a 'much more rigid and hierarchical structure' and efficient operational behaviour than before (Emsley 1996: 26).

It was also largely born out of a perceived necessity to distinguish this new policing force from the regular military, and from any views that this force was being engaged in a 'system of espionage', associated in England at the time with the French police system (Emsley 1996: 24–25). Importantly for our argument, a crucial element for distinguishing the police from the above municipal and military state forces was that this force had to be articulated as a system of signification that was different from the latter. Focusing on the civil/military distinction, Clive Emsley (1996: 26) shows how

[r]ecognising the English antipathy to a standing army quartered at home, efforts were made to ensure that the new police did not look like soldiers: they were given top hats, uniforms of blue, swallow-tail coats with the minimum of decoration, in contrast to the short scarlet tunics with coloured facings and piping of the British infantry; the constable's weaponry was limited to a wooden truncheon, though cutlasses were available for emergencies and for patrolling dangerous beats, and inspectors and above could carry pocket pistols.

As the Whig history of the English/British police of the nineteenth century puts it, the English model police man was characterized as being 'civilian, restrained, free of corruption, [thus] superior to a generalized European model, military, arbitrary, political, secretive' (Emsley 1999: 30), a European model best exemplified in the English imagination by 'military state' forces such as the French gendarmes (Luc 2008).

Moreover, from the perspective of the police officers, uniforms also perform the symbolic function of 'promoting obedience, comradeship, and a display of strength' (Pfanner 2004: 123; see also Foucault 1975: 190–199), and produce self-identity as well as specific modes of being and action among the police forces (see, for instance, Fassin 2011: 91–93, 139–141, 173–174). In this way, uniforms perform both the formal *and* symbolic function of identification and distinction – inside and outside the ranks alike. Uniforms adorn colours and they can be coloured one way or another. Police uniforms are also full of specific signs – epaulettes, numbered collars (to identify, for instance, and possibly file a complaint against a police officer), ranks, and so on – that are markers both within and outside the specific institution of the police and make the deployment of the state visible (Luc 2008: 396–397). But when you encounter the police in the street, what you see first is largely the colour and type of uniform.

The colours of, or on a police uniform however do not stand by themselves; they are not just visible because of their inherent salience, they are visible because they convey meanings. 'One does not simply wear blue, white, or khaki; instead one's dress indicates membership in a police force, medical group, or military service' (Joseph and Alex 1972: 720). So, it is impossible to decouple the visual saliency of a specific semiotic vehicle linked to an institution, such as the police, from what this institution represents, does, and interpellates politically. This means that we need to reflect on the link between visibility and colour-use in order to understand what the types of police spaces police interventions, patrols, and the ensuing encounters are.

Of major importance here is that semiotic sign-vehicles, such as uniforms, are coloured markers associated with certain formal expectations, norm-fulfilments, and values. The bearers of such signs are considered to be liable for the norms they represent, but also, and importantly, for certain expectations linked with the police spaces constituted by the presence of such semiotic vehicles. If the bearer of a police uniform does not abide by the set of norms attached to them, s/he is viewed as usurping the uniform, whether because s/he is an impersonating imposter for some other purposes, or because s/he is 'betraying the uniform' by not abiding to the attached set of rules (see Joseph and Alex 1972: 723, 726). This was one of the logics behind the introduction of the uniform for the French gendarmes in the nineteenth century, as an 1854 decree made clear by stating that the military uniform of the gendarme has to compel him to act 'openly and without any manoeuvres which would discredit' the corps (quoted in Luc 2008: 396).

An illustration is provided by Joseph and Alex (1972: 725): the presence of a uniformed police officer with a non-uniformed detective in the early hours of the morning during a door-to-door search for a missing child was not necessary from a procedural perspective. Yet, the uniformed policeman was seen as a form of assurance that the non-uniformed individual is linked to the police. 'The reluctance to admit a stranger to one's apartment in the early morning hours was obviated by the sight of a uniform; the uniformed patrolman was wearing credentials for both'. Of course, these credentials would depend on many other contextual elements, such as race, gender, trust, or whether, for instance, the door-to-door search happened in a predominantly African-American neighbourhood in South Side Chicago, and was done by white officers.

As colours by themselves are characterized by their potential ambiguity (Kress and van Leeuwen 2002), uniforms are usually elaborated combinations of colour, design, and insignia codified to form unambiguous systems of signification and 'sets of norms'. A specific modality of the uniform might change, but the system of signification remains unambiguous. This was the case in the 2014 Sochi Olympic's security apparatus, when police and security forces visible inside or around the Olympic park were provided with purple-coloured uniforms 'to make the operation seem warm and fuzzy, a rarity in a place where police often come across as intimidating' (Sonne and Troianovski 2014); yet, at the same time, there was no ambiguity behind the deployment of such forces. Alternatively, if the uniform becomes ambiguous or does not convey this unambiguous system of signification, then one wearing such uniform would not necessarily feel compelled to abide, and would not necessarily be expected to abide, to the attached set of rules.

For instance, from 2014 to 2015, but replicating a practice dating back at least to 2008, the unionized police officers of the province of Québec in Canada have worn camouflaged battlefield pants, their colouration ranging from more military-like green or sand to bright pink or orange camouflages. This practice has been a political one, as they have done this in order to protest changes in their pension plans despite not having the right to go on strike; the police have not had the right to protest, but have done this none the less by subverting their uniforms. Political officials have called on the officers to take back their normal uniforms, as this display of camouflaged battlefield pants indicated a disrespect for their function, and the risk of losing credibility in the public's eyes (see Hamilton 2014; Peritz 2015). 'As far back as 2008, Montreal's police chief said officers in camo pants presented an image of "confrontation" and "repression" that could frighten immigrants who had survived military dictatorships' (Peritz 2015).

Making norms visible 161

Importantly, however, beyond the specific case connected to a social mobilization by the police forces of Québec, the ambiguity of the police uniform may also affect one's selfhood, as there is an identification between what the uniform may represent and how one's modes of being and action are correlated with it. Didier Fassin (2011: 97–100), for instance in his ethnographic account[8] of police work in some suburbs in Paris, details how the policemen from the *Brigade Anti-Criminalité* (lit. anti-crime squad), wearing the 'civilian uniforms', identified themselves with TV series or movies that portrayed policemen who

> benefited from a large autonomy from their hierarchy to conduct intervention, with almost no accountability for their acts, ... as with these [fictional characters], they can enfranchise themselves, to an extent, from legality to impose their law, with this idea that their legitimate objective justified their prospective irregular means.

This transgressive dimension of the absence of uniforms on the behaviour of police forces is even attested to in historical sources. Aurélien Lignereux (2008: 407–409), for instance, describes how not only the practice of disguise by gendarmes was badly perceived by the population in the nineteenth century, but how it was correlated with irregular conduct by the gendarmes themselves. Paying attention to the transgressions in the visual interpellation of a social order and the actual or expected modes of being and action of the police forces is precisely what we now want to turn to in the case of the 2014 events in Ferguson, Missouri. We do this to highlight how paying attention to colour-use is an important analytical window about the effects and modalities of the expansion of the militarization of the police.

Tactical transgression: police splendour in Ferguson, Missouri

In their conclusion to an edited volume concerned with the question of what it meant to be a police officer in Europe between the eighteenth and the twentieth centuries, Dominique Kalifa and Vincent Milliot (2008: 553) note how transgression is a potential starting point for analysing modes of being and action of the police. In effect, transgression is an analytical way to comprehend either the 'police/population relations, [or] the modalities of the legitimation of the police action'. Kalifa and Milliot highlight two transgressions that are usually linked to the legal (e.g. situations of exception) or infra-legal (e.g. actions taken by police officers outside the boundaries of legality) spheres. We add to these symbolic transgressions linked to the visual modality of security representations and signs, which are used to make security norms visible.

When local police first responded to protests over the police shooting of Michael Brown in Ferguson in August 2014, they did so with an unusual display of vehicles, uniforms, and weapons. While the colour of the police uniforms and vehicles was hardly the only thing that differed from a more orthodox police response, the turn towards military tactical and even camouflaged uniforms, and completely black armoured vehicles[9] is a turn that interpellates an anticipation of violence and repression behind what remains a democratic right of demonstration. What happened in Ferguson, with such deployment of local police forces (before the appearance of traditionally clad state troopers), participates in the process of paramilitarization of civil state forces in the United States already identified in the literature (see Kraska 1996; Kraska and Kappeler 1997). Paramilitarization, following Tony Jefferson's (1987, 1993) and Peter Kraska's work, refers here to the borrowing by the police, whether through a social imaginary and/or actual circulation of knowledge, of 'characteristics of the military, notably the hierarchical structure (chain of command), technologies and mentality' (Lemieux and Dupont 2005: 1–2).

Rather than a mentality, we view this kind of borrowing as the adoption of a social imaginary – modes of being and action – that connects to a specific regime of visibility. This social imaginary is apparent in changes in weaponry, training, language, tactics, and uniforms (see Kraska 1996), and effectively modifies the modes of being and action usually identified with the development of civil state forces by making them akin – in their own imaginary[10] and in the visual encounter – to military state forces. In the United States (Kraska and Kappeler 1997), and in France (Jobard 2008: 103), there is a multiplication of police paramilitary units (PPUs; popularly known in the United States as SWAT – Special Weapons And Tactics – teams). In the United Kingdom too, some researchers have identified a militarization of the policing of (potentially violent) demonstrations during the 1980s struggles against the Thatcher government policies (Jefferson 1987, 1993).

While there is, 'historically, politically and sociologically', a clear connection between the military and the police, it is only in recent decades that an increase in PPUs has been witnessed. These units not only possess militaristic equipment and technologies, they also adopt the organizational structure of the military (Kraska and Kappeler 1997: 2–4). In his ethnographic account of a 'training session' with such PPU, Kraska (1996) also highlights the highly masculinist and 'militaristic' social imaginary at work in these units. PPUs interventions have increased in the United States from about 3,000 a year in 1980 to about 50,000 in the last few years. 'By 2007 more than 80% of police departments in cities with between 25,000 and 50,000 people had them, up from 20% in the mid-1980s' (*The Economist* 2014). This is a clear indication of police militarization. However, even though the traditional scope of PPUs in situations such as terrorist attacks, hostage taking, a 'lone sniper', and so on, has been expanded, what happened in Ferguson is different. What transpired was not a SWAT team responding to the demonstrations, but local police forces with access to military equipment that adopted militarized tactics towards the demonstrators. A government programme for police forces to buy second-hand military equipment facilitated this appearance, yet it remains an active choice of the police to deploy such equipment in the situation in question.

In light of Rancière's aesthetics of politics, this visual display – black or camouflaged tactical battlefield uniforms poignantly among them – highlights

Making norms visible 163

the importance of the way in which both the local authorities and the citizen is enacted in the meeting between police and citizen. As argued by Radley Balko, a Washington Post journalist specialized in police equipment, equipping police with gear and vehicles that interpellates a situation of war rather than peace means that police officers are 'going to start seeing themselves as soldiers, and seeing the people they serve less as citizens with rights and more as potential threats, and that's what we're seeing' (Curry and Martinez 2014). The turn away from standard police equipment does not only possibly impact police officers' understanding of the situation, but does the same for the citizen.

Commenting on the Ferguson display of police force, an ACLU spokesman argued that equipping police forces to look like a military contingent 'tends to escalate the risk of violence, makes people less safe, and undermines the public's trust in law enforcement' (Curry and Martinez 2014). The point here is that it matters how the police looks, and that it matters that the police looks different from the military, as it has been a defining trait of the functional *and* political differentiation between civil and municipal or military state forces (see, for instance, Singer and Singer 2001 on civilian vs. uniform police clothing).

As discussed above, the trend in police uniform colouring is that they use colours linked to the wearing of the uniform that (problematic as that may be) historically evoke authority, cleanliness, and civility[11] (see, for instance, Freyssinet-Dominjon 2003: 78). The appearance in Ferguson of traditionally clad police forces, Missouri state highway patrol forces taking over the management of the operations from the St. Louis county local forces, and the demilitarization of their presence on the ground led to an effective de-escalation of the situation (Swaine 2014).

The visibility of the uniform, and thus the different regime of visibility it may pertain to depending on its design and colouring, is even a specific strategy of public recognition in different policing spaces (see, for instance, Paperman 2003). A turn away from 'traditional' designs and colour-schemes towards those used in military or militarized operations – tactical battlefield pants and camouflage colouring – changes the expectations of the encounter. It communicates a change in expectations for the encounter, and interpellates a modification of the police spaces performed through such encounters and interventions (a situation that has been noted by the different actors commenting on or present during the events in Ferguson; see, for instance, Levs 2014; Swaine 2014).

As recently reported by *The New Yorker* (Konnikova 2014), psychological studies on the link between perception of trust, safety, competence, and the colours of uniforms worn by police officers clearly showed that an overwhelming majority of respondents preferred darker colours – identified with traditional police uniforms – over the lighter ones – identified with military ones (see, for instance, Nickels 2008). The same preference is found among those wearing the uniforms. To wear a certain gear – military or civilian – induces different behaviours and self-perceptions. As Nicolas Camerati (2006: 79) notes in his ethnography of beat police practicing in a Parisian neighbourhood:

As soon as the police is in a public space, it is as an image of order and control presented itself. The police officer, with his uniform, expresses the idea that he carries with him social characteristics and demands and, as a consequence, that he carries in him an expectation, that others recognise, valorize [*sic*], and act upon appropriately. This image implies, explicitly or implicitly, that police officers have to be treated in specific and appropriate manners corresponding to their function (…). As people have to behave in a certain way toward them, police officers have duties, that is to say that they have to behave in a manner *that conforms to their image*.

The strong connection between uniform colour and normative expectations explains the negative reactions to the form of protest used by 'striking' police officers in Québec as wearing colourful or militarized camouflage battlefield pants interpellate a different police space than a traditional uniform would.

This image, or rather the modality that is expressed with colour-use and design in a uniform, that we associate with the splendour of the state, is a performative force as the arrival, presence, and departure of police forces carries with it 'a series of symbolic information' to the actors present in the public space; to the point that one can say that 'a police arrival communicates by itself' as it 'provides the necessary signal and time for this space to adjust itself to this new situation' by ordering the different actors to take their appropriate places in that space according to that encounter (Camerati 2006: 80). Indeed, for Rancière (2014), a police space is one where everyone has a set role and position: it is clear who matters, and who is allowed to speak; the consensus that police interventions assume reduces political subjects into populations, and transforms politics into activities of professionals and experts (Corcoran 2014: 5). In this way, what the police officer adorns interpellates a specific encounter, which for Rancière is actually the effacement of the possibility for dissensus as the encounter invites us not to see.

Yet, in a more nuanced fashion than Rancière, we argue that the interpellations at the source of the shape of the police space vary depending on – in our case – the ways in which the public, citizens and non-citizens alike, are invited *to see* something specific. Police spaces vary too. Dark, militarized local police forces as seen in Ferguson performed a different kind of encounter than the 'kinder blue' of liaison teams designed to 'enhance the quality of police protester communication and interaction' in the UK (Waddington 2013: 46), or than the state troopers in Ferguson that came in days later. While both kinds of uniforms turn a site of demonstration into a police intervention and a demonstration of state authority, their effects differed. Adorning different colours interpellates different social orders and makes different norms visible.

As the tragic example of Ferguson illustrates, when police forces project an image of themselves that does not conform with the expectations of their regime of visibility, that does not conform to the modalities usually associated with the splendour of the state as the legitimate wielder of force, then another set of subjectivities is interpellated. The conjunction of different modalities in the design, the use of military tactical uniforms rather than traditional uniforms, and the colours of such uniforms, as well as the use of camouflage patterns, have clear effects on the police space that is produced by such modalities.

The symbolic transformation of the social imaginary of the police: from legitimate policing to violent ordering

Police operations 'establish the visibility of objects and make them available for thought' (Corcoran 2014: 22). By paying attention to this, we have put forward the importance of a chromatology of policing in highlighting the colour-use in police uniforms in certain encounters between civil state forces and the public. While avoiding a singling out of this dimension as a causal factor in a shift from a more legitimized form of policing to a more violent ordering in the constitution of specific police spaces, the chapter furthers our understanding of what authors have identified as the paramilitarization of civil state forces (see Jefferson 1987, 1993; Kraska 1996; Kraska and Kappeler 1997). Our chapter identifies another sphere of transgression of the norms expected in policing beyond those identified by Kalifa and Milliot: the legal (e.g. situations of exception) or infra-legal (e.g. actions taken by police officers outside the boundaries of legality) spheres. Using the case of Ferguson, Missouri, we have shown how the symbolic transgressions linked to the visual modality of security representations and signs, is another way by which security norms are made visible and interpellate specific political spaces. As should be clear, and although we have concentrated on an example taken from the United States, this more militarized and war-like transformation of the civil state forces is not necessarily limited to the case of the United States.

Though it is important to avoid generalizing in regard to a topic such as policing, which is multifarious (Moreau de Bellaing 2012) not only internationally but domestically, it is worth noting that in other countries, such as France, researchers have noted a 'relational rupture' between specific segments of the population and civil state forces, where the latter have developed, over the past fifteen years in the French case, a largely repressive mode of action and being when in uniformed service that led one researcher to speak of the predominance of a 'police of war' over 'a police of peace' (Boucher 2014). This is important, as when we speak of (para)militarization, we do not limit ourselves to the material and technological transfer from one to the other, and to the possible correlation between equipment availability, lack of proper training, and so on that might result in a more violent ordering of social life than was previously the case. Nor do we limit ourselves to the circulations of knowledge that may occur from a transfer of competences and skills either from former military personals moving to an employment in civil state forces after leaving the military or from specific public or private trainings (Partlow 2009; Vick 2009; Ingersoll 2013; Winston 2014).

We have highlighted the importance and relevance to consider what is the place of specific visual semiotic vehicles of the civil state forces, such as police uniforms or vehicles, in order to understand how the state and its representatives – bearing in mind that police forces often are rather autonomous from the state – are producing specific police spaces in differentiated sites (a town in Missouri, the streets of Paris' suburbs, the alleys of an Olympic event, and so on). Interpellations, however, are not solely performative to the extent that a regime of visibility is produced and projected upon individuals and groups; it is performative to the extent that, and how, it is reacted to. Further investigations in the splendour of the state and the police spaces it interpellates should thus also foray into the type of interactions that are produced by such interpellations.

Notes

1 We would like to thank Cyril Magnon-pujo for some reading suggestions. All translations and quirks are ours.
2 We take here the notion of interpellation in Louis Althusser's sense of the process by which individuals are constituted as subjects via 'a quotidian practice, submitted to a precise ritual' (Althusser 1995: 226 note 116), and through such a process are subjected to an ideology. Butler (1997) makes the point that interpellation 'cites', rather than 'does' the work of hailing the subject as subject, introducing an element of uncertainty to the act and easing the ideas of causality sometimes read into interpellation.
3 For a critical, and salutary, discussion on Foucault's relevance for an analytics of the police, see Denis (2013).
4 For Rancière, 'the void is an-archy, the absence of any legitimacy of power and itself constitutive of the very nature of political space' (Rancière, 2014: 34).
5 Another transformation in police attire has been the expanded use of neon and dayglow reflective gear. This expansion coincides with the increased use of such apparel in civilian contexts too. While previously neon was worn by professionals in high risk situations (such as dock workers or firemen), it has become a commonplace for cyclists and kindergarten children. In this way, the use of neon subtracts from the authority of the police as they do not stand out among the neon citizens and appear like any other out on the streets who embodies risk society through their apparel.
6 Uniforms can also be transgressive and subversive when they are 'appropriated in a range of transgressive subversive contexts – such as in pornography, prostitution, sadomasochism, transvestism, cross-dressing, vaudeville, mardi gras, gay cultures, subcultures, choirs, and stripograms' (see Craik 2003: 129, 2005).
7 The Metropolitan Police of London has been an important source of discussion, inspiration and influence, not always successful (see, for instance, Johansen 2012), throughout Europe, and within England itself (Emsley 1996, chapters 2 and 3), in the transformation of policing, without necessarily leading to greater connections between European police institutions that came to develop fairly similar functions (see Lawrence 2012) though there was a clear circulation of knowledge between countries and regions over policing matters in the nineteenth century (see, for instance, Emsley 1999).
8 For a critical review of Fassin's at times problematic ethnographic methodology, see Moreau de Bellaing (2012).
9 Police vehicles are rarely if ever pitch black as high visibility is the preferred mode for police vehicles, see Thomas and Williams 2012; for a more comprehensive discussion about police vehicles, see Vuori *et al.*, manuscript.
10 US army veterans interviewed by several news medias during the events criticized the Ferguson police forces not only for the mismatched tactics used in a policing

operation but also for playing at being soldiers rather than having a soldiery attitude, with one commenting that 'The general consensus here: if this is militarization, it's the s***iest, least-trained, least professional military in the world, using weapons far beyond what they need, or what the military would use when doing crowd control' (Levs 2014).

11 While the expanded use of neon on police uniforms reduces the authority of the uniform (it is like any other working outfit), it does make it appear more civil and clean.

References

Althusser, L. (1995). *Sur la Reproduction*. Paris: Presses Universitaires de France.
Andersen, R. S., Vuori, J. A., and Mutlu, C. E. (2015). Visuality. In: C. Aradau, J. Huysmans, A. Neal, and N. Voelkner, eds., *Critical Security Methods: New Frameworks for Analysis*. London and New York, Routledge, pp. 85–117.
Andersen, R. S., Guillaume, X., and Vuori, J. A. (2016). Flags. In: M. B. Salter, ed., *Making Things International 2: Catalysts and Reactions*. Minneapolis, Minnesota University Press, pp. 137–152.
Anievas, A., Manchanda, N., and Shilliam, R. eds. (2014). *Race and Racism in International Relations. Confronting the Global Colour Line*. London: Routledge.
Bal, M. and Bryson, N. (1991). Semiotics and Art History. *Art Bulletin*, 73(2), pp. 174–208.
Barthes, R. (1973[1964]). *Elements of Semiology*. Trans. Lavers, A. and Smith, C. New York: Hill and Wang.
Berlière, J-M. (2011). *Naissance de la police moderne*. Nouvelle édition. Paris: Perrin.
Boucher, M. (2014). Police de rue, habitants des quartiers populaires et usage de la force. Analyse d'un processus de défiance réciproque. *Pensée plurielle*, 36, pp. 77–109.
Bowling, B. and Sheptycki, J. (2012). *Global Policing*. London: SAGE Publications.
Butler, J. (1997). *Excitable Speech: A Politics of the Performative*. London: Routledge.
Camerati, N. (2006). La «performance» de la police dans l'espace public. *Sociétés*, 94 (4), pp. 77–90.
Corcoran, S. (2014 [2010]). Editor's Introduction. In: Jacques Rancière, *Dissensus: On Politics and Aesthetics*. London, Bloomsbury, pp. 1–24.
Craik, J. (2003). The Cultural Politics of the Uniform. *Fashion Theory*, 7(2), pp. 127–148.
Craik, J. (2005). *Uniforms Exposed: From Conformity to Transgression*. New York: Berg.
Curry, C. and Martinez, L. (2014). Ferguson Police's Show of Force Highlights Militarization of America's Cops. *ABC News*. 14 August 2014. URL: http://abcnews.go.com/US/ferguson-police-small-army-thousands-police-departments/story?id=24977299 [Accessed 8 February 2015].
Deluermoz, Q. (2008a). Être sergent de ville à Paris entre 1854 et 1880: le bricolage d'une identité. In: J.-M. Berlière, C. Denys, D. Kalifa, and V. Milliot, eds., *Métiers de police. Être policier en Europe, XVIIIe–XXe sicèle*. Rennes: Presses Universitaires de Rennes, pp. 415–426.
Deluermoz, Q. (2008b). Circulations et élaborations d'un mode d'action policier: la police en tenue à Paris, d'une police 'londonienne' au 'modèle parisien' (1850–1914). *Revue d'Histoire des Sciences Humaines*, 19(2), pp. 75–90.
Denis, V. (2013). L'histoire de la police après Foucault. Un parcours historien. *Revue d'histoire moderne et contemporaine*, 60(4), pp. 139–155.

Deroux, M. (2010). The Blackness Within: Early Modern Color-concept, Physiology and Aaron the Moor in Shakespeare's *Titus Andronicus*. *Mediterranean Studies*, 19(1), pp. 86–101.

Emsley, C. (1996). *The English Police: A Political and Social History*, 2nd edn. London: Routledge.

Emsley, C. (1999). A Typology of Nineteenth-century Police. *Crime, Histoire & Sociétés/ Crime, History & Societies*, 3(1), pp. 29–44.

Fassin, D. (2011). *La force de l'ordre. Une anthropologie de la police des quartiers.* Paris: Seuil.

Favre, P. (2009). Quand la police fabrique l'ordre social. Un *en deçà* des politiques publiques de la police? *Revue française de science politique*, 59(6), pp. 1231–1219.

Foucault, M. (1975). *Surveiller et punir*. Paris: Gallimard.

Foucault, M. (2004). *Sécurité, territoire, population. Cours au Collège de France (1977–1978)*. Paris: Hautes Etudes/Gallimard/Seuil.

Freyssinet-Dominjon, J. (2003). En bleu et noir? L'image visuelle du gendarme dans la communication affichée de la gendarmerie (1958–2002). *Sociétés & Représentations*, 16 (2), pp. 77–19.

Gage, J. (1990). Colour in Western Art: An Issue? *Art Bulletin* LXXII(4), pp. 518–42.

Guillaume, X., Andersen, R. S., and Vuori, J. A. (2016). Paint it Black: Colours and the Social Meaning of the Battlefield. *European Journal of International Relations*, 22(1), pp. 49–71.

Gregory, D. (2010). Seeing Red: Baghdad and the Eventful City. *Political Geography*, 29(5), pp. 266–279.

Hamilton, G. (2014). Harmless Protest or Threat to Public Safety? Quebec City Wants to Force Police Officers to Ditch Outrageous Pants. *National Post*. 14 August 2014. URL: http://news.nationalpost.com/news/canada/harmless-protest-or-threat-to-public-safety-quebec-city-wants-to-force-police-officers-to-ditch-outrageous-pants [Accessed 24 June 2016].

Harris, C. (2006). The Omniscient Eye: Satellite Imagery, 'Battlespace Awareness' and the Structures of the Imperial Gaze. *Surveillance and Society*, 4(1–2), pp. 101–122.

Ingersoll, G. (2013). Police Bring Iraq-style 'Counter Insurgency' Strategy to US City. *Business Insider*. 6 May 2013. www.businessinsider.com/police-bring-iraq-counter-insurgency-strategy-to-us-city-2013-5?IR=T [Accessed 15 May 2016].

Jefferson, T. (1987). Beyond Paramilitarism. *The British Journal of Criminology*, 27(1), pp. 47–53.

Jefferson, T. (1993). Pondering Paramilitarism: A Question of Standpoints? *The British Journal of Criminology*, 33(3), pp. 374–381.

Jobard, F. (2008). La militarisation du maintien de l'ordre, entre sociologie et histoire. *Déviance et Société*, 32, pp. 101–109.

Johansen, A. (2012). Être tout pour tous: Le Bobby anglais au cœur des débats sur les réformes policières en Allemagne, 1848–1914. In: C. Denys, ed., *Circulations policières. 1759–1914*. Villeneuve d'Ascq: Presses Universitaires du Septentrion, pp. 119–135.

Joseph, N. and Alex, N. (1972). The Uniform: A Sociological Perspective. *American Journal of Sociology*, 77(4), pp. 719–730.

Kalifa, D. and Milliot, V. 2008. Les voies de la professionnalisation. In: J.-M. Berlière, C. Denys, D. Kalifa, and V. Milliot, eds., *Métiers de police. Être policier en Europe, XVIIIe–XXe sicèle*. Rennes: Presses Universitaires de Rennes, pp. 545–553.

Koller, V. (2008). Not Just a Colour: Pink as a Gender and Sexuality Marker in Visual Communication. *Visual Communication*, 7(4), pp. 395–423.

Konnikova, M. (2014). Dressed to Suppress. *The New Yorker*. 3 December 2014. URL: www.newyorker.com/science/maria-konnikova/will-decreasing-police-use-military-gear-prevent-another-ferguson?mbid=social_twitter [Accessed 8 February 2015].
Kraska, P. B. (1996). Enjoying Militarism: Political/Personal Dilemmas in Studying U.S. Police Paramilitary Units. *Justice Quarterly*, 13(3), pp. 405–429.
Kraska, P. B. and Kappeler, V. E. (1997). Militarizing American Police: the Rise and Normalization of Paramilitary Units. *Social Problems*, 44(1), pp. 1–18.
Kress, G. (2011). What is a mode? In: C. Jewitt, ed., *The Routledge Handbook of Multimodal Analysis*. London: Routledge, pp. 40–53.
Kress, G. and van Leeuwen, T. (2002). Colour as a Semiotic Mode: Notes for a Grammar of Colour. *Visual Communication*, 1(3), pp. 343–368.
Lawrence, P. (2012). They Have an Admirable Police at Paris, but they Pay for it Dear Enough. La police européenne vue d'Angleterre au XIXe siècle. In: C. Denys, ed., *Circulations policières. 1759–1914*. Villeneuve d'Ascq: Presses Universitaires du Septentrion, pp. 103–117.
Lemieux, F. and Dupont, B. (2005). Introduction. La militarisation de la police: un réalignement des perspectives. In: F. Lemieux and B. Dupoint, eds., *La militarisation des appareils policiers*. Saint-Nicolas: Les Presses de l'Université de Laval, pp. 1–14.
Levs, J. (2014). Ferguson Violence: Critics Rip Police Tactics, Use of Military Equipment. *CNN*. 15 August 2014. URL: http://edition.cnn.com/2014/08/14/us/missouri-ferguson-police-tactics/ [Accessed 24 June 2016]
Liang, H.-H. (1992). *The Rise of Modern Police and the European State System from Metternich to the Second World War*. Cambridge: Cambridge University Press.
Lignereux, A. (2008). Être ou ne pas être gendarme. L'usage du déguisement dans la gendarmerie française au premier XIXe siècle. In: J.-M. Berlière, C. Denys, D. Kalifa, and V. Milliot, eds., *Métiers de police. Être policier en Europe, XVIIIe-XXe sicèle*. Rennes: Presses Universitaires de Rennes, pp. 403–414.
Loader, I. and Walker, N. (2001). Policing as a Public Good: Reconstituting the Connections between Policing and the State. *Theoretical Criminology*, 5(1), pp. 9–35.
Luc, J-N. (2008). Anthropologie du policier: le corps, le temps, l'espace. In: J.-M. Berlière, C. Denys, D. Kalifa, and V. Milliot, eds., *Métiers de police. Être policier en Europe, XVIIIe–XXe sicèle*. Rennes: Presses Universitaires de Rennes, pp. 393–402.
McNevin, A. (2006). Political Belonging in a Neoliberal Era: The Struggle of the Sans-papiers. *Citizenship Studies*, 10(2), pp. 135–151.
Moreau de Bellaing, C. (2012). Comment (ne pas) produire une critique sociologique de la police. *Revue française de science politique*, 62(4), pp. 665–673.
Mouhanna, C. (2011). *La police contre les citoyens?* Nîmes: Champ social éditions.
Nickels, E. (2008). Good Guys Wear Black: Uniform Color and Citizen Impressions of Police. *Policing: An International Journal of Police Strategies and Management*, 31(1), pp. 77–92.
Paperman, P. (2003). Surveillance Underground. The Uniform as an Interaction Device. *Ethnography*, 4 (3), pp. 397–419.
Partlow, J. (2009). To Rid Slums of Drug Gangs, Police in Rio de Janeiro Try War Tactics. *Washington Post*. 6 January 2009. www.washingtonpost.com/wp-dyn/content/article/2009/01/05/AR2009010502741.html [Accessed 15 May 2016].
Pastoureau, M. (2000). *Bleu. Histoire d'une couleur*. Paris: Seuil.
Pastoureau, M. (2008). *Noir. Histoire d'une couleur*. Paris: Seuil.
Pedersen, A. (2001). Governing Images of the Australian Police Trooper. In: G. Wickham and G. Pavlich, eds., *Rethinking Law, Society and Governance. Foucault's Bequest*. Oxford: Hart Publishing, pp. 27–42.

Peritz, I. (2015). Quebec Loses Patience with Fancy-pants Police Protest. *The Globe and Mail*. 11 June 2015. URL: www.theglobeandmail.com/news/national/montreal-police-pension-pants-protest-tests-premiers-patience/article24929803/ [Accessed 24 June 2016].

Pfanner, T. (2004). Military Uniforms and the Law of War. *International Review of the Red Cross*, 86(853), pp. 93–130.

Rancière, J. 2009. *Aesthetics and its Discontents*. Trans. S. Concoran. Cambridge: Polity Press.

Rancière, J. (2011[2008]). *The Emancipated Spectator*. Trans. G. Elliott. London: Verso.

Rancière, J. (2014 [2010]. *Dissensus: On Politics and Aesthetics*. Ed. and translated by Steven Corcoran. London: Bloomsbury.

Reynolds, E. (1998). *Before the Bobbies: The Night Watch and Police Reform in Metropolitan London, 1720–1830*. London: Macmillan.

Singer, M. S. and Singer, A. E. (2001). The Effect of Police Uniform on Interpersonal Perception. *The Journal of Psychology*, 119(2), pp. 157–161.

Sonne, P. and Troianovski, A. (2014). Sochi's Softened State of Security. A Ring of Steel Outside These Games Gives Way to a Softer Security Presence Inside. *The Wall Street Journal*. 9 February 2014. URL: www.wsj.com/articles/SB10001424052702303874504579373180074621124 [Accessed 24 June 2016].

Swaine, J. (2014). Ferguson: Disarming Tactics of Highway Patrol Pay Dividends as Calm Descends. *Guardian*. 15 August 2014. URL: www.theguardian.com/world/2014/aug/15/ferguson-disarming-tactics-of-highway-patrol-pay-dividends-as-calm-descends [Accessed 24 June 2016].

Taylor, C. (2004). *Modern Social Imaginaries*. Durham, NC: Duke University Press.

The Economist. (2014). Cops or Soldiers? America's Police have Become too Militarised. *The Economist*. 22 March 2014. URL: www.economist.com/news/united-states/21599349-americas-police-have-become-too-militarised-cops-or-soldiers [Accessed 25 June 2016].

Thomas, M. D. and Williams, C. C. (2012). Police Car Visibility: Detection, Categorization, and Defining Components. *The Journal of Law Enforcement* 2(3), pp. 1–29.

Van Veeren, E. (2011). Captured by the Camera's Eye: Guantánamo and the Shifting Frame of the Global War on Terror. *Review of International Studies*, 37(4), pp. 1721–1749.

Van Veeren, E. (2016). Orange Prison Jumpsuit. In: M. Salter, ed., *Making Things International 2*. Minneapolis, MN: Minnesota University Press, pp. 122–136.

Vick, K. (2009). Calif. City Tries Counterinsurgency to Stem Gang Problem. *Washington Post*. 15 November 2009. www.washingtonpost.com/wp-dyn/content/article/2009/11/14/AR2009111400915.html [Accessed 15 May 2016].

Waddington, D. (2013). A 'kinder blue': analysing the police management of the Sheffield anti-'Lib Dem' protest of March 2011. *Policing and Society*, 23(1), pp. 46–64.

Winston, A. (2014). US Police Get Antiterror Training in Israel on Privately Funded Trips. *Reveal: The Center for Investigative Reporting*. 16 September 2014. www.revealnews.org/article-legacy/us-police-get-antiterror-training-in-israel-on-privately-funded-trips/ [Accessed 15 May 2016]

10 Auto-photographing (in)securities
Former young female soldiers' post-war struggles in Monrovia[1]

Leena Vastapuu

Introduction

More than a quarter of a century ago Gayatri Spivak (1988: 66) posed her famous question: 'Can the Subaltern Speak?' After critically observing the works of Marx, Gramsci, Foucault, and Deleuze, among others, Spivak's answer was 'No' – at the end of the day the subaltern cannot speak if academics and other intellectuals continue to scrutinize the 'other' only through their own 'universal' paradigms. According to Spivak, these paradigms have two implicit problems: on the one hand, the heterogeneity of the subaltern mass is not recognized, and the intellectual is, on the other hand, considered as someone who can 'speak for' the subaltern. By leaning on the work of Foucault, she thus argues that intellectuals (herself included) inevitably practice epistemic violence when they force the subaltern either to speak the language of the dominant elite or to remain virtually unheard. Spivak's essay has had a fair amount of criticism and not least for the author's complicated usage of language, yet has remained among the most influential texts in postcolonial studies (see e.g. Didur and Heffernan 2003). Maybe one reason for this success is that her main concern still remains pertinent throughout the spectrum of social sciences: how can we investigate the 'other', the 'subaltern', without imposing our implicit ontological and epistemological preconceptions towards the subjects and topics we are trying to comprehend?

In this chapter, I suggest that the auto-photographic research approach can provide one alternative for shifting agency from the researcher to the research participants, hence amplifying the voices of the 'others'. I am not, indeed, arguing that this research approach would somehow magically solve the problems of representation, nor that any research setting could ever be value-free. However, I claim that when the auto-photographic method and the photo-elicitation technique are combined as a methodological set, they have potential to reduce epistemic violence especially in risky environments or in places where cultural biases and unequal power relations between the researcher and research participants may unintentionally distort research results. In the chapter at hand, I test these arguments with a visual case study among former girl soldiers in Liberia.

I begin my analysis by explaining why no photographs can be found in a chapter that argues for the usage of photographic research methods. After this, I detail how the main characters of this chapter, named here as *Amy*, *Teta*, and *Priscilla* ended up in the Liberian warzone, and detail the main principles of the auto-photographic research approach. I maintain that this methodological set is a logical newcomer in critical studies of security (CSS), a field that has recently undergone both ethnographic (Salter and Mutlu 2013: 51–80) and visual (Andersen *et al.* 2015) expansions. The empirical relevance of the research approach is finally demonstrated with case studies from the streets of Monrovia. Here, the Monrovian street milieu is understood as a complicated (in)security environment, an interconnected web of rivers and rivulets, where each small stream has its specific task in the production of (in)securities.[2]

Drawing from the concept of social navigation (Vigh 2006a, 2009), my three interviewees are considered as *social rafters* whose tactic agency (Utas 2005; Vigh 2006a) is severely limited in comparison with their more fortunate peers by the inadequate resources they most often have at their disposal. Hence, time and again, social rafters are forced to resort to peculiar and potentially dangerous security arrangements that are visualized in the auto-photographic pictures and verbalized through photo-elicitation interviews.[3]

Making security visible sans visuals?

The reader might find it surprising that no photographs are presented in a chapter that champions the auto-photographic research approach. This is first and foremost an ethical choice, since being a female war veteran in Liberia entails a very strong stigma, one that research images can involuntarily perpetuate. One late evening in November 2012 I received a phone call from Monrovia. It was Juliet calling, a former frontline fighter who now sounded anxious and asked me to 'tell the BBC' to take her picture out of the internet.[4] Juliet had just found out that a close facial photograph of her holding an AK-47 was online. According to Juliet, the picture was taken during the second Liberian civil war from a helicopter that had suddenly appeared above her. As quickly as the helicopter had arrived, it had disappeared, and Juliet had already forgotten the whole incident. But now, when she found her face in the picture in question, she remembered the whole incident again. Juliet was extremely worried that this 'BBC effect' might first prevent her from travelling abroad. Second, and more importantly, she was concerned about the stigma the photo might still cause for her and her children, some nine years after the war had ceased. I thus promised Juliet that I would see what I could do and call her back at the first possible opportunity. Soon, however, it became evident that my abilities were very limited in this matter, since the picture was already on countless personal websites, news sites, and blogs. Because of this, and a few similar incidents, I have since then decided to be extremely cautious in publishing any photographs of the women with whom I am working.

In relation to research ethics, *the looking/not looking dilemma* (Möller 2009) poses constant challenges to the observer/reader if ethically problematic photographs or other visuals are presented alongside textual material. In the chapter at hand, I have been able to overcome this challenge, since in the setting of my research the photographs themselves do not 'speak security' (Hansen 2011: 51), but have instead acted as a medium, a visual method, for prompting the interviewees to illuminate, through their personal pictures, their life-worlds (Husserl 1970) to the researcher. For these overlapping reasons, I have been able to follow the example of the celebrated writer Susan Sontag, whose main volumes on photography – *On Photography* (1977) and *Regarding the Pain of Others* (2003) – contain no images.

Background: how civilian girls turn into soldiers

The main characters of this chapter are Amy, Teta, and Priscilla; former young female soldiers[5], who took part in Liberia's civil war(s) (1989–1996 and 1999–2003) in different kinds of capacities. Amy acted as a commander in the first civil war, whereas Teta and Priscilla participated in the second war – the former in combat service support tasks and the latter in frontline fighting.[6] After the fighting ceased, all these three women ended up living in one of Monrovia's numerous shanty towns.

Amy, the oldest of the three, had been extremely lucky as a young girl, since she had been given a chance to help a 'Congo woman'[7] with her housekeeping duties. Amy's tasks included a massive amount of household chores, but she became literate in return, and learned all the other necessities of being 'civilized' (Bledshoe 1980; Moran 1990, 2006). However, her freshly developed skills turned against her when she was captured while visiting the village of her parents in 1990. As a literate and in many ways capable sixteen-year-old young woman, she attracted the attention of the leaders of the main opposition force called the National Patriotic Front of Liberia (NPFL) and was captured. Later, when the group divided into two (Prince Johnson's INPFL and Charles Taylor's NPFL), Amy chose Taylor's forces and ended up commanding her own unit, which comprised of around fifty young women and men. Altogether, she spent more than ten years in various warring factions on the warfront.

While Amy enjoyed the short lull between the two civil wars during the last years of the century, *Teta* decided to run away from her home. Her aunt, the owner of the house, had recently realized that Teta's beautiful young body could be used as a commodity and had therefore made Teta perform sexual services to those who paid enough. Being forced into prostitution, Teta escaped the house at the age of fifteen and ended up, first, on the streets of Monrovia, and, in the following months, as a 'general's wife' in the Armed Forces of Liberia (AFL). After being elected as president in 1997, the ('former') warlord Charles Taylor had made plenty of effort to reform the AFL. When the second Liberian civil war broke out in 1999, Taylor and his forces were ready to face the rebels who would soon try to overthrow the newly elected government. Besides 'loving business', Teta's wartime *combat service support* duties included cooking, cleaning, and carrying services, as well as selling looted goods in the street corners of Monrovia for the benefit of her 'bush husband's' small unit.

At the turn of the new millennium, *Priscilla*'s house was attacked in another part of war-torn Monrovia. Priscilla's parents were brutally executed in front of her, and the ten-year-old girl was captured by some members of the Liberians United for Reconciliation and Democracy (LURD), one of the two main rebel groups fighting against Taylor's AFL. Priscilla was trained as a *fighter* so she headed for the frontline with her AK-47, alongside her new boyfriend, whom she had decided to hook up with during the training phase of her service. In addition to being a 'regular' relationship, this move was also a clever security arrangement for Priscilla that provided protection against hazardous rapes perpetrated by random male soldiers of her own unit.

As Amy's, Teta's, and Priscilla's examples aptly reveal, young women were often recruited to the Liberian warzone in a combination of haphazard coincidences and bad luck.[8] Surviving in these dangerous fields required, as a minimum, social skills, luck, and stamina; qualities that would also prove useful in post-war Liberia. Besides learning new skills and perseverance, the years in the warfront also brought about deep traumas that were typically treated with substance abuse and magic, *juju*. When the second civil war finally ceased in 2003, traumas and addictions prevailed. Many young female and male soldiers then ended up on the streets of Monrovia, from where they could easily find peer support and cheap narcotics to erase – at least temporarily – the haunting memories of war.[9]

Situating auto-photographic research practice in visual security studies

Considering the attention given to visuals in critical international relations theory in the recent years[10], it is rather surprising that the *production of visuals* as a research method still remains underexplored in Visual Security Studies, with only a few exceptions (e.g. Bleiker and Kay 2007). Although some researchers (e.g. Särmä 2014; Andersen 2015) have used pre-existing visuals and combined them in new, innovative ways, they have done so in a categorically different manner than what is pursued with the auto-photographic research approach. Whereas in the former the researchers utilize existing visuals in their visual analyses and academic artworks, the aim of the researchers in the latter is rather to act as assistants to the de facto artists of the research, the research participants.

My initial interest in visual research methods did not grow in academia, however, but in another country in western Africa, Senegal. Whilst returning to Dakar for the first time after having lived for six months in one of the city's poor neighbourhoods, I decided to ask my local friend Sire to take over my camera and photograph his daily activities. I did not expect much of the photos, especially since this was the first time Sire had used a digital SLR camera. In addition, I had already taken thousands of pictures of my small home quartier called Santhiaba, and was quite convinced that even in the best scenario he would bring me the kinds of pictures I already had in my possession. Then, later that same evening, Sire came back with well over 100 pictures in the camera. The photographs revealed that I had been right in assuming that the surroundings were already familiar to me. Nonetheless, it was just as evident that I had been completely wrong about the insights of the pictures: in front of my eyes I saw the everyday lives of Santhiabans in a way I had never witnessed before. I was able to see Sire's whereabouts during an ordinary day and observe the ways he navigated Santhiaba and its surroundings. In addition, the themes and details he considered fascinating and worth picturing were in many instances of totally different topics than I had found interesting in my own set of pictures. I was also astounded by the manner in which individuals looked at Sire through the lens of the camera; somehow, it seemed, I was able to see through the eyes of Sire.

When a few years later I then tried to find a suitable way for collecting data for my future dissertation, the memory from Santhiaba returned. I wanted to understand the post-war realities of female war veterans in Liberia, but was simultaneously painfully aware that even through participant observation I could never truly assimilate into, let alone 'be the other'.

Then I remembered what had happened in Santhiaba with Sire: maybe through auto-photographic research data I could try to 'see' like the 'other', as had been the case in Senegal. In addition, by providing a camera to each woman and by asking them to take pictures of their daily realities and aspirations, they would be the ones setting the agenda for the interviews instead of myself. Thus, from the autumn of 2012 to the summer of 2014, I spent altogether five months in Liberia in three separate field research trips. With the help of my two wonderful research assistants, Glorious Neoh and Jessica Doe, I conducted some 160 background interviews and spread around thirty-five cameras to four counties in Liberia. Many cameras got broken in the process and a few were stolen. Furthermore, I decided to discard some material, either because the profiles of the interviewees did not match my research setting (e.g. some were older women) or the data seemed unreliable (e.g. some gave contradictory information on their movements within the warring factions). Finally, I had at hand 133 background interviews and twenty-five photo-interviews. For the purpose of this chapter, I have chosen three cases from these data that to some extent illustrate the life-worlds of several other interviewed individuals in Monrovia.

In academia, the usage of photographs in research interviews was first described by John Collier Jr. (1957), a documentary photographer, who had been involved in a multidisciplinary research project investigating the relationship between the environment and mental health in Canada in the mid-1950s. As a part of this project, Collier photographed the living surroundings of chosen research participants. The resulting pictures were placed in interview situations that Collier (1957) labelled in his article as *photo-interviews*. When this initial experiment seemed to produce deeper information than 'ordinary' interviews had done previously, the practice of *photo elicitation* spread and Collier's later works (Collier 1967; Collier and Collier 1986) became standardized introductions to visual anthropology and sociology (Harper 2002: 14).

Building on the methods and ideas of John Collier, some anthropologists began to question their own subject positions within their research settings in the 1960s and 70s. It was understood that researchers' race, gender, and social position, among other things, had a deep impact on what was studied and which methods were chosen (Thomas 2009: 245). A revealing example on the impact of subject positions can be found from my own experiences in Santhiaba: the photographs I had taken differed at times radically from the pictures by Sire, since we had an utterly dissimilar understanding of what was interesting in that particular social environment.

After the findings of John Collier Jr., the next huge step in the development of participatory visual research came about in 1966 when a film and communications scholar, Sol Worth, and an anthropologist, John Adair, launched a collaborative experimental research project in North America. Worth and Adair gave 16mm film cameras to Navajo Native Americans, taught the research participants to utilize the cameras and edit film, and asked them to film their living surroundings. The scholars maintained that their method was able to capture the 'Navajo' ways of experiencing the world. Although some critics argued that Worth and Adair's work was placing too much emphasis on ethnic and racial differences at the cost of other social identities, their research nevertheless was an important benchmark in the development of auto-photography as a visual method (Thomas 2009: 245).

There are numerous variations within the field of participatory photography (see e.g. Balomenou and Garrod 2015), such as photovoice (e.g. Ruby 1992); photo essay (e.g. Grusky 2004); photo-interview (e.g. Vila 2013); and photo-communication (e.g. Dinklage and Ziller 1989). Therefore, for the sake of clarity, I have decided to utilize the term 'auto-photographic research practice' to describe the methodological combination of participant-generated auto-photographs and photo-elicitation interviews. Thus, with auto-photography, I refer to the process of taking photographs. Photo-elicitation, on the other hand, refers to the interview processes in which the participant-generated photographs are placed one by one in front of the research participant, who details the insights and meaning of each picture for the interviewer. Together, these two steps form the auto-photographic research approach.

Social rafting on the streets of Monrovia

Monrovia is the bustling capital of Liberia, situated between the Atlantic Ocean and the Mesurado River. With its more than one million inhabitants, Monrovia is the home for a little less than every third Liberian and for numerous expatriates ranging from thousands of NGO staff and UN employees to small- and large-scale entrepreneurs.[11] Although post-war Liberia has undoubtedly enjoyed rapid economic and infrastructural development, the everyday realities in the numerous shanty towns of Monrovia have barely improved, if not worsened, in recent years. For example, the World Bank (2014) estimates that 83.8 per cent of Liberians still live on less than $1.25 a day and the Gender Inequality Index

2016 (UNDP 2017) ranks Liberia as 177th out of 188 countries. In addition, the 2014–2015 Ebola epidemic unfortunately reinforced the already existing discrimination patterns in the country (Vastapuu 2015).

In this chapter, the security environment of the streets and slums of Monrovia is understood as a web of rivers, streams, and rivulets, where droughts and floods occasionally occur, and where a steady rivulet might suddenly turn into a bursting stream. In these (in)secure rivers, Amy, Teta, and Priscilla can be thought of as managing their lives through *social rafting*, a term that builds upon the popular idea of *social navigation* – brought to general attention by anthropologist Henrik E. Vigh (2006a: 51; see also Vigh 2006b) to explain the lives and struggles of marginalized youth in Bissau, the capital of Guinea-Bissau. Vigh's young research participants explained to him that in the hardships experienced by urban, marginalized youth, the way to get by was through *dubriagem*, an ancient Portuguese word still used in Guinea-Bissau today. From *dubriagem*, and with the clarifications provided to him by his research participants, Vigh then developed the term 'social navigation' for describing urban youth's survival strategies in Bissau, where 'possibilities and life chances are limited in the extreme' (ibid.: 56). Since then, the term has gained wide support, especially in youth studies, but 'despite its increasing popularity, the concept is most often used in an unspecified and misunderstood manner – it is generally not well defined!' (Vigh 2009: 419). However, in this specific context, I have chosen to reformulate Vigh's innovative term 'social navigation' as *social rafting* (see also Vastapuu 2018). Whereas the first emphasizes tactics, intentions, and targets, the latter is more haphazard and coincidental. Hence, where navigation can be considered as mainly goal-oriented and instrumental (one navigates in order to get somewhere), the main purpose of rafting is to stay afloat, to try to manoeuvre in the water and enjoy the thrill of the ride. In addition, the material of the raft, the scale of the stream, and the level of professionalism matters in rafting: sometimes the journey can be rather calm and enjoyable, whereas at other times the ride can prove fatal to an inexperienced or a badly equipped rafter.

In July 2014, I was exposed to a very concrete example of social rafting in one of Monrovia's numerous slums called West Point. When I arrived there one early morning, I found many of my respondents devastated and ill: a flood had occurred the previous week, and the water had not only entered a number of houses but had also washed away many of the ramshackle buildings. Floods are very typical during the rainy season in the world's most rainy capital, but since West Point is situated in a narrow peninsula between the Mesurado and Saint Paul rivers, floods and huge waves can potentially have extremely devastating effects in the area. Some of the residents had lost almost all their possessions and were aided by their 'street' sisters and brothers. Some slept rough under their *lappa* clothes with their children. Most suffered from colds and other infections since they were not able to get warm during the night-time. Individuals and families collected a piece of cardboard from here, another from there, a third one from a friend; received clothes from benevolent neighbours and friends, bought food on credit, and tried to contact whoever they thought might be of help.

Indeed, their actions and manoeuvring on that particular morning can probably be best described as social rafting.

To survive in post-war Monrovia's various slums as a disadvantaged individual thus requires, among other things, social skills, intelligence, luck, and the ability to manoeuvre smartly through the various obstacles brought about by the constant lack of resources. Therefore, the various skills the (young) soldiers learnt on the frontlines during the war(s) are of high value even today. How, then, do Amy, Teta, and Priscilla themselves manoeuvre in the (in)secure streams of post-conflict Monrovia, and what types of rafts do they have at their disposal?

My first encounter with Teta happened in a small room in a Monrovian slum, a room that had cardboard walls and was owned by a shopkeeper living in the same 'zinc round'. The shopkeeper allowed idle youth to spend time in that room; sometimes they bought liquor or other commodities from him, and other times he just liked to have them around to provide him with company. In addition, by allowing these youngsters to stay in his shop, he created a small-scale security network and a resource base, should he one day need some services. It took a while, and numerous encounters, to get Teta to trust me, but finally she agreed to take a camera along and photograph her daily activities and aspirations. Through Teta's pictures, it became evident that she was a small-scale drug dealer who saw prostitution or selling drugs as her only livelihood options. She had been in jail numerous times, she lived in a tarpaulin house that was almost collapsing, and most of her family members had either abandoned her or were dead. In many ways, Priscilla's realities resemble those of Teta's. Like Priscilla, Teta too earns the majority of her income with a combination of petty drug business and prostitution; her living conditions are deprived; and she does not have good relationships with her remaining family members.

Both Teta and Priscilla are extremely underprivileged, even in the context of Liberia. Their *rafts of survival* can therefore be thought of as collections of random pieces of junk that they have hastily assembled together. Teta and Priscilla have no proper steering mechanism in their rafts, let alone resources or know-how to significantly improve their vessels. Both Teta and Priscilla are nonetheless expert at manoeuvring in their personal rivers of (in)securities. An outsider or someone from an upper social class who visits these specific rivers would most likely be in trouble if she was only given Teta's or Priscilla's raft to survive with. It is therefore important to keep in mind that these women are definitely not only victims, but also social survivors who manage to endure the storms of life.

In comparison to Teta and Priscilla, Amy's raft is a bit more stable and sophisticated. After the second civil war of Liberia, Amy succeeded in subscribing to a Disarmament, Demobilization, and Rehabilitation (DDR) programme in three separate locations with weapons she had hidden in different phases of the civil wars.[12] From the money acquired through these processes, she was able to save a few hundred US dollars and build a small zinc house on an abandoned strip of land in the capital. Today, the community is one of the numerous slum areas of

Monrovia. Even though Amy's living environment seems very poor in her pictures – for instance, the majority of residents defecate into plastic bags and throw those bags into the nearby swamp – she is still doing rather well in comparison to Teta and Priscilla. Attached to her 'zinc round', inhabited by Amy and her youngest daughter, Amy has a very modest shop. From there, a random passer-by can purchase a shot of *gana gana*, local 'whisky' made from fermented cane juice; a cigarette 'from China'; a roll of toilet paper; or occasionally a small bottle of 'egg-nog' spiced with cannabis leaves. Amy has also acquired some crooked benches where customers and random individuals can 'lecture' about everyday life or enjoy the overtly distorted *hipco* music that keeps on blasting from Amy's precious boom box. These arrangements not only provide a small income, but are also a source of security to Amy and her daughter since the customers have an incentive to keep the business going.

Security in violence, violence in security

The complexity of security arrangements one has to master as a poor person in Monrovia really struck me during my second field research period in 2013. In my previous field trip in Liberia, I had lived with two families residing in different shanty towns of the capital, and found an excellent research assistant, *Glorious*. Thus, when organizing my second research trip, Glorious and I had planned that I would live with Glorious and her daughter in a small house she had just rented in one of the disenfranchised neighbourhoods of the capital. However, because her sister had suddenly come to visit Monrovia, we had to alter our plans at the last minute since four persons could simply not fit in one double bed.

Then, just two weeks into my second field research trip, I met Glorious one morning with deep worry on her face. During the previous night, armed robbers had entered her neighbouring house, killed a person, and wounded two others. The quarter's unofficial 'security guards' had caught one of the robbers, killed him, and thrown his body into the river. When the policemen came later that morning to the quarter, none of the residents confessed to having known the person who had executed the robber. Afterwards, the 'security guards' were celebrated as heroes since nobody trusted the police anymore. Because of these events, Glorious had slept only a few hours during the night and she was extremely worried about the safety of her household since she could not afford an iron door at the moment. Even though she had agreed with a bunch of young boys that they would be her 'street brothers', and come to her help at any time, she still did not feel safe and secure. Although I too was extremely worried about Glorious and her daughter's safety, at the same time I felt very relieved that I had not been living in her house as we had originally planned. If I had been there, I realized, our house would have definitely been one of the preferred targets in the slum since no other white residents lived in the neighbourhood. This way, as a researcher who was seeking to be as close to her interviewees as possible, I would have not only put myself in danger, but also Glorious along with her daughter.

How, then, to deal with security issues in an environment where the police and other authorities are anything but trustworthy, if one cannot afford concrete walls or an iron door, let alone private security services? To stay afloat in this type of river of (in)security, human relations are the key; the *wealth is in people* (Bledshoe 1980), as the example of Glorious reveals.

Social networks can have two faces, however. Once, I met Teta while she was still in the process of taking photographs. She expressed worry over the fact that her right hand was completely swollen and had two deep cuts in it. Because of this injury, she was unable to finalize her set of pictures. Teta nonetheless asked me to photograph her hand on her behalf, since 'you people need to know what is going on in our country today'. Teta explained that the reason for her condition was her current boyfriend, who had beaten her up for some trivial reason. Similar kinds of instances were also familiar to Priscilla, who, while observing the picture of her current boyfriend, explained that he was frequently violent towards her, mainly out of jealousy. Interestingly, neither of the men had complained about the fact that their girlfriends had to turn to prostitution for their basic income, but instead had problems with 'outside boyfriends'. They thus seemed to be fine with 'professional promiscuity', a quite normal profession in their particular neighbourhoods, but even a rumour of 'intimate promiscuity' was enough for a violent attack.

There are countless explanations as to why so many battered women cannot end their abusive relationships (see e.g. Ferraro and Johnson 1983; Rhodes and McKenzie 1998). Although some of these reasons are relevant in the case of my interviewees, an interesting practical motivation for the numerous Tetas and Priscillas of Liberia to stay with their violent partners is the need to increase their everyday security. To put it simply, a disadvantaged woman who is in a relationship with a well-respected and street-smart man is generally much safer and better off than someone who is either single or with someone who is incapable of 'providing for' his family – in terms of income, or, as a minimum, increased physical security. The apparent flipside is that as a bargain for general safety in the streets, there are numerous women who need to endure occasional violence inside their homes. Amy, on the other hand, can afford to be picky when it comes to partner candidates since she does not need a boyfriend for strengthening her security arrangements. Her security is sufficiently guaranteed by the fact that a huge group of young men and women from her neighbourhood utilize her small shop as a local 'entertainment spot' and have an incentive to keep the business going by keeping it secure.

The threat of violence in these neighbourhoods is abundant even in the daytime. On one occasion, during Any's interview, we had to stop the discussion and go to fetch her twelve-year-old daughter from the local police station. She had had a violent quarrel with a drunken man, who apparently did not agree to take responsibility for the baby that Amy's daughter was now carrying. To free her daughter, who now also carried bruises on her swollen body, Amy had to provide US$20 to the police officer as a 'contribution', and give a promise that she would keep her daughter next to her in the future.

Many disputes in these areas are drug-related. Cannabis is produced in Liberia and can be found in various forms practically anywhere in the country. One portion, a 'wrap', of marijuana costs around US$0.2 in the street market. In addition, West Africa is one of the transit points in the smuggling of heroin and cocaine to Europe and North America (Carrier and Klantschnig 2012: 41; UNODC 2014). Many of my interviewees, such as Teta and Priscilla, have 'gained' from the spillover of this trafficking in the form of cheap heroin. In the slums of Monrovia, a portion of *tar-white* (brown heroin that is usually smoked through a metal pipe from a foil) costs about US$1.1, whereas a gram is sold for approximately US$14. Among my research participants, cocaine usage is rather rare, since the cost of one gram can be as high as US$50.[13]

Teta's set of pictures was extremely revealing about the realities of substance abusers in Monrovia. In addition to having taken detailed photographs of the users of different kinds of narcotics, she gave detailed accounts of how those drugs were consumed, what their costs were, and what effects they had. In many of her pictures, former child soldiers, obviously now adults, were completely high on drugs, leaning on walls with an empty look in their eyes. While observing one of these pictures, Teta explained: 'They are all ex-combatants. Some of them fought, some of their families were killed, some people lost their legs; they are all traumatized.'

Although Liberia has recently reformed its legislation on drug and substance abuse (Legislature of Liberia 2014), severe weaknesses prevail in the law enforcement sector (US Department of State 2014). In practice, corruption is ubiquitous and police officers are deeply distrusted; in some of the pictures taken by my interviewees, there are DEA officers in their uniforms inhaling the catch of the night. In the following excerpts, Teta and Priscilla exemplify some of the everyday worries of substance abusers in the shanty towns of Monrovia.

LEENA (L): What is happening in this picture?

TETA (T): We were thinking about the police in this picture. When I went inside the room, they all looked sad and so I asked them: 'But what has happened?' And they told that it will not be easy today since the police is arriving.

L: But how were you able to tell in advance that the police is coming?

T: Someone called them! It is funny [laughing] but also serious. Because when the police is coming, they can capture you and take your picture in the station. After, they will ask money from you: 40, 30, 20, 10, 15 USD. It all depends. So when they are coming, everybody is in worry. You see, me and you it is not the same [gives me her hand]. Now smell my hand. Smell it? So if they smell the drugs on you, next they will ask you to show your teeth. You can also tell from the teeth if a person is smoking.

LEENA (L): Priscilla, the last time when I was here, you had your small business. Can you tell me once again what happened with your bucket? Why don't you have it anymore in your pictures? [Priscilla had had a small bucket that she carried around on top of her head. It contained cigarettes, matches, candies and, on occasion, drugs.[14]]

PRISCILLA (P): The police people came and took my bucket. They said that I've got drugs in the bucket.
L: Did you have [at the time]?
P: No. But they took it and beat me and put me to jail. I spent two days there and then my boyfriend came and freed me [paid a bribe]. They took my bucket, took my small money, turned me around and took my picture.
L: But why?
P: They took it to tell people that I am a drug seller. If you will pay, they can take your picture off the wall.
JESSICA: The reason they are putting these pictures up is that if they are taking your picture three times, the first two times someone can come and free you with some money. But with the third one they will carry you straight to South Beach [central prison in Monrovia with a very bad reputation]. That is where armed robbers, the rapists, the murderers, all those are kept.

After hearing Teta's and Priscilla's stories on the pictures, I visited two local police stations in two different slums and had a meeting with the heads of the stations. On both of their office walls there were numerous photographs of mostly young men and women, with handwritten captions on each picture stating 'drug addict', 'armed robber', 'thief', 'prostitute', and so on. In addition, the other officer asked for 'a kind contribution' in order for me to receive some information on Liberian street drugs. In Teta's words, the situation was indeed 'funny but also serious'.

Street sisters and brothers as security providers

> [Street brothers and sisters are] the people that can protect us in the street. If somebody is beating me, he comes and fights with me. If somebody is cursing to me, he can come and put his mouth there.
>
> Priscilla

All of my research participants had numerous pictures of their 'sisters' and 'brothers'. At first, I did not give the issue much thought, but then started to wonder how it was possible. Where did all these sisters and brothers come from? After all, many of my interviewees had in fact lost contact with their families and some were orphans. When enquiring about the matter, it soon became apparent that the majority of sisters, brothers, and even mothers were not biological relatives, but 'street sisters', 'street brothers', and 'play mothers'. These were individuals who would take care of each other when in need, by providing one another food, shelter, small favours, or advice, among other things. Together they formed small-scale security networks, huge rafts of survival, which were sturdier than the fragile rafts of vulnerable individuals. Basically, the more *wealth in people* (Bledshoe 1980) one had, the better one's chances of managing different types of daily struggles.

These types of informal security arrangements have been well-theorized in the context of Africa. For example, *patrimonialism/neopatrimonialism* (e.g.

Pitcher *et al.* 2009), *clientelism* (e.g. Van de Walle 2014), and *bigmanity* (e.g. Utas 2012) have become standard concepts when trying to unveil the informal power relations ubiquitous in the continent. AbdouMaliq Simone's (2004) idea of *people as infrastructure* is a fresh take on the issue, since it captures not only human relations themselves, but also 'the ability of residents to engage complex combinations of objects, spaces, persons, and practices'; conjunctions that 'become infrastructure – a platform providing for and reproducing life in the city'. Simone emphasizes that the critical question for researchers and policymakers is: how to 'practice ways of seeing and engaging urban spaces that are characterized simultaneously by regularity and provisionality'? (Simone 2004: 408). In other words: how to make sense, how to understand and grasp these multi-layered infrastructures of spaces, objects, people, and their social relations? How to unravel life-worlds of individuals and their social arrangements, arrangements such as *street-sisterhood* or *rafts of survival*?

It seems to me that the auto-photographic research approach indeed provides the researcher with ways of seeing and understanding what might, at first glance, appear to be invisible or inaccessible life-worlds. First, the method can facilitate communication where neither the interviewer nor the interviewee can easily dictate the topics of conversation. Second, the method can provide access to possibly dangerous arenas, and, finally, provoke understanding beyond verbal encounters: seeing is believing, but seeing is also understanding. Let me provide a final practical example from my interview material.

In one of Priscilla's pictures there is a small child, probably about two years old, posing for the camera in a beautiful print dress in front of an almost-collapsing thatched wall. With eyes filled with joy, Priscilla explained in her photo interview session the context of the photograph.

PRISCILLA (P): This is my [street] brother's baby here. The other people, I don't really know them.
LEEN (L): What is the child doing?
P: She is playing on the ground. That is why I took the picture.
JESSICA: What are you thinking of when you see this picture?
P: If I will have a good home someday, that is how I want to take care of my children.
L: And how is that?
P: I will bathe him, feed the baby, see that he is not sick, make sure that the baby has a good health.
L: So you want a baby one day?
P: Yes. That is why I took the picture.
L: When you look at the picture, how do you see her future?
P: Well, the baby's mother ran away and left the baby with her father. Nobody really knows where she went. We are the ones who can take care of the baby, especially me, I am the one taking care of her.
L: So how do you see this girl's future?
P: I hope she will have a good future.

L: What is a good future?
P: She will have her own house, her own car, a job, she will be working and helping people.

As the example hopefully demonstrates, street sisters and street brothers help one another, not only in acute crises, but also in small and bigger everyday challenges. Nobody forced Priscilla and her friends to take the baby under their care, but they did so out of humanity, of kindness and solidarity. Like the majority of biological siblings, they watch each other's backs and give advice, or, if needed, can very concretely fight by their sides. Also, like 'ordinary' siblings, they can have arguments over trivial matters, gossip, or just share good times. It must be brought to attention here that regardless of all their enormous daily struggles, numerous pictures taken by my interviewees reveal situations of joy and laughter, of good times shared with loved ones.

Conclusion

At the beginning of this chapter I quoted Gayatri Spivak (1988: 66), who asks: 'Can the subaltern speak?' In this chapter, I have tried to examine Spivak's concern through auto-photographic research data produced by Amy, Teta, and Priscilla; three young female veterans from Liberia's capital Monrovia. What I have learnt from the *life-worlds* of these highly disenfranchised, yet extremely persistent individuals, is that maybe the 'subaltern', the 'other', cannot speak the language of the dominant elite, but that is not the problem of the subaltern mass but rather of the ignorant scholar. It is, and should be, the struggle of the privileged to challenge her own life-world, to critically scrutinize her own ontological and epistemological assumptions, if that is what it takes to achieve a better understanding between the scholar and the 'other'. I have tried to exemplify in this chapter that one way to *lessen epistemic violence* (Spivak 1988) in research carried out in dangerous environments, such as Monrovian slums, and at the same time a promising way to amplify silent voices, can be found in methodological choices such as the auto-photographic research practice. Pictures in this specific context, and with these particular individuals, indeed tend to be worth a thousand words – at least when the contents of these photographs are illuminated and explained by the photographers themselves. In this way, it seems, the *subaltern* can speak via pictures to the arrogant scholar; the *subaltern* can visualize.

Notes

1. A different version of this chapter has been published in *Liberia's Women Veterans: War, Roles and Reintegration* (Zed Books 2018) by Leena Vastapuu and Emmi Nieminen.
2. The metaphor of river fits perfectly to the Liberian (post-)conflict zone, since some researchers (e.g. Hoffman 2011) argue that the Liberian civil wars should be scrutinized and understood in the regional Mano River context.
3. For a detailed description of *social rafting*, please see Vastapuu (2018).

4 'The BBC' is an umbrella term used in Liberia for international media, so the reference to this broadcasting company does not mean that 'the BBC' had actually published the picture.
5 According to a widely accepted definition, a child soldier is 'any person under 18 years of age who is part of any kind of regular or irregular armed force or armed group in any capacity, including but not limited to cooks, porters, messengers and anyone accompanying such groups, other than family members. The definition includes girls recruited for sexual purposes and for forced marriage. It does not, therefore, only refer to a child who is carrying or has carried arms' (UNICEF 1997).
6 See Vastapuu (2018) for a detailed description on the roles of Liberia's female soldiers in the wars.
7 The *Congo People* refers to the descendants of freed American blacks, many of them former slaves, who began to arrive to the area of current Liberia in the 1820s. Earlier, many slave ships had arrived from the Congo River, hence all the newcomers were named as Congo People. In turn, the newcomers started to call the native residents *Country People*, of whom many yearned to become 'civilized'; to learn the manners of the Congo People, in the following decades. The independence of Liberia was declared on 26 July 1847, and by then it had become clear that the new immigrants had gained supremacy in the area. Their True Whig Party held political power until 1980, when the first indigenous head of state, Master Sergeant Samuel Doe, seized the regime from the former Americo-Liberian president, William Tolbert.
8 See also Utas 2003 and 2005; Specht 2006;; Hoffman 2011; Vastapuu 2018.
9 Ibid.
10 E.g. Campbell and Shapiro 2007; Shapiro 2009; Vuori 2010; Hansen 2011; Andersen and Möller 2013; Aradau and Hill 2013; Heck and Schlag 2013; Hansen 2014; Särmä 2014; Andersen *et al.* 2015.
11 In a 2008 census, there were 1,010,970 inhabitants in Monrovia, whereas the population of whole Liberia was 3,489,072.
12 These kinds of wrongdoings were extremely prevalent in Liberia's disarmament processes; naturally, the idea was that a soldier could only subscribe once. See also Vastapuu (2018).
13 Communication with Monrovian drug users and the Deputy Chief of Investigation from the Drug Enforcement Agency (DEA) of Liberia in July 2014. To put these prices into perspective, in 2007 the average retail price of a gram of brown heroin in the UK was USD 90 (EMCDDA 2014).
14 I did not have a chance to ask Priscilla in private if she had drugs among her selling items on that particular day and wanted to respect her right to deny it. However, since Priscilla was a substance abuser and had previously told me about her small-scale drug business, it is likely that she had drugs in her bucket also on this occasion.

References

Andersen, R. S. (2015). *Remediating Security: A Semiotic Framework for Analyzing how Video Speaks Security*. Doctoral dissertation. Copenhagen: University of Copenhagen.
Andersen, R. S., Vuori, J. A., and Mutlu, C. E. (2015). Visuality. In C. Aradau, J. Huysmans, A. Neal, and N. Voelkner, eds., *Critical Security Methods: New Frameworks for Analysis*. London and New York. Routledge, pp. 85–117.
Andersen, R. S. and Möller, F. (2013). Engaging the Limits of Visibility: Photography, Security and Surveillance. *Security Dialogue*, 44(3): 203–221.
Aradau, C. and Hill A. (2013). The Politics of Drawing: Children, Evidence, and the Darfur Conflict. *International Political Sociology*, 7(4): 368–387.

Balomenou, N. and Garrod, B. (2015). A Review of Participant-Generated Image Methods in the Social Sciences. *Journal of Mixed Methods Research*, 10(4): 335–351.

Bledsoe, C. H. (1980). *Women and Marriage in Kpelle Society.* Stanford, CA: Stanford University Press.

Bleiker, R. and Kay, A. (2007). Representing HIV/AIDS in Africa: Pluralist Photography and Local Empowerment. *International Studies Quarterly*, 51(1): 139–163.

Campbell, D. and Shapiro, M. J. (2007). Guest Editors' Introduction [in special issue on securitization, militarization and visual culture in the worlds of post-9/11]. *Security Dialogue*, 38(2): 131–137.

Carrier, N. and Klantschnig, G. (2012). *Africa and the War on Drugs.* London: Zed Books.

Collier, J. (1957). Photography in Anthropology: A Report on Two Experiments. *American Anthropologist.* 59(5): 843–859.

Collier, J. (1967). *Visual Anthropology: Photography as a Research Method.* New York: Holt, Rinehart and Winston.

Collier, J. and Collier, M. (1986). *Visual Anthropology: Photography as a Research Method.* Albuquerque, NM: University of New Mexico Press.

Didur, J. and Heffernan, T. (2003). Revisiting the Subaltern in the New Empire. *Cultural Studies*, 17(1): 1–15.

Dinklage, R. I. and Ziller, R.C. (1989). Explicating Cognitive Conflict through Photo-Communication: The Meaning of War and Peace in Germany and the United States. *The Journal of Conflict Resolution*, 33(2): pp. 309–317.

EMCDDA – The European Monitoring Centre for Drugs and Drug Addiction (2014). *Price of Heroin at Retail Level, 2007.*

Ferraro, K. J. and Johnson, J. M. (1983). How Women Experience Battering: The Process of Victimization. *Social Problems*, 30: 325–339.

Grusky, O. (2004). Signs of HIV. *Contexts*, 3(1): 52–59.

Hansen, L. (2011). Theorizing the Image for Security Studies: Visual Securitization and the Muhammad Cartoon Crisis. *European Journal of International Relations*, 17(1): 51–74.

Hansen, L. (2014). How Images Make World Politics: International Icons and the Case of Abu Ghraib. *Review of International Studies*: 41(02) 1–26.

Harper, D. (2002). Talking about Pictures: A Case for Photo Elicitation. *Visual Studies*, 17(1): 13–26.

Heck, A. and Schlag, G. (2013). Securitizing Images: The Female Body and the war in Afghanistan. *European Journal of International Relations*, 19(4): 891–913.

Hoffman, D. (2011). *The War Machines: Young Men and Violence in Sierra Leone and Liberia* [Kindle eBook]. Durham NC: Duke University Press.

Husserl, E. (1970). *The Crisis of European Sciences and Transcendental Phenomenology: An Introduction to Phenomenological Philosophy.* Evanston, IL: Northwestern University Press.

Legislature of Liberia (2014). *Senate has Passed Controlled Drug and Substances Act.*

Möller, F. (2009). The Looking/Not Looking Dilemma. *Review of International Studies*, 35(04): 781–794.

Moran, M. H. (1990). *Civilized Women: Gender and Prestige in Southeastern Liberia.* Ithaca, NY and London: Cornell University Press.

Moran, M. H. (2006). *Liberia: The Violence of Democracy.* Philadelphia, PA: University of Pennsylvania Press.

Pitcher, A., Moran, M. H., and Johnston, M. (2009). Rethinking Patrimonialism and Neo-patrimonialism in Africa. *African Studies Review*, 52(01): 125–156.

Rhodes, N. R. and McKenzie, E. B. (1998). Why Do Battered Women Stay? Three Decades of Research. *Aggression and Violent Behavior*, 3(4): 391–406.

Ruby, J. (1992). Speaking for, Speaking about, Speaking with, or Speaking alongside: an Anthropological and Documentary Dilemma. *Journal of Film and Video*, 44(1/2, International Issues): 42–66.

Salter, M. B. and Mutlu, C. E. (2013). *Research Methods in Critical Security Studies: An Introduction*. London: Routledge.

Särmä, S. (2014). Junk Feminism and Nuclear Wannabes – Collaging Parodies of Iran and North Korea. Doctoral dissertation. Tampere: Tampere University Press.

Shapiro, M. J. (2009). *Cinematic Geopolitics*. London: Routledge.

Simone, A. (2004). People as Infrastructure: Intersecting Fragments in Johannesburg. *Public Culture* 16(03): 407–429.

Sontag, S. (2003). *Regarding the Pain of Others*. London: Hamish Hamilton.

Sontag, S. (1977). *On Photography*. New York: Farrar, Straus and Giroux.

Specht, I. (2006). *Red Shoes: Experiences of Girl-Combatants in Liberia*. Geneva: International Labour Office.

Spivak, G. C. (1988). Can the Subaltern Speak? In: C. Nelson and L. Grossberg, eds., *Marxism and the Interpretation of Culture*. Basingstoke: Macmillan Education.

Thomas, M. E. (2009). Auto-Photography. In: R. Kitchin and N. Thrift, eds., *International Encyclopedia of Human Geography*. Oxford: Elsevier, pp. 244–251.

UNDP (2017). Gender Inequality Index 2016. *Human Development Reports*, March. Available at: http://hdr.undp.org/en/composite/GII [Accessed 9 March 2018].

UNICEF (1997). *Cape Town Principles and Best Practices: Adopted at the Symposium on the Prevention of Recruitment of Children into the Armed Forces and on Demobilization and Social Reintegration of Child Soldiers in Africa*. Cape Town: UNICEF.

UNODC (2014). *World Drug Report 2014*. Vienna: United Nations Office on Drugs and Crime (UNODC).

US Department of State (2014). *Country Report: Liberia. Bureau of International Narcotics and Law Enforcement Affairs*.

Utas, M. (2003). *Sweet Battlefields: Youth and the Liberian Civil War*. Uppsala: Uppsala University.

Utas, M. (2005). Victimcy, Girlfriending, Soldiering: Tactic Agency in a Young Woman's Social Navigation of the Liberian War Zone. *Anthropological Quarterly* 78(2): 403–430.

Utas, M. ed. (2012). *African Conflicts and Informal Power: Big Men and Networks*. London: Zed Books & The Nordic Africa Institute.

Van de Walle, N. (2014). The Democratization of Clientelism in Sub-Saharan Africa. In: B. D. Abente and L. J. Diamond, eds., *Clientelism, Social Policy, and the Quality of Democracy*. Baltimore, MD: The Johns Hopkins University Press, pp. 230–252.

Vastapuu, L. (2015). Study on the Gendered Impacts of Ebola in Liberia. Independent assessment commissioned by Finn Church Aid, February 2015. [Published as L. Kotilainen.]

Vastapuu, L. (2017). Hope is Not Gone Altogether: The Roles and Reintegration of Young Female War Veterans in Liberia. Doctoral dissertation. University of Turku: Department of Philosophy, Contemporary History and Political Science.

Vastapuu, L. (2018). *Liberia's Women Veterans: War, Roles and Reintegration*. Illustrated by Emmi Nieminen. London: Zed Books.

Vigh, H. (2006a). *Navigating Terrains of War: Youth and Soldiering in Guinea-Bissau.* New York/Oxford: Berghahn Books.

Vigh, H. E. (2006b). Social Death and Violent Life Chances. In: C. Christiansen, M. Utas and H. E. Vigh, eds., *Navigating Youth, Generating Adulthood: Social Becoming in an African Context.* Uppsala: The Nordic Africa Institute, pp. 31–60.

Vigh, H. (2009). Motion Squared: A Second Look at the Concept of Social Navigation. *Anthropological Theory*, 9(4): 419–438.

Vila, P. (2013). The Importance of Photo-interviewing as a Research Method in the Study of Identity Construction Processes: An Illustration from the U.S.–Mexico Border. *Visual Anthropology*, 26(1): 51–68.

Vuori, J. A. (2010). A Timely Prophet? The Doomsday Clock as a Visualization of Securitization Moves with a Global Referent Object. *Security Dialogue*, 41(3): 255–277.

World Bank (2014). *Poverty & Equity: Country Dashboard Liberia.*

11 Visual security
Patterns and prospects

Roland Bleiker

The chapters in this book make a clear and compelling central point: the visual is absolutely central to the issues that define and drive security.[1] 'Think of a major conflict or security issue where visuality is not important?' Rune S. Andersen and Juha A. Vuori (this volume) asked us to contemplate this question in their introduction. It is impossible to do so, and not just since the Vietnam War, when a mass audience around the world was exposed to horrific images of war and suffering. Every aspect of security, from terrorist attacks to civil wars and border controls, contains visual dimensions, which, in turn, inevitably become political. This is as much the case with conflicts that are not visualized, which is why the UN Secretary General urged photojournalists to produce more images, particularly of atrocities that seem to exist in silence and demand urgent action (Pronk 2005; Devereux 2010: 124–134).

The second theme that comes across clearly in this book is how incredibly diverse and complex the links between visuality and security are. They range across all aspects of security, from terrorism and war to policing and surveillance. They reach from the state level to the everyday and cover all visual dimensions: photography, film, television, new media, drones, art, internet memes. The chapters in this book address countless aspects of this constellation, including – just to name a few examples – state surveillance of citizens; media coverage of terrorism and war; the role of popular culture in generating militarized values; the potential of art to challenge prevailing conceptions of security; the gendered dimensions of prevailing depictions of nuclear issues; and the visual performance of state power through uniforms, parades, and election campaign rallies.

The various criss-crossing links among these visuality-security constellations are so numerous and complex that Vuori and Andersen (this volume) rightly stress that 'security is something that we cannot fully grasp'. I fully agree. We should not – and cannot – arrive at a kind of grand explanation that can capture the essence of visual security in an all-encompassing and ahistorical manner. But analyse and explain we must, not least because of how crucial questions of visuality are to understanding the nature, practice, and impact of security.

My concluding remarks aim to contribute to such a conceptualization of visual security in two ways. First, I identify a number of key patterns that exist across the complex visuality-security nexus. I make a distinction between visual images and visual artefacts and performances and then examine a number of crucial communalities between them, most notably how they delineate what we see and what we do not and how this shapes the contours and content of security politics. I offer this conceptualization in addition – or, rather, in reinforcement – of the triptych that Vuori and Andersen present at the outset: the differentiation of visual security as a modality, a practice, and a method. Second, I identify two challenges that I believe are particularly important: (1) The need to better understand the role played by emotions in visual security and (2) the centrality of pursuing experimental – including visual – research while, at the same time, retaining the ability to communicate in accessible and compelling ways.

The visual turn in security studies

The authors in this volume have clearly made what W. J. T. Mitchell (1986, 1994) called the 'visual' or 'pictorial' turn. They recognize that people often perceive and remember key events more through images than through verbal accounts. Mitchell writes of a 'new heightened awareness' of the role of visuality, even of how the problem of our time is the 'problem of the image' (Mitchell 2018).

There are few realms where the importance of the visual is more pronounced than in security. Our understanding of terrorism, just to take one example, is inevitably intertwined with how images dramatically depict the events in question, how these images circulate worldwide, and how politicians and the public respond to these visual impressions. Take the terrorist attacks of 11 September 2001. There is no way to understand the origin, nature, and impact of the event without understanding the role of images. The attack was designed for visual impact. Images circulated immediately worldwide, giving audiences a sense of how traumatic and how terrible the event was. Many of these images not only shaped subsequent public debates and policy responses, including the War on Terror, but also remain engrained in our collective consciousness.

Images are, of course, not new, nor have they necessarily replaced words as the main means of communication. Images have been around from the beginning of time. The visual has always been part of life. Images were produced not only to capture key aspects of human existence, but also to communicate these aspects to others, going all the way back to prehistoric cave paintings.

But there are two ways in which the politics of images has changed fundamentally and the chapters in this volume do an excellent job in highlighting the issues at stake.

First is the speed at which images circulate and the reach they have. Not that long ago, during the time of the Vietnam War, it would have taken days if not weeks for a photograph taken in the war zone to reach the front page of, say, the *New York Times*. In today's digital world, a photograph or a video can reach audiences worldwide immediately after it has been taken. Media networks can now make a local event almost instantaneously global. The issue goes well beyond the influential CNN-effect (Robinson 2002). The circulation of news has changed fundamentally. Consider how Saara Särmä (this volume) compellingly shows why seemingly mundane internet parodies can take on important political features: they circulate with incredible speed, sometimes so fast that they reach the audience before the depiction of the actual political event they seek to parody does. She highlights how crucial it is to understand how new technical features, such as mobile apps, provide people with the ability to view and circulate material from a range of different devices and no matter where they are.

Second is what one could call the democratization of visual security and visual politics in general. It used to be that very few actors – states or global media networks – had access to images and the power to distribute them to a global audience. Today, everyone can take a photograph with a smartphone, upload it on social media, and circulate it immediately with a potential worldwide reach (Vuori and Andersen, this volume). The result is an unprecedented visualization of both our private lives and our security landscape: a global communication dynamic that is fundamentally new and rooted in various networks and webs of relations (Kaempf 2018). Consider how the terrorist organization Islamic State is using beheading videos, recorded in and diffused from undisclosed and unknown locations, as part of a carefully orchestrated and well organized social media strategy, aiming at numerous audiences simultaneously (Friis 2015). The result is nothing less than a visual communication revolution that has shaken the foundations of established media networks. We see a dismantling of the division between broadcaster and viewer, producer and consumer, which, ultimately, and as flagged by Vuori and Andersen (this volume), 'erodes long-established hierarchies of who gets to speak about security and how'.

Visual security: images, artefacts, performances

To appreciate the wide range and far-reaching consequences of visual politics it is important to look not only at two-dimensional images but also at three-dimensional visual artefacts and performances (see Callahan 2018).

Two-dimensional images refer to, for instance, television shows (Shapiro, this volume), CCTV cameras (Cardullo and Steven, this volume), photographs (Möller, this volume; Vastapuu, this volume), videos (Fish, this volume) or internet memes (Särmä, this volume). Three-dimensional artefacts refer to phenomena such as border installations, national monuments, rallies and parades (Sandor, this volume), and uniforms (Guillaume, Vuori and Andersen, this volume). It is, as a result, important to explore the politics of the visual beyond images. This is why Vuori and Andersen (this volume) rightly stress the need to understand how images influence security issues, but also 'how sight and appearance' itself is integral to security practices.

Visual images and visual artefacts differ in their nature and function. For one, images have the potential to circulate rapidly while some artefacts and performances are limited by their physical nature and location. But at a time of globalization and global communication these boundaries become more and more blurred. Consider the Vietnam Veterans Memorial in Washington DC, designed by Maya Lin. It is one of the most influential visual artefacts in the realm of security and war, a monument visited by millions of people who often leave with deeply emotional impressions. But most people around the world have 'seen' the monument not as a result of a personal visit, but through images that circulate online, in newspapers, on TV, and in movies. The same is the case with almost any influential visual artefact or performance, from flags to military parades and presidential election debates: they are always more than localized three-dimensional objects or phenomena. They are artefact-performance-constellations that circulate politically through still and moving images.

Möller (this volume) analyses Trevor Paglen's photographs of military installations. They evoke fixed installations that cannot move. But Paglen's photographs reproduce and circulate these installations, even if they deal with the invisible, rather than the visible. Likewise, police uniforms and their symbolic colours, analysed by Guillaume, Vuori and Andersen (this volume), are three-dimensional artefacts limited in their direct impact to a particular time and place. But they too travel through the spread of images. Most of us know of the powerful symbolism of Nazi Germany not because we have directly witnessed the atrocities of the Third Reich, but because we have seen – with the benefit of hindsight – chilling still and moving images of uniformed German men doing goose-steps and Nazi salutes. Even people in Germany at the time experienced the politico-aesthetic power of uniforms not only directly but also through the spread of images, such as through Leni Riefenstahl's powerful films of Nazi rallies. Her *Triumph of the Will* or *Olympia* helped the Nazi regime turn mere propaganda into a broader aesthetic-mythology that was instrumental in gaining popular support for a racist and militaristic state apparatus: 'Fascinating Fascism', as Susan Sontag called it (Sontag 1975; Bach 2007).

Security politics and the distribution of the sensible

The links between images and security work gradually and across time and space. They transgress numerous borders – spatial, linguistic, psychological, and other. They work inaudibly but powerfully: by slowly entrenching – or challenging – how we view and think of security and thus how security is articulated and implemented.

Understanding the exact role – and especially the impact – of images and visual artefacts is, as a result, no easy task. I do not pretend to have an easy answer here but I think a good start is with a suggestion advanced by Jacques Rancière. It is no surprise that several contributors to this volume relied on his work (Chouliaraki, this volume; Guillaume, Vuori, and Andersen, this volume).

Rancière offers a very useful way to understand the politics of images. He speaks of the 'distribution of the sensible', that is, of how in any given society and at any given time, there are boundaries between what can be seen and not, felt and not, thought and not and, as a result, between what is politically possible and not. These boundaries are arbitrarily but often accepted self-evidently as common sense (Rancière 2004: 13; see also Rockhill 2009: 199–200). Images influence the distribution of the sensible. They frame or reframe the political, either by entrenching existing configurations of seeing, sensing, and thinking, or by challenging them. The boundaries between what is sensible and not sometimes shift rapidly but mostly they evolve gradually as the visual world around us shifts and evolves.

Images and visual artefacts are neither progressive nor regressive. They can entrench existing power relations or they can uproot them. This volume offers plenty of examples how visuality is implicated with and enforces current political practices. Shapiro (this volume) focuses on television shows, such as *Homeland*, and shows how they depict and enact and entrench a 'militarized security-oriented gaze'. This is manifest, for instance, in a tendency towards anonymous drone killings in which those who operate and those who authorize the weapons are located at a remote distance. Sandor (this volume) reveals how visual rituals – from government ceremonies to parades – are ways of staging and exerting state power. They are influential visual routines that represent and legitimize the very substance of security: what a threat is and who is able to offer protection from it.

Visual practices can also uproot and change security practices. Chouliaraki (this volume) shows in a compelling way how gradual changes in photojournalistic practices also lead to changes in long-term collective attitudes towards war and its role in society. She stresses, with Rancière, that the visual depictions of war is inevitably linked to power since they frame what can be seen and what is legitimate, a kind of 'collective moralization'. She shows how recent visualizations of war, which focus on trauma and intense psychological experiences, replace earlier photojournalistic practices that revolved around more masculine portrayals of brave heroic soldiers, battling for survival under horrific circumstances. While these changes took place over decades, other visual engagements with security are more immediate. Särmä (this volume), for instance, reveals how collage and internet parodies can make visible the gendered norms associated with nuclear politics. Although seemingly mundane and apolitical, these memes can not only circulate rapidly but are also a part of popular culture and thus part of the shared cultural values that surround us and frame our politics (see also Hamilton 2016).

Visibility and invisibility in security politics

An added layer of complexity emerges when one explores the security politics of what is visualized and what not. An immediate and normal reaction is: what happens to people, issues, and phenomena that we do not see? What happens when we do not see violence, human rights violations, mass rape during war? The genocide in Rwanda, for instance, killed up to a million people in a few months in 1994. Because there were very few images circulating in global media at that time it was possible to dismiss the tragedy as a mere local conflict (Robinson, 2018). Even today, many of the world's most deadly conflicts, particularly in Africa, are not covered by global media because there are no Western geopolitical interests at stake (Kirkpatrick 2016: 91, 97).

The evolution of warfare has very much been intertwined with what we see and what we don't – from emerging camouflage practices in the nineteenth century (Guillaume *et al.* 2016) to attempts at controlling the spread of images during the Vietnam War (van Veeren 2018). But recent conflicts, most notably in Afghanistan and Iraq, have shown that control over the flow of images is almost impossible to retain in the face of social media, which allows any individual or group to take images of the war zone and circulate them immediately (see Dauphinee, 2018).

But invisibility is, as Möller (this volume) convincingly shows, not inevitably always a negative. He advances a complex notion of invisibility, one that suggests people can be stimulated not by what they see but, paradoxically, by what they cannot see. Obscurity, here, is a way of stimulating the imagination of the viewer. Look at how suppressing photographic evidence of the killing of Osama Bin Laden only spurred on the public's imagination and generated suspicion and conspiracy theories (see also Mitchell 2011). This is why invisibility can actually 'activate the imagination', because the process of alluding to, rather than showing in full, shatters the illusion that images somehow are an authentic representation of reality (Andersen and Möller 2013: 207). Möller looks at several artists who directly depart from the traditional photojournalistic practice of war reporting that seeks to visually reveal the realities of the battlefield. But, as Möller (this volume) points out, such visual practices are always and inevitably concealing as much as they are revealing: they depict war from a certain angle and thus already contain a politics. This is why Möller explores what he calls 'obscure photography' and its ability to point to things that are in principle not visible: military installations that are not accessible to the public, or more abstract notions of security and defence. While important and potentially of significance to security politics one caveat is necessary, though: for 'obscure photography' to have a social impact it would need to circulate outside of the art scene and create a substantial amount of public awareness.

The image-emotions-security nexus

I would like to end my short commentary by drawing attention to two challenges that are particularly pertinent in the study of visual security. The first is, I believe, the need for more and more systematic work on the role that emotions play in the links between visuality and security.

Several chapters in this book flag the crucial role of emotions and affect. Chouliaraki (this volume) stresses how photojournalism moves towards an 'increasingly explicit visualization of war' which emphasizes the emotional over the physical impact that war has on soldiers and civilians. Sandor (this volume) points towards the importance of emotional connection in the political role that visual rituals play. Some of the practices he refers to are indeed intensely emotional, such as 'singing, drumming, and the performance of customary dance'. Likewise, when analysing the symbolic burning of narcotics seized by the police Sandor (this volume) stresses how this practice touches on the 'emotional and affective registers' of spectators.

More enquiries and more systematic ones are needed to understand the complex role that emotions play in visual security. In many ways, the power of images is very much linked to their emotional dimensions. Images generate excitement and anxieties, which is why, as Mitchell (2005: 7), put it, 'people have such strange attitudes towards images'.

Why is it that audiences are given a stern warning before they see shocking images of, say, war or terror or bodily mutilation? Why, Lene Hansen (2014) asks, do we not get the same warning with verbal depictions? Consider how news outlets that published images of the bombing of the Boston marathon in 2013 felt compelled to add notes that read 'Warning: This image may contain graphic or objectionable content' (Haugney 2013). No such warning was given with language-based articles of the same event, even though they described the horror of the attack in equally great detail. What makes images seemingly more dangerous and powerful than words?

Part of what makes images unique is that they often evoke, appeal to, and generate emotions. Pictures of traumatic events, such as terrorist attacks, seem able to capture the unimaginable. This is why news coverage of such traumas is frequently accompanied by images, as if they could provide audiences with a type of emotional insight that words cannot convey. Images seem to convey the pain and distress of victims better than words do. They are thus central to how audiences worldwide perceive and thus also understand and respond to crises (Hutchison 2014, 2016).

Film and television are visual media that appeal to feelings and emotions in a particularly powerful way. Cinematic depictions of political issues offer the viewer a very visceral experience, in part because they combine narratives, visual images, and sound. But such depictions are also powerful because they are based on individual characters and the moral choices they make, offering the viewer not just an abstract depiction of politics but a form of cinematic storytelling that allows them to identify with particular individuals and their situations. As a result, distant and complex political topics become accessible through personal stories (see Shapiro, this volume).

There is no space here to elaborate on how an understanding of emotions can illuminate the links between images and security. I have explored the issue elsewhere (Bleiker and Hutchison 2008; Hutchison and Bleiker 2014) but would like to encourage visual security scholars to engage with the vibrant literature on emotions and politics and, in particular, with scholarship that explicitly explores the role of emotions in security. There are, meanwhile, many compelling studies that do so (see, for instance, Callahan 2004; Hutchison 2010; Solomon 2012; Fierke 2013; Mercer 2013; Ross 2014; Åhäll and Gregory 2015; Holmes 2015).

Exploring alternative visual methods

The final point I would like to make is a strong endorsement of how Vuori and Andersen (this volume) advocate visuality as a research method itself or, as they put it, a form of 'visual knowledge production'. In order to explore the complexity of security we need to explore new ways of thinking, seeing, hearing, and sensing the political. We need to break free of disciplinary boundaries, write creatively, and explore other ways of communicating, including visual ones.

Although we live in a visual age, knowledge conventions – both in academia and in the wider realm – are still very much focused on texts and textual analysis (see Williams 2003). What would a true political appreciation of the visual security look like? What would it mean to communicate and think and act in visual ways? How would the media, books, classrooms, and other realms be transformed if we were to treat images not just as illustrations or as representations but as political forces in themselves?

Numerous international relations scholars have meanwhile started to tackle security and other political issues through alternative modes of knowing and communicating, such as art, photo essays, novels, music, or documentary films. Several prominent writers have also used film as a way of communicating security issues (see, for instance, Weber 2007; Der Derian *et al.* 2009; Weber 2011; Song *et al.* 2012; Callahan 2015a, 2015b; Gara and Der Derian 2015).

The contributors to this volume continue these practices of visual research and push it in new directions. Särmä (this volume) uses a 'playful visual method', in this case internet parody images that challenge commonsensical assumptions about nuclear politics. Cardullo and Steven (this volume) explore the use of art as a way to challenge the role of CCTV cameras as a 'technology of surveillance'. They seek to push an understanding of the complex role of CCTV systems beyond the prevailing 'discourse of power and control'. Through artistic engagements we see how CCTV cameras can also make visible aspects and people that otherwise tend not to be noticed.

It is no surprise that art is at the forefront of exploring new ways of understanding security. For Rancière (2004: 9), art is the very meeting point between existing configurations of the sensible and attempts to reconfigure our sensory experience of the world (Rancière 2004: 9; Rockhill 2009: 200). This is to say that he attributes to art the ability to challenge existing political narratives and push the boundaries of what can be seen, thought, and done.

A particular compelling example of such a visual exploration of security is Vastapuu's chapter in this volume. She uses a method that is alternatively called 'photo-elicitation' (Harper 2010); 'participatory photography' (Bleiker and Kay 2007) or, as she calls it, 'auto-photography'. Vastapuu observes what becomes visualized when she provides former Liberian girl soldiers, now living in the urban slums of Monrovia, with cameras to document their lives. What are revealed as a result are not only threats that tend to be invisible to Western researchers, but also particular security structures, such as those linked to social networks. In addition, Vastapuu addresses one of the thorniest issues in postcolonial studies: Gayatri

Spivak's argument that the 'subaltern cannot speak', because they have to always do so through the epistemic framework of privileged Western (and Southern) intellectual elites. By providing her research 'objects' with cameras to document their own lives, she turns them into subjects and researchers themselves. Vastapuu knows very well that there is no magical solution to the problem that Spivak articulated, but she also believes, and I think compellingly shows, that the 'subaltern can speak via pictures to the arrogant scholar' because the 'subaltern can visualize'.

Visualizing and communicating security

Opening up thinking space through alternative visual methods inevitably involves risks. It is to embrace creativity, and the uncertainty associated with it, over the comfort of time-honoured procedures and disciplinary conventions. It is to never stand still and to search for ever newer ways of writing, sensing, seeing, and hearing the political. Taking such risks is well worthwhile but also comes with challenges and responsibilities.

Särmä (this volume) makes a very important point when talking about collage as a research methodology: she stresses the need for accessibility when approaching academic discussions. In her case this refers to making accessible, to a broad audience, feminist critiques of nuclear policies. She wants to show how 'gender and sexuality underpin the thinking about nuclear proliferation'. The two experimental chapters in this volume – Särmä's and Vastapuu's – are very powerful examples of research that does this successfully. They are innovative and push the boundaries of what we see and know, but they are also very clearly and compellingly written. They avoid academic jargon and, in doing so, take the reader on new journeys that are theoretically informed but do not get caught in and become confined in sub-disciplinary quarrels.

Taken together, the chapters in this volume convincingly show not only that visuality is absolutely central to questions of security, but also that there is great value in pursuing experimental visual research into security. This is most effectively done when communicated in sophisticated but intelligible ways. Doing so is far from easy. Exploring new forms of visual communication harks back to a dilemma that poets have sought to deal with for time immemorial: that we need to stretch the boundaries of language so that we can speak and think anew, but do so in ways that still allows us to communicate, reach people, and change how they think about the world.

Note

1 I draw on and expand some of my previous work on this topic, most notably Bleiker 2001, 2015, 2016, 2018; Bleiker and Kay 2007; Bleiker and Butler 2016.

References

Åhäll, L. and Gregory, T. eds. (2015). *Emotions, Politics and War*. New York: Routledge.

Andersen R. S. and Möller F. (2013). Engaging the Limits of Visibility. *Security Dialogue*, 44 (3), pp. 203–221.

Bach, S. (2007). *Leni: The Life and Work of Leni Riefenstahl*. New York: Alfred A. Knopf.

Bleiker, R. (2001). The Aesthetic Turn in International Political Theory. *Millennium: Journal of International Studies*, 30(3), pp. 509–533.

Bleiker, R. (2015). Pluralist Methods for Visual Global Politics. *Millennium*, 43(3), pp. 872–890.

Bleiker, R. (2016). Visuality and Creativity: In Memory of Alex Danchev. *New Perspectives*, 24(2), pp. 13–21.

Bleiker, R. ed. (2018). *Visual Global Politics*. London: Routledge.

Bleiker, R. and Kay, A. (2007). Representing HIV/AIDS in Africa: Pluralist Photography and Local Empowerment. *International Studies Quarterly*, 51(1), pp. 139–163.

Bleiker, R. and Butler, S. (2016). Radical Dreaming: Indigenous Art and Cultural Diplomacy. *International Political Sociology*, 10(1), pp. 56–74.

Bleiker, R. and Hutchison, E. (2008). Fear No More: Emotions and World Politics. *Review of International Studies*, 34(S1), pp. 115–135.

Callahan, W. A. (2004). National Insecurities: Humiliation, Salvation and Chinese Nationalism. *Alternatives: Global, Local, Political*, 29(2), pp. 199–218.

Callahan, W. A. (2015a). The Visual Turn in IR: Documentary Filmmaking as a Critical Method. *Millennium*, 43(3), pp. 891–910.

Callahan, W. A. (2015b). *Toilet Adventures in China: A Film about Transnational Encounters*. Australian Center on China and the World www.thechinastory.org/2015/08/toilet-adventures-in-china-making-sense-of-transnational-encounters/ [Accessed 5 April 2017].

Callahan, W. A. (2018). Culture. In: R. Bleiker, ed., *Visual Global Politics*. London: Routledge.

Dauphinee, E. (2018). Body. In: R. Bleiker, ed., *Visual Global Politics*. London: Routledge.

Der Derian, J., Udris, D., and Udris, M. (2009). *Human Terrain: War Becomes Academic*. http://humanterrainmovie.com [Accessed 5 April 2017].

Devereux, L. (2010). From Congo: Newspaper Photographs, Public Images and Personal Memories. *Visual Studies*, 25(2), pp. 124–134.

Fierke, K. M. (2013). *Political Self-Sacrifice: Agency, Body and Emotion in International Relations*. Cambridge: Cambridge University Press.

Friis, S. M. (2015). Beyond Anything We Have Ever Seen: Beheading Videos and the Visibility of Violence in the War against ISIS. *International Affairs*, 91(4), pp. 725–746.

Gara P. and Der Derian, J. (2015). *Project Z* (Bullfrog Films) www.bullfrogfilms.com/catalog/pz.html [Accessed 5 April 2017].

Guillaume, X., Andersen, R. S. and Vuori, J. A. (2016). Paint it Black: Colours and the Social Meaning of the Battlefield. *European Journal of International Relations*, 22(1), pp. 49–71.

Hamilton, C. (2016). *The Everyday Artefacts of World Politics: Why Graphic Novels, Textiles and Internet Memes Matter in World Politics*. Sydney: PhD Thesis, University of New South Wales.

Hansen, L. (2014). Annual Michael Hintze Lecture in International Security. Lecture presented at the University of Sydney, 20 February.
Harper, D. (2010). Talking about Pictures: A Case for Photo Elicitation. *Visual Studies*, Vol 17, No 1, pp. 13–26.
Haugney, C. (2013). News Media Weigh Use of Photos of Carnage. *New York Times*, 17 April, available at: www.nytimes.com/2013/04/18/business/media/news-media-weigh-use-of-photos-of-carnage.html [Accessed 5 April 2017].
Holmes, M. (2015). Believing This and Alieving That: Theorizing Affect and Intuitions in International Politics. *International Studies Quarterly*, 59(4), pp. 706–720.
Hutchison, E. (2010). Trauma and the Politics of Emotions: Constituting Identity, Security and Community After the Bali Bombing. *International Relations*, 24(1), pp. 65–86.
Hutchison, E. (2014). A Global Politics of Pity? Disaster Imagery and the Emotional Construction of Solidarity after the 2004 Asian Tsunami. *International Political Sociology*, 8(1), pp. 1–19.
Hutchison, E. (2016). *Affective Communities in World Politics: Collective Emotions After Trauma*. Cambridge: Cambridge University Press.
Hutchison, E. and Bleiker, R. (2014). Theorizing Emotions in World Politics. *International Theory*, 6(3), pp. 491–514.
Kaempf, S. (2018). Digital Media. In: R. Bleiker, ed., *Visual Global Politics*. London: Routledge.
Kirkpatrick, M. (2016). *Photography, the State and War: Mapping the Contemporary War Photography Landscape*. Ph.D. Thesis, University of Ottawa.
Mercer, J. (2013). Emotion and Strategy in the Korean War. *International Organization*, 67(2), pp. 221–252.
Mitchell, W. J. T. (1986). *Iconology: Image, Text, Ideology*. Chicago, IL: The University of Chicago Press.
Mitchell, W. J. T. (1994). *Picture Theory: Essays on Verbal and Visual Representation*. Chicago: The University of Chicago Press.
Mitchell, W. J. T. (2005). The Unspeakable and the Unimaginable: Word and Image in a Time of Terror. *ELH*, 72(2), pp. 291–308.
Mitchell, W. J. T. (2011). *Cloning Terror: The War of Images, 9/11 to the Present*. Chicago, IL: University of Chicago Press.
Mitchell, W. J. T. (2018). Pictorial Turn. In: R. Bleiker, ed., *Visual Global Politics*. London: Routledge.
Pronk, J. (2005). We Need More Stories and More Pictures. 8 October, available at: www.janpronk.nl/speeches/english/we-need-more-stories-and-more-pictures.html [Accessed 5 April 2017].
Rancière, J. (2004). *The Politics of Aesthetics: The Distribution of the Sensible*. Trans. G. Rockhill. London: Continuum.
Robinson, P. (2002). *The CNN Effect: The Myth of News Foreign Policy and Intervention*. New York: Routledge.
Robinson, P. (2018). CNN Effect. In: R. Bleiker, ed., *Visual Global Politics*. London: Routledge.
Rockhill, G. (2009). The Politics of Aesthetics: Political History and the Hermeneutics of Art. In: G. Rockhill, ed., *Jacques Rancière*. Durham, NC: Duke University Press, pp. 195–215.
Ross, A. A. G. (2014). *Mixed Emotions: Beyond Hatred in International Conflict*. Chicago, IL: Chicago University Press.

Solomon, T. (2012). 'I wasn't angry because I couldn't believe it was happening': Affect and Discourse in Response to 9/11. *Review of International Studies*, 38(4), pp. 907–928.

Song, K., Nabers. D. and Shim, D. (2012). *Seeing is Believing*. Unpublished short film. www.dropbox.com/s/wv7rovfd5ybj449/Song%2C%20K.%2C%20Nabers.%20D.%20and%20Shim%2C%20D.%20%282012%29.%20Seeing%20is%20Believing.wmv?dl=0 [Accessed 5 April 2017].

Sontag, S. (1975). Fascinating Fascism. *New York Review of Books*, 6 February, available at: www.nybooks.com/articles/1975/02/06/fascinating-fascism/ [Accessed 5 April 2017].

Van Veeren, E. (2018). Invisibility. In: R. Bleiker, ed., *Visual Global Politics*. London: Routledge.

Weber, C. (2007). I Am an American: Portraits of Post-9/11 US Citizens, www.iamanAmericanproject.com [Accessed 5 April 2017].

Weber, C. (2011). *I Am An American: Filming the Fear of Difference*. Bristol, UK: Intellect Books and Chicago, IL: University of Chicago Press.

Williams, M. C. (2003). Words, Images, Enemies: Securitization and International Politics. *International Studies Quarterly*, 47(4), pp. 511–531.

Index

Page numbers in **bold** denote tables, those in *italics* denote figures.

Abu Ghraib atrocities 85, *86*; 'ghost of Abu Ghraib 4
abusive relationships 180
accessibility, of visual collaging 118
Adair, John 176
aesthetics: CCTV 52, 55, 62–63, 65; collage 122; of politics 152–153, 162–163; propaganda 192; of quality of war photography 75–79, 81–84, 142–143; subject 41–41; turn 1–2
affective expressivity in war photojournalism 85, 86
Afghanistan 83–84, *83*, 85, 142, 194
Agathangelou, A.M. 119
agonistic politics 35
airfield photography 140–141
Alex, N. 159, 160
Alexander, J.C. 95
American Anthropological Association 42
American Civil War 76
Amy (former Liberian soldier) 173, 174, 177, 178–179, 180
Andersen, R.S. 8, 9
Anderson, B. 64
Anonymous 8, 23–36; desecuritization discourse 24, 34–36; macrosecuritization discourse 24, 29–30, 34, 35–36; Operation Last Resort 23, 24, 26, 31–34, *32*, *33*, 35, 36; securitization discourse 26–29; use of military imagery 23–24, 25, 31–34
anti-terrorist manhunts *see* drone *dispositif*
Arab Spring activists 24
Aradau, Claudia 118
Armed Forces of Liberia (AFL) 173–174
art-veillance 55
Ascension Island 141, 142

Assiz, Tariq 47–49, *48*, 50
Aumont, J. 34
Australia 155
auto-photographic research 171–184, 196–197; domestic violence 180; drugs and substance abuse 181–182; ethics of publishing photographs 172–173; situating in visual security studies 174–176; social rafting in Monrovia 172, 176–179; street sisters and brothers as security providers 182–184; violence and security 179–182; young female soldiers in Liberia 172, 173–174

Back, L. 59
Balko, Radley 163
battlefield photojournalism *see* photojournalism
Bayart, J.-F. 97
Beardsley, J. 140, 141
Bell, C. 84
Bell, V. 64
Berger, Arthur Asa 14
Berger, J. 13
Bigelow, Kathryn 39
bigmanity 183
Bin Laden, Osama 194
Bleiker, Roland 126
Blitz of London 78
bodies, in photojournalism 74, 75–78, *77*, 81–82, *82*
Boltanski, L. 78, *86*
Bosnia 142
Boston marathon bombing 195
Bousquet, A. 78
Bratunac soccer stadium, Bosnia 142
Brennan, William 42, 50

Bridle, J. 133
Brown, Michael 150, 161
Bryant, Brandon 47, *48*
Burke, John 142
'Burning Man' festival 107
Bussolini, J. 53
Butler, J. 74

Caldicott, Helen 121
Camerati, Nicolas 163–164
Campany, David 138, 139, 141
Campbell, D. 9
Canada 94, 160, 164
cannabis 102, 181
Capa, Robert 77, 80
Carmichael, J. 75
Carruthers, S. 75, 76
Castoriadis C. 73
CCTV *see* video surveillance and artistic interventions
CCTV Sniffing performance 54–55, 61–63, *62*, *63*
Chamayou, Gregoire 43, 45, 47, 50
change.org petition 35
Chapelle, Dickey 76
Chomsky, N. 72
chromatology of policing 150–151, 153, 154–157, *157*, 159–160, 161–165
Church of Scientology 24, 31
CIA 42, 48–49, 50
city bombing imagery 78, *79*
civilian fatalities in war 83
clientelism 183
Clinton, Hillary 29
cocaine 91, 102, 105–106, 181
Cohen, A. 94
Cohn, Carol 119–120, 124
Coker, C. 83, 85
collaging 116–119, 120, 197; Iranian missile tests 121–122, 124–125, 127; thematic 117; theoretical 116–117; visual 117–119
Collier, John, Jr. 175–176
colour-use in police uniforms 150–151, 153, 154–157, *157*, 159–160, 161–165
common sense 156–157, 192–193
communitarianism 29
Corcoran, S. 165
cosmopolitanism 29, 30, 35
Craik, J. 158
'CTRL [SPACE]' exhibition 55
cultural memory, war as 72, 73
Curry, C. 163
cyborg soldier 81–82

Dallaire, Roméo 142
data-veillance 55
D-Day landing 77
de Young, Karen 50
'Death the Reaper' (photograph) 76, *77*
Deleuze, G. 30
DeLillo, Don 40
Deluermoz, Quentin 153, 155
democratization of visual security 191
Deptford.TV 54–55, 61–63, *62*, *63*
Der Derian, J. 9, 76, 83, 88
Derrida, J. 1, 3
desecuritization discourse, Anonymous 24, 34–36
Deseriis, M. 25
Dillon, M. 85
Disarmament, Demobilization, and Rehabilitation (DDR) programmes, Liberia 178
disciplinary society 53
dispositif 53; health 39, 46; military 39–40; of surveillance 55, 56; *see also* drone *dispositif*
distribution of the sensible 192–193
domestic violence 180
Doob, L. 34
Dower, J. 80
Drew, Richard 135
drone *dispositif* 8, 40–43, 193; 'The Drone Queen' 40–41, 42, 47; necro-biographies 45–47; return of gaze and 8, 40, 41–42, 44–45, 50; *Unmanned: America's Drone War* 44–45, 47–50, *48*, *49*, *50*
drug incineration ceremonies 102–108, *104*, *105*, *106*
drug trafficking: West Africa 91, 181; World Drug Day 92, 98, 99–108, *104*, *105*, *106*
dubriagem 177

Ebola epidemic 177
ecology concept 63–64
Eisenstein, Sergei 34
Elkins, J. 139
Ellul, J. 34
emotions 194–195
Emsley, Clive 155, 158–159
Enloe, Cynthia 118, 125, 128
Ernst, Max 117
ethical killing machine 43–44
exclusive universalism 29
existing order universalism 29
extraversion concept 97

Facebook 115
'Falling man' (photograph) 135
Falzone, J. 35
Farish, M. 75
Fassin, Didier 161
Ferenbok, J. 65
Ferguson, Missouri 150, 161–165
Foucault, Michel 3, 39, 45, 46, 53, 151, 171
France, police 153, 155–156, 158, 159, 160, 162, 163–164, 165
Frazer, E. 74
Fuller, M. 53–54, 63–64
Fussell, Paul 73, 77

gaming, gender and 123–124
Garfinkel, Harold 41
gaze 38–41, 53; ethics of 43–45; medical 39, 46; mutual 56, 61; return of 8, 38–39, 40, 41–42, 44–45, 50; *see also* video surveillance and artistic interventions
geek culture, gender and 123–124
gender: gaming and geek culture 123–124; nuclear proliferation and 119–125
Gender Inequality Index 176–177
Ghana 100–101, 106–107
Gibbs, Philip 80
Gilgen, Peter 137, 139, 140
Glorious (Liberian research assistant) 175, 179–180
Goffman, E. 94, 95
Goldsmiths, University of London 54, 57
Google 126, 127
Gray, C.H. 81
Great War and Modern Memory, The (Fussell) 73
Greenwald, Robert 44–45, 47–50
Gregory, D. 155
Guantánamo 4, 154
Guattari F. 30
Guinea 105–106
Guinea-Bissau 177
Gulf War 81
Gurevich, A.J. 46
Gustafsson, H. 146

hacktivist activism *see* Anonymous
hacktivist art projects 52; *#OCTV* art installation 54, 56–61, *57*, *60*; *CCTV Sniffing* performance 54–55, 61–63, *62*, *63*
Halberstam, Judith 115, 116
Hansen, Lene 8, 195

Hardt, M. 36
Harris, C. 156
Hasselhoff, David 121, 122
Haugney, C. 195
HBGary 24
health *dispositif* 39, 46
Heck, A. 93
Hello Militarized Kitty (collage) 124–125
Herman, E. 72
heroin 102, 181
heroism 75, 76, 80
Hiroshima 78, 79, *79*, 80
Holmqvist, C. 85
Holocaust 73
Homeland (television series) 40–41, 42, 47
Hooper-Greenhill, E. 93
horror film genre 135–136
Hosseini, Massoud 84
Howard, M. 71
humanitarian action 82–83, *83*
humanity of war *see* photojournalism
Huppauf, B. 78, 80
Hurley, Frank *77*
Hurt Locker, The (film) 39
Hutchings, K. 74
Huysmans, Jef 118

image-emotions-security nexus 194–195
inclusive universalism 29, 30
informal security arrangements 182–184
intellectual stereoscopic effect 137
Inter-Ministerial Committee in the Fight Against Drugs (CILD), Senegal 101–102
international diplomacy, as ritual 95
International Visual Sociology Association 54, 57
internet content, personalization of 127
internet freedom *see* Anonymous
internet parody images and memes 114–128, 191, 193, 196; collaging 116–119, 120, 121–122, 124–125, 127, 197; gender, sexuality and nuclear proliferation 119–125; of Iranian missile tests 114, 119–120, 121–125; masculinity game of nuclear proliferation 119–125; reverse snowballing method 126; studying 114–116
invisibility 193–194; obscure photography and 133, 134–135, 136, 141, 144, 194
Iranian missile tests: collages of 121–122, 124–125, 127; internet parody images of 114, 119–120, 121–125; nuclear ambitions 116

Iraq Afghanistan Deployment Impact Fund 85
Iraq War 81–82, *82*, 83–84, 85, *86*, 194
Islamic State group 4, 191

Jefferson, Tony 154, 162
jirga drone attack, Pakistan 44, 49–50, *50*
Joseph, N. 159, 160
Juliet (former Liberian soldier) 172

Kalifa, Dominique 161
Kant, Immanuel 44
Keenan, T. 144
Kitchin, R. 58
Knight Rider (television series) 121, 122
Koskela, H. 56, 64–65
Kraska, Peter 154, 162

Lacan, Jacques 38–39
landscapes, in photojournalism 78–79, *79*, 82–84, *83*
Lasswell, Harold 72
Lawrence, X. 80
Leavy, Patricia 117, 125
Lee, A. 34
Lee E. 34
Leed, E. 76, 78
Legg, S. 54
Leonardo da Vinci 133, 134
Levin, T.Y. 53
liberal paradox of war 71–72
Liberia: domestic violence 180; drugs and substance abuse 181–182; police 179, 180, 181–182; social rafting in Monrovia 172, 176–179; street sisters and brothers as security providers 182–184; violence and security 179–182; young female soldiers 172, 173–174
Liberians United for Reconciliation and Democracy (LURD) 174
Life magazine 77
Lignereux, Aurélien 161
Limit Telephotography (photography series) 143–144
Lin, Maya 191–192
Linfield, Susan 71, 87, 137
Ling, L.H.M. 119
Lisle, D. 9
Lister, M. 139
Loader, I. 152
Logos Technologies 45
Luc, J-N. 155–156

MacDougall, D. 137, 138

McFarlane, C. 64
McGrath, J. 53, 55
macrosecuritization discourse, Anonymous 24, 29–30, 34, 35–36
making security visible 3, 5, **6**, 7; *see also* auto-photographic research; obscure photography; police uniforms
Mann, S. 65
Manufacturing Consent (Herman and Chomsky) 72
Martinez, L. 163
Martins, Edgar 139, 140–141
masculinity game of nuclear proliferation 119–125
mass digital surveillance 26–27
Masters, C. 82, 116
Mbembe, A. 97
Media, War and Conflict (journal) 1
media studies 1
mediatised conflict 81
mediatization 27
medical gaze 39, 46
memes *see* internet parody images and memes
memory studies 72, 73
metaphors 36, 116
Metropolitan Police of London 158
Miettinen, M. 122
militarization: of the internet 24, 35, 36; of the police 151, 154, 161–165
military *dispositif* 39–40
military humanitarianism 82–83, *83*
Milliot, Vincent 161
mirroring 27–28
Mirzoeff, N. 9
Missile Envy (collage) 122
Mitchell, C. 14
Mitchell, W.J.T. 1, 133, 135, 136, 190, 195
Möller, F. 9
moral agency of war photography 75, 79–81, 84–87, *86*
mutual gaze 56, 61

National Patriotic Front of Liberia (NPFL) 173
Navajo Native Americans 176
Nazi Germany 192
'necklacing' 108
necro-biographies 45–47
Negri, A. 36
neopatrimonialism 182–183
New York Times 81
New Yorker, The 163

No Man's Land imagery 78
Norfolk, Simon 134, 139, 141–143
Nuclear Non-proliferation Treaty 116
nuclear proliferation: gender, sexuality and 119–125; Iranian ambitions 116; masculinity game of 119–125; missile envy 121–123
nuclear war imagery: Hiroshima 78, 79, *79*, 80; *see also* Operation Last Resort
Nuremberg trials 44

obscure photography 9–10, 133–146, 194; Martins 139, 140–141; Norfolk 134, 139, 141–143; Paglen 139, 141, 143–144, 192; participant witness and 133, 144–145
#OCTV art installation 54, 56–61, *57, 60*
O'Hagan, Sean 139
online mediation of security 4
Operation Last Resort 23, 24, 26, 31–34, *32, 33*, 35, 36
Orange Iran (collage) 121–122

Paglen, Trevor 139, 141, 143–144, 192
Pakistan 44, 49–50, *50*
Palin, Sarah 24
Panopticon 53
parody images *see* internet parody images and memes
participant witness 133, 144–145
participatory photography 175–176; *see also* auto-photographic research
patrimonialism 182–183
Pauwels, Luc 14
Pedersen, Annette 155
people as infrastructure 183
Peritz, I. 160
personalization of internet content 127
Pfanner, T. 159
photo-elicitation interviews 171, 175–176; *see also* auto-photographic research
photography *see* auto-photographic research; obscure photography
photojournalism 9, 71–88, 134, 135, 137, 193, 194; aesthetic quality 75–79, *77, 79*, 81–84, *82, 83*; amateur 84; bodies in battle 74, 75–78, *77*, 81–82, *82*; landscapes 78–79, *79*, 82–84, *83*; moral agency 75, 79–81, 84–87, *86*; twentieth century World Wars 75–81, *77, 79*; twenty-first century War on Terror 81–87, *82, 83, 86*; war imaginary 9, 71–72, 73–75, 78–79, 84, 86, 87
The Pirate Bay (TPB) 27–28

police: aesthetics of politics and 152–153, 162–163; Liberia 179, 180, 181–182; militarization of 151, 154, 161–165
police paramilitary units (PPUs) 162
police uniforms 150–166, 192; colour-use in 150–151, 153, 154–157, *157*, 159–160, 161–165; Ferguson, Missouri 150, 161–165; functions of 158–161; impact of absence on behaviour of police 161–165; origins of 155–156, 158–159; as systems of signification 156, *157*, 159–160; transgression of norms 161–165; World Drug Day 101, 103, *104*
politics of representation 7
Priscilla (former Liberian soldier) 174, 177, 178, 180, 183–184
propaganda 4, 34; Anonymous 28, 34, 35; Nazi Germany 192; war as 72
Propaganda Technique in World War I (Lasswell) 72
psychologization of the soldier 82
public health *dispositif* 39, 46
Puwar, N. 59

Québec, Canada 160, 164

Rancière, Jacques 152–153, 156, 157, 162, 192–193, 196
Reagan, Ronald 121
Reid, J. 85
Remembering to Forget (Zelizer) 73
reverse snowballing method 126
Riefenstahl, Leni 192
Ritchin, F. 138, 140
rituals of security *see* visual rituals of security
Roosevelt, Franklin D. 76
Rwanda 142, 193

Sahlins, Marshall 42–43
Salman, Muzaffar 137
Salter, M.B. 94
Saltzman, Lisa 135–136
Sauer, F. 43
Schirato, T. 135
Schlag, G. 93
Schörnig, N. 43
securitization discourse 34; Anonymous 26–29
securitization theory 8, 26–29, 92–96; macrosecuritization 8, 24, 26–34; *see also* desecuritization 9, 24, 34–36, 94
security rituals *see* visual rituals of security

Index

security spectacles and spectatorship 3, 5, 6, 7; *see also* internet parody images and memes; photojournalism; visual rituals of security
security technology 3, 5, 6; *see also* Anonymous; drone *dispositif*; video surveillance and artistic interventions
Senegal 174–175; Inter-Ministerial Committee in the Fight Against Drugs (CILD) 101–102; World Drug Day 101–107, *104*, *105*, *106*
sexuality, nuclear proliferation and 119–125
Shapiro, M.J. 7, 9
Simone, AbdouMaliq 183
Simpson, D. 144
Singer, P.W. 43–44
Sites of Memory, Sites of Mourning (Winter) 73
Situationist International 55
Snow, N. 34
snowballing method, reverse 126
Snowden, Edward 26–27
Sochi Olympic Games 160
social construction of security threats 92–96
social meaning of policing *see* police uniforms
social media 115, 191
social navigation 172, 177
social rafting 172, 176–179
soldier as machine 76, 77, 81, 82, 84, 85
Sonne, P. 160
Sontag, Susan 136, 137, 173, 192
sous-veillance 61, 65
Spanish Civil War 71
Spivak, Gayatri 171, 184, 196–197
SpongeBob SquarePants 115
Stanford-NYU investigation of drone use 42
Stevenson, Julia 81
Steyerl, H. 62
Strauss, D.L. 142
Stritzel, H. 94
Strutt, William 155
Sturken, M. 73
subjectivist aesthetic, in war photojournalism 82, 84, 86, 87
sublime aesthetic, in war photojournalism 78–79, 80, 84, 85, 86
substance abuse, Liberia 181–182
surveillance: drone targeting and 45–47; mass digital 26–27; *see also* video surveillance and artistic interventions

Surveillance Camera Players 55
surveillance studies 2
Swartz, Aaron 23, 24, 26, 31
SWAT (Special Weapons And Tactics) teams 162
Sylvester, Christine 116, 117
systems of signification 156, *157*, 159–160
systems of the sensible 156–157, *157*, 192–193

Taylor, Charles (Liberian president) 173–174
Taylor, Charles (philosopher) 73, 155
Taylor, D. 133
terrorist attacks 83–84, 190, 195
Teta (former Liberian soldier) 173–174, 177, 178, 180
thematic collaging 117
theoretical collaging 116–117
threat construction in securitization theory 92–96
Troianovski, A. 160
Tumbler, David 82
Twitter 56–58, 59

uniforms *see* police uniforms
United Kingdom, police 154, 158–159, 162
United States: CIA 42, 48–49, 50; police 150, 154, 161–165; Sentencing Commission website 26, 31, *32*; 'State of the Union' address 94; Supreme Court Justices 26; *see also* drone *dispositif*
Unmanned: America's Drone War (documentary) 44–45, 47–50, *48*, *49*, *50*

van Alphen, Ernst 142–143
van Veeren, Elspeth 4, 154
video surveillance and artistic interventions 52–65, 196; #*OCTV* art installation 54, 56–61, *57*, *60*; *CCTV Sniffing* performance 54–55, 61–63, *62*, *63*; ecologies of 63–64
videos, hacktivist *see* Anonymous
Vietnam Veterans Memorial, Washington DC 191–192
Vietnam War 81, 190, 194
Vigh, Henrik E. 177
vigilante justice, Africa 108
viral replication 27–28
visual artefacts 191–192
visual collaging 117–119
visual culture studies 1–2

visual performances 191–192
visual rituals of security 91–109, 193, 194–195; drug incineration ceremonies 102–108, *104*, *105*, *106*; importance of in West Africa 92, 96–98; social construction of security threats 92–96; World Drug Day 92, 98, 99–108, *104*, *105*, *106*
visual turn in security studies 190–191
visuality as a method 3, **6**, 12–14; *see also* auto-photographic research; internet parody images and memes; video surveillance and artistic interventions
visuality as a modality 3, **6**, 7–10; *see also* Anonymous; obscure photography; photojournalism
visuality as a practice 3, **6**, 10–12; *see also* drone *dispositif*; police uniforms; visual rituals of security

Walker, Craig 82
Walker, N. 152
Walzer, M. 80
war as memory 72, 73
war as propaganda 72
war communication studies 72–73
war crimes 44
war imaginary 9, 71–72, 73–75, 78–79, 84, 86, 87
war neurosis 76
War on Terror: photojournalism 81–87, *82*, *83*, *86*; *see also* drone *dispositif*
war photojournalism *see* photojournalism
warnings, of shocking images 195
Washington Post 50, 163
Webb, J. 135
Weber, C. 9
West Africa: drug incineration ceremonies 102–108, *104*, *105*, *106*; drug trafficking 91, 181; importance of visual rituals of security 92, 96–98; World Drug Day 92, 98, 99–108, *104*, *105*, *106*; *see also* Liberia
WikiLeaks 24, 28
Winter, Jay 73
World Bank 176
World Drug Day 92, 98, 99–108, *104*, *105*, *106*
World War I, photojournalism 75–76, 77–81, *77*
World War II, photojournalism 76–81, *79*
Worth, Sol 176
Wylie, Donovan 139

YouTube 25, 30, 31

Zelizer, Barbie 73
Zinn, Howard 32, *33*